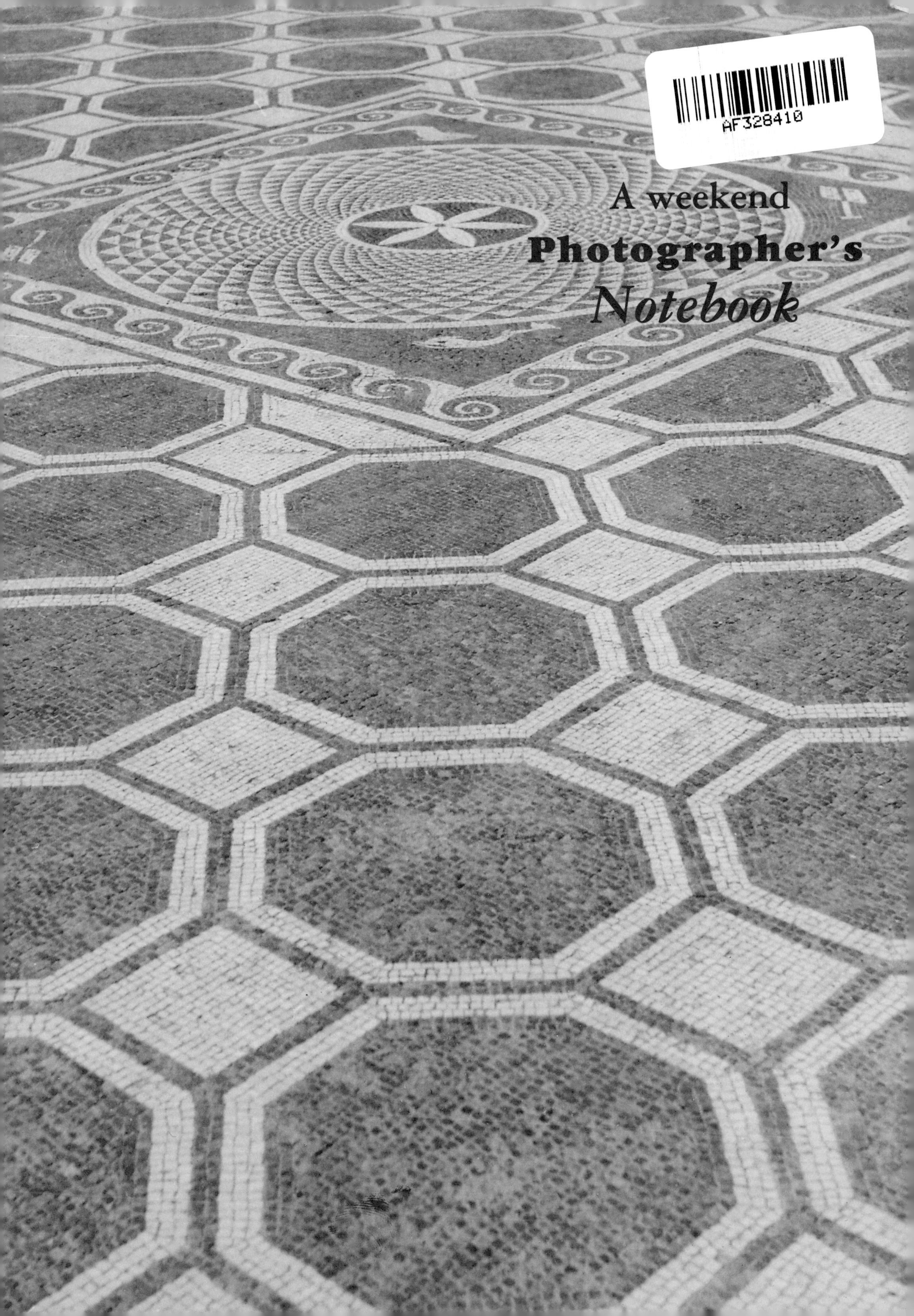

A weekend
Photographer's
Notebook

For my dear friend

Hans Deichmann

A weekend **Photographer's** *Notebook*

170 Photographs by

Vernon Richards

FREEDOM PRESS

London 1996

First published 1996
by Freedom Press
84b Whitechapel High Street
London E1 7QX

© Freedom Press

ISBN 0 900384 87 5

Printed in Great Britain by
Aldgate Press, 3 Gunthorpe Street, London E1 7RQ

CONTENTS

Followed by Notes on the photographs

INTRODUCTION

I hope that not only the title of this volume but a quick glance through its pages will make it abundantly clear that it is intended as a collection of photographs *to be enjoyed as photographs*, as black-and-white 'colours', as 'textures', irrespective of location, explanations or dates and photographic data.

With the title *A Weekend Photographer's Notebook* I think I explain honestly this photographer's lack of professional expertise or pretensions. But I say this *without modesty*! For the advantage the weekend button-presser has over the professional is that it's not his bread and butter and so he/she can indulge as and when the fancy takes him/her, and not on orders from the picture editor or the publisher wanting a particular picture or volume, or the travel agencies their technicolour brochures of Paradise!

From 1946 when I decided no longer to be a 'professional' (a civil engineer in my case) one of the potential freelance occupations included photography. At that time (the post-war years) all kinds of magazines were appearing in Europe and not least in this country, and in the 1950s continental travel took off. That was all short-lived. The magazines disappeared and the travel agencies got all their pictures in colour from the national agencies for free!

So in the 1950s, apart from being an editor of the weekly *Freedom* for free, I worked as a freelance courier for two or three travel agencies, and since I was only responsible for the passengers' comfort on the journey from London by train and boat to their destinations on the continent or for their return journey to London, I had hours, sometimes even a day, to wander on the continent alone ... with my camera!

If the photos involving people have any claim for your enjoyment it is that *not one was posed*. They were strangers, some looking at me, and their expressions recorded simply by pressing the button (mainly on a very early Rolleicord camera).

In view of all the publicity about Doisneau's *Le Baiser* which apparently earned him some $50,000 in fees and which immediately attracted claims by the subjects of *Le Baiser*, Doisneau, to defend himself, had to admit that *it was a posed picture* and named the paid models! Fair enough, so long as one recognises that the professional photographer is not invariably concerned with recording *a moment of truth*! I believe that my photo (28) was a moment of truth, as well as offering me a photographic framework. *It was there* and I observed it for *minutes* and nothing changed. Such is a true kiss, as well as the indifference of that academic gentleman!

Both professional and weekend photographers depend on equipment and chemistry. To see the professionals always reminds me of Daudet's *Tartarin de Tarascon*, the intrepid mountaineer. In their case they are laden with all the gadgets from spare cameras, long-focus lenses and light-meters to tripods and assistants. And the top-notchers wouldn't dream of processing the film and making the enlargements, which is not surprising. Part of my pleasure as a 'weekend photographer' was to process my films and print the enlargements using my eye to focus the image on the printing paper — no automatic focusing enlarger for the likes of me. Only the other day I read of a professional photographer who had just died and who apparently had taken 65,000 photographs in his professional lifetime. It made me think back to a long time ago when I was a boy, to an illustrated feature in the *Sunday Express* by one Ripley, in which he showed a number of chimpanzees busily tapping away at typewriters, and he pointed out that if enough of them went on typing long enough they would produce the Encyclopaedia Britannica! I didn't understand then but have since realised what he was driving at in connection with professional photography. Television news programmes capturing the clamouring photographers outside Downing Street and elsewhere explains that not one photograph that eventually appears in the newspapers *is necessarily a genuine one*. The news and features editors have *thousands* to choose from. They can make a minister, or anyone they are targeting, either to be shown picking his nose or holding his head in 'desperation', or 'smiling' at his political enemy! Even when one is not taking pictures of people by a hundred exposures an hour, the result can lie (see photos 88 and 89 and Notes XIV in this volume).

Apart from the brief period referred to at the beginning, all these photographs were taken without the intention of publishing them. Only recently, at the end of a long life, I thought it was time not to leave others to clear up my accumulated 'rubbish'. I won't bore you, dear reader, with the details of non-photographic 'rubbish', but I have, in selecting prints for this volume, 'dumped' hundreds not because they were 'bad' photos but simply because they were minor records, snapshots. Nevertheless, this volume of 170 photos is not a selection from 65,000 prints but probably from 1,500 taken over a period of twenty years. Since I started up as an organic grower (on a hectare) in 1968, I have only taken a few photographs to illustrate anything I may yet write on the subject. But I still hope to produce a smaller, more intimate volume of photographs with the provisional title *Instead of an Autobiography*, of people (alas not all) I have known, many I have loved and admired. It could happen soon. If interested get in touch with Freedom Press to keep you informed.

Last but not least, two acknowledgements. First, more than a word of thanks to my dear friend Hans Deichmann, who will be 90 years young next year, who has contributed a half of the printing costs of this volume which, with my contributing the other half from the sale of my books and papers, means that all the income from sales of this volume will go to the new Freedom Press Solidarity Fund to help 'subsidise' those virtually full-time voluntary workers at Freedom Press who don't get the dole and so need a helping hand.

Secondly a warm word of thanks to Charles Hall who has been the valuable liaison between photographer and printer. Though I am responsible for the selection of photographs and their sequence (for better or for worse), Charles has 'translated' my intentions into the language of printing. And when I learn what all this involves, I am humbled! After all, I saw a picture, pressed a button and then in the dark-room processed the film and eventually made the enlargement. Printing these photographs that you are about to see is much more complicated, so thanks also to our colleagues at Aldgate Press.

Vernon Richards
Colchester 1996

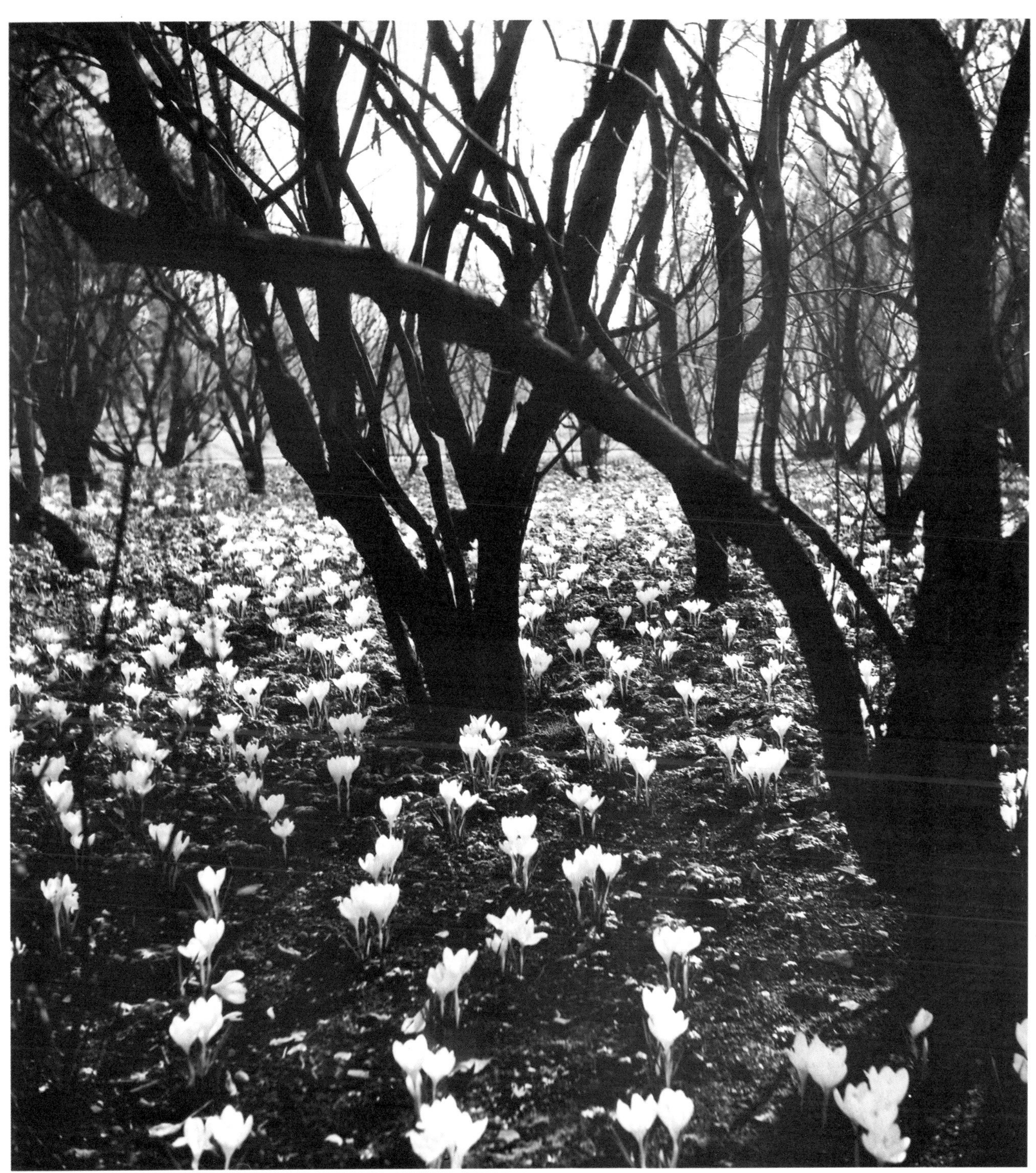

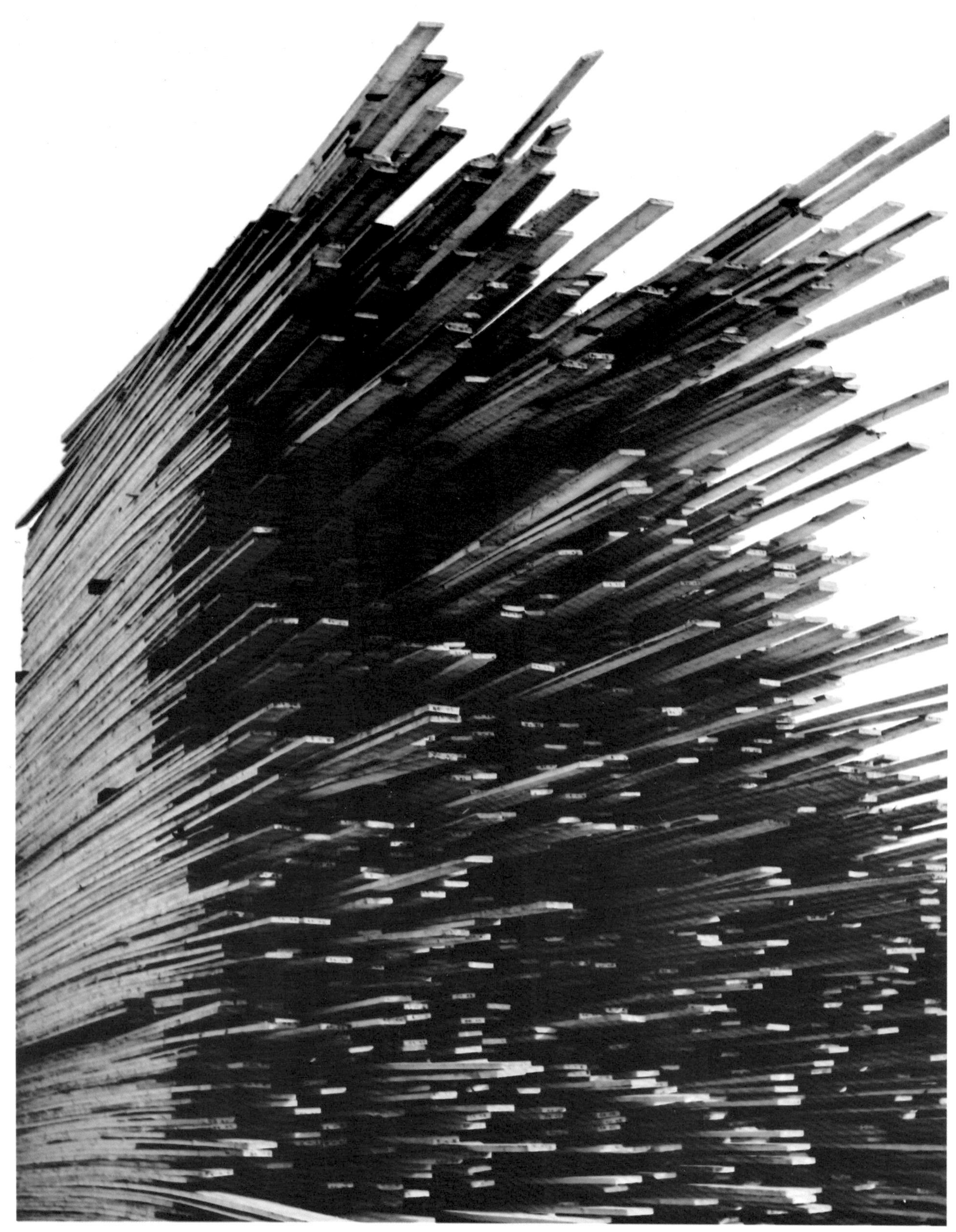

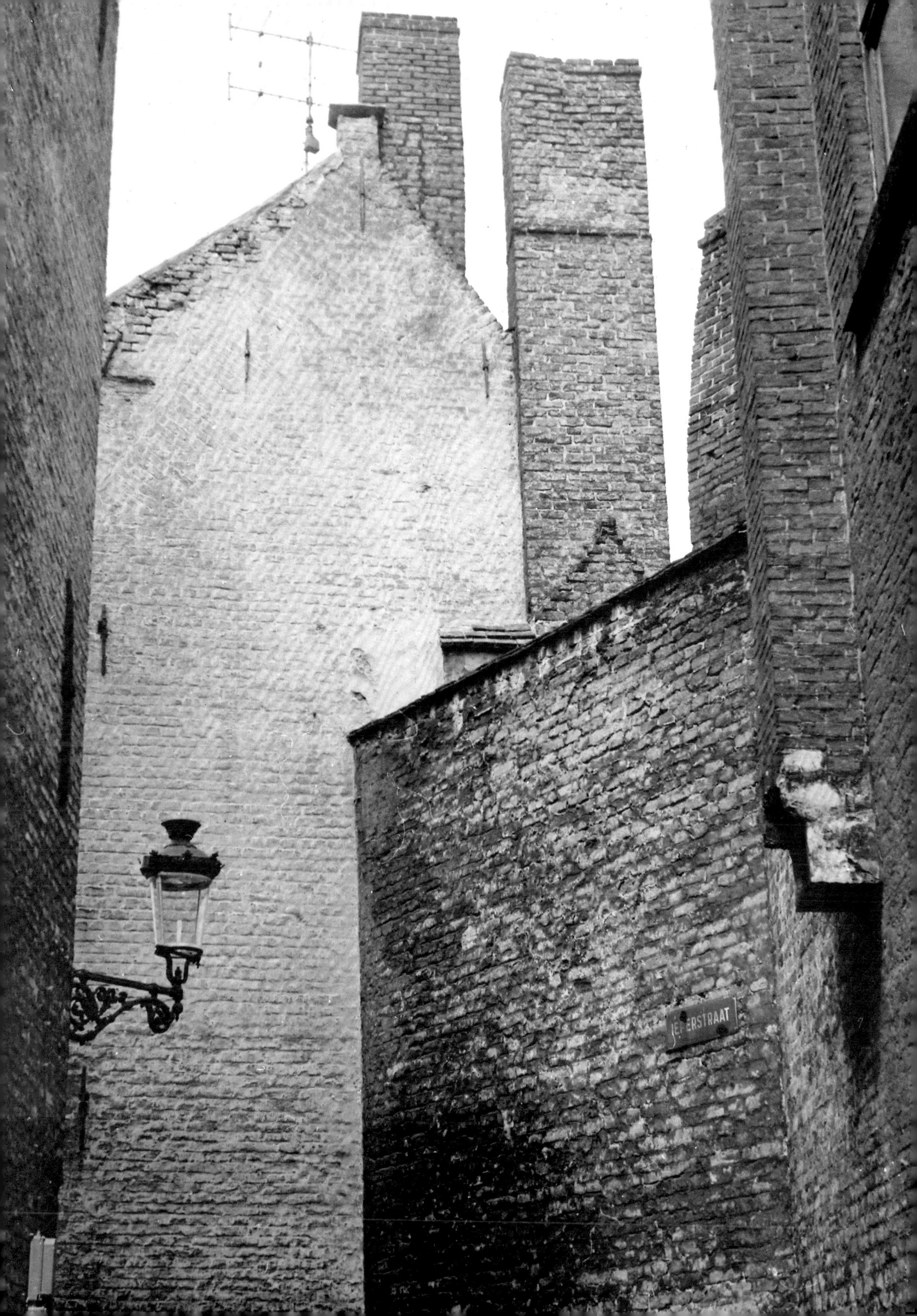

EPERSTRAAT

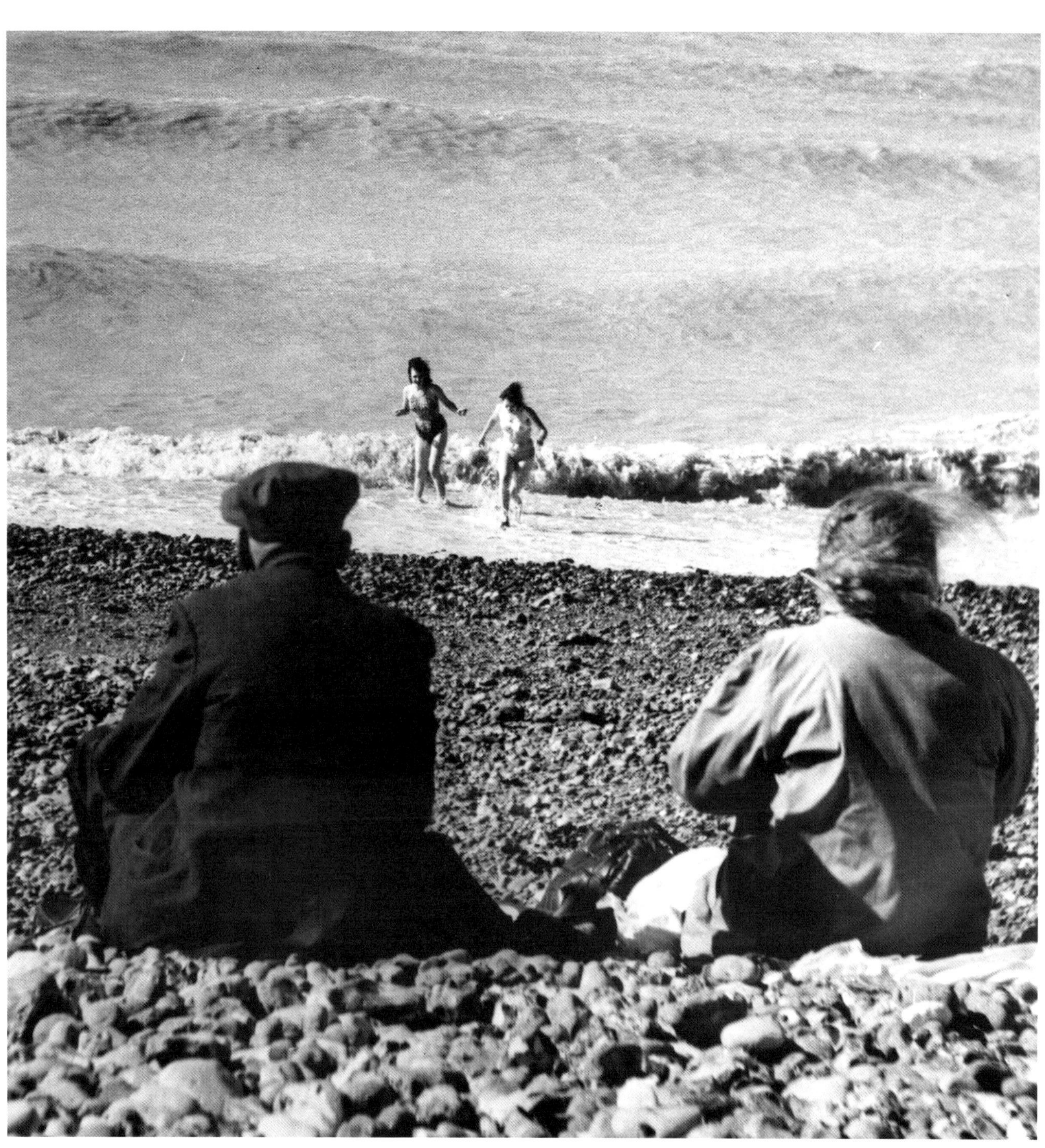

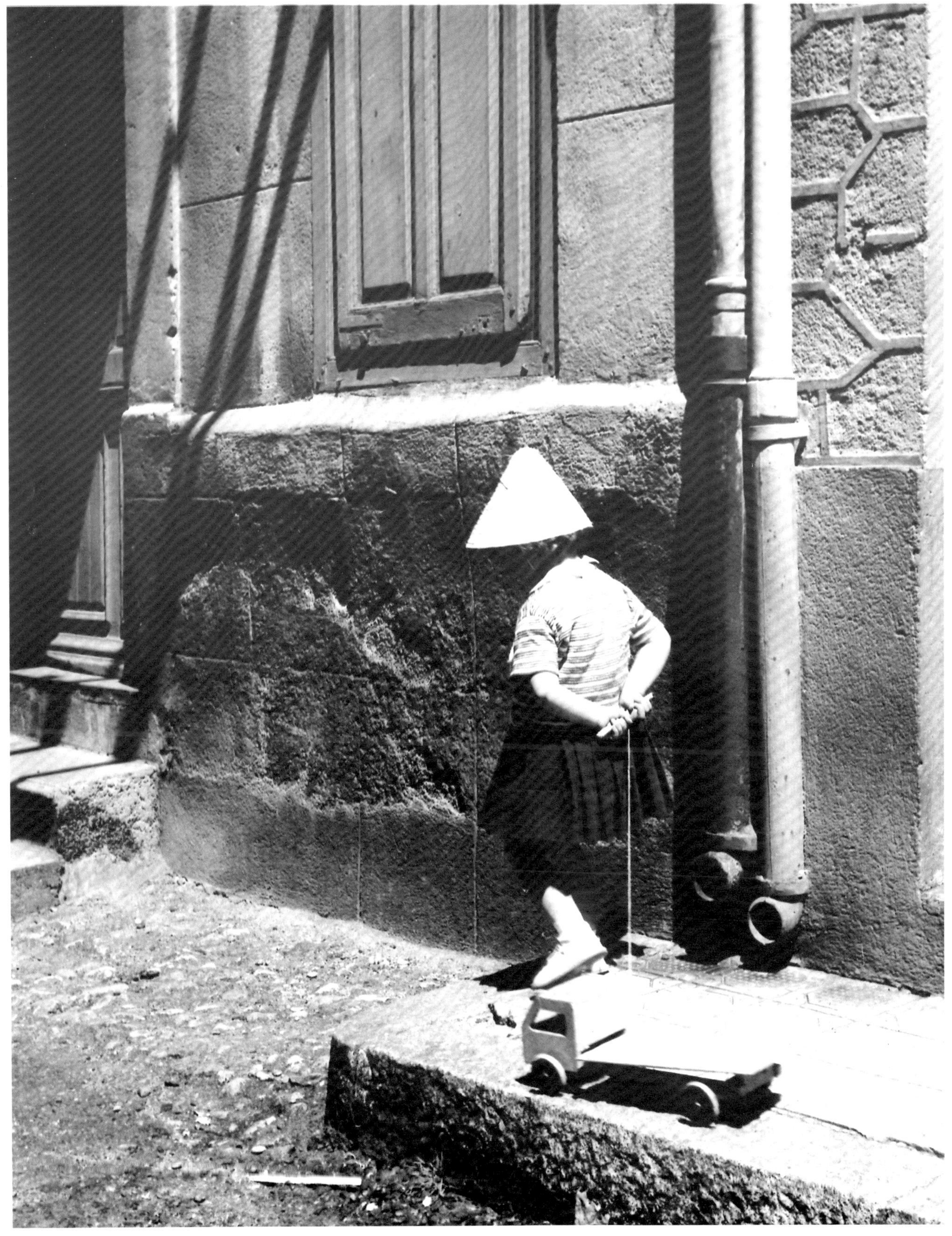

5

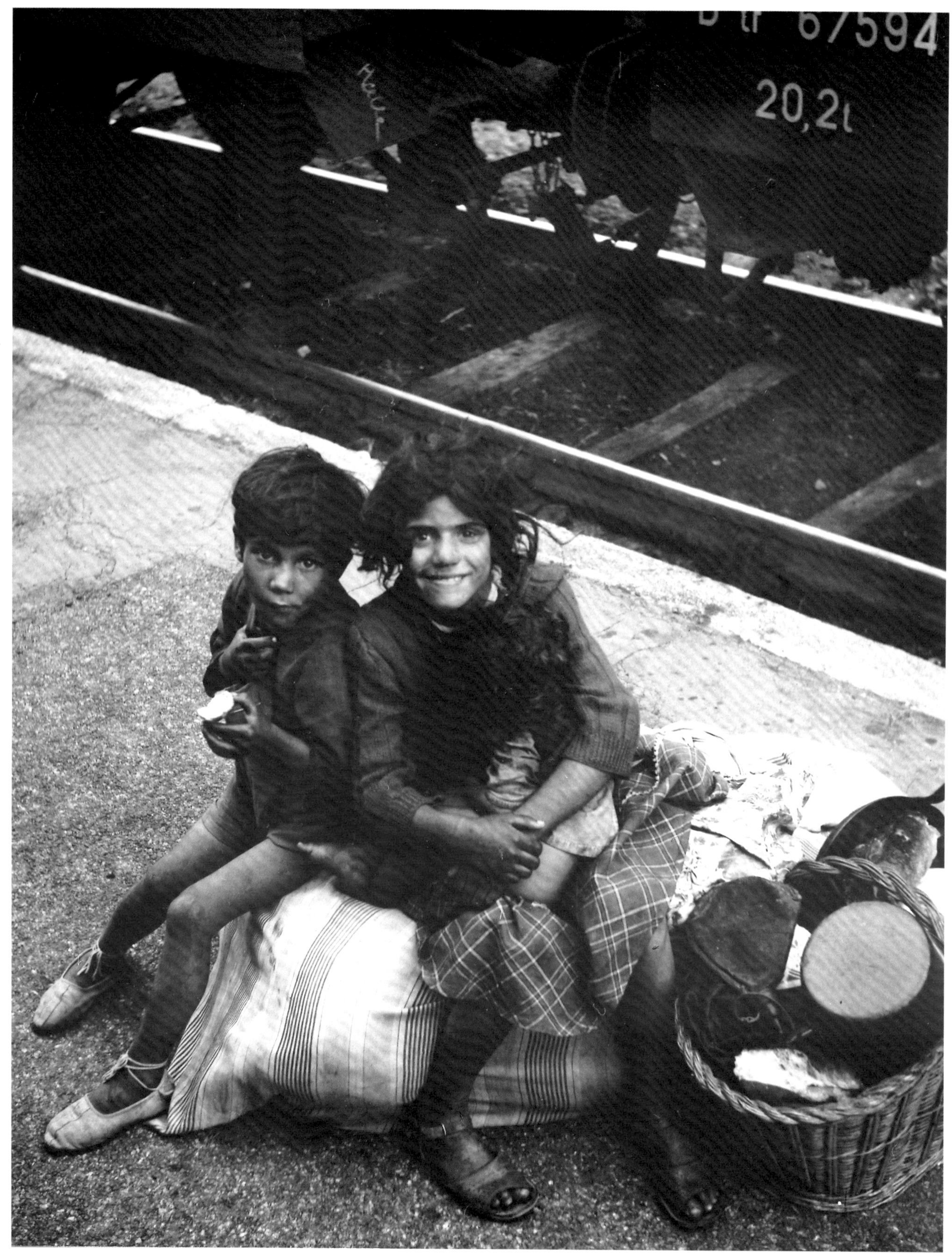

6/594
20,2t

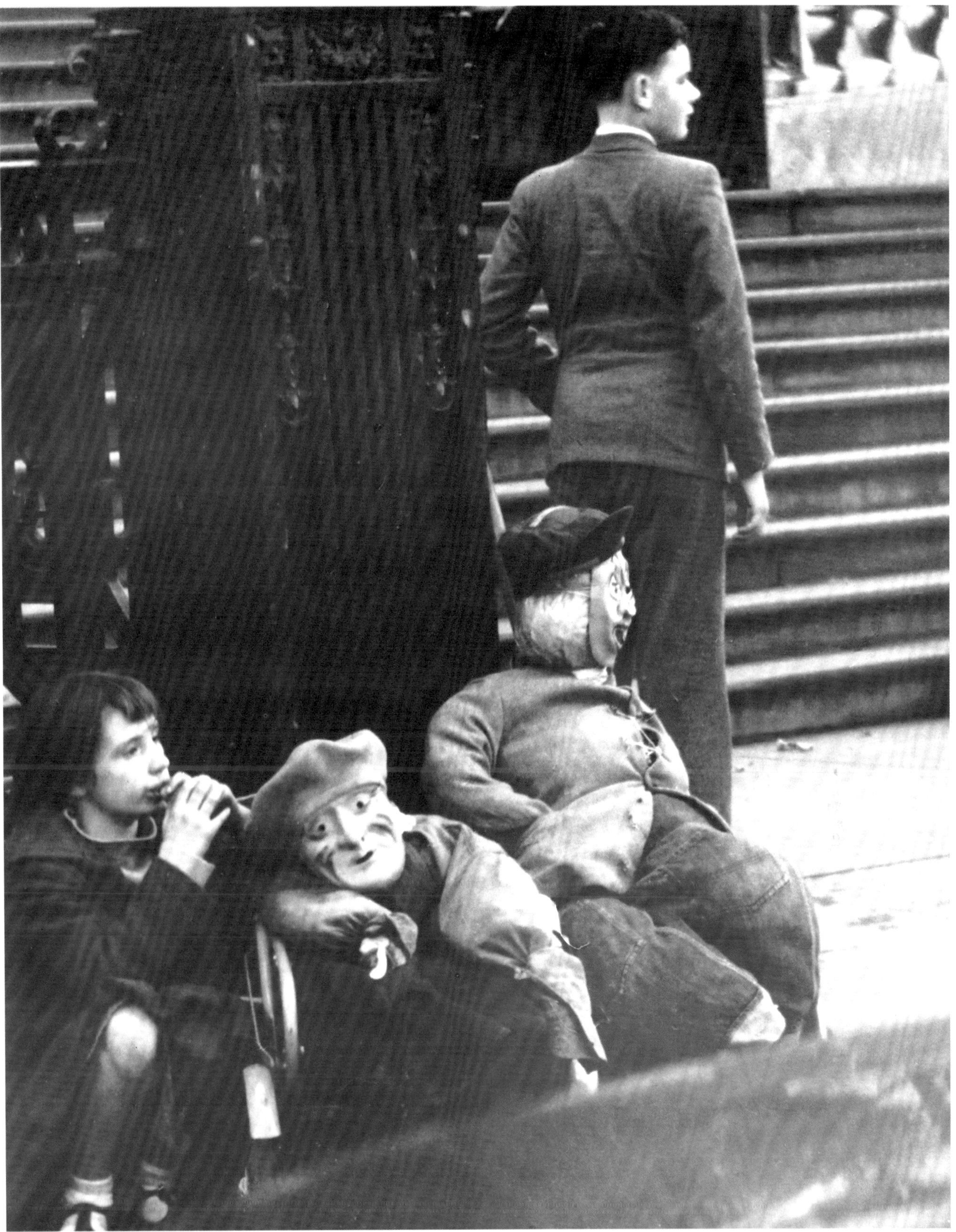

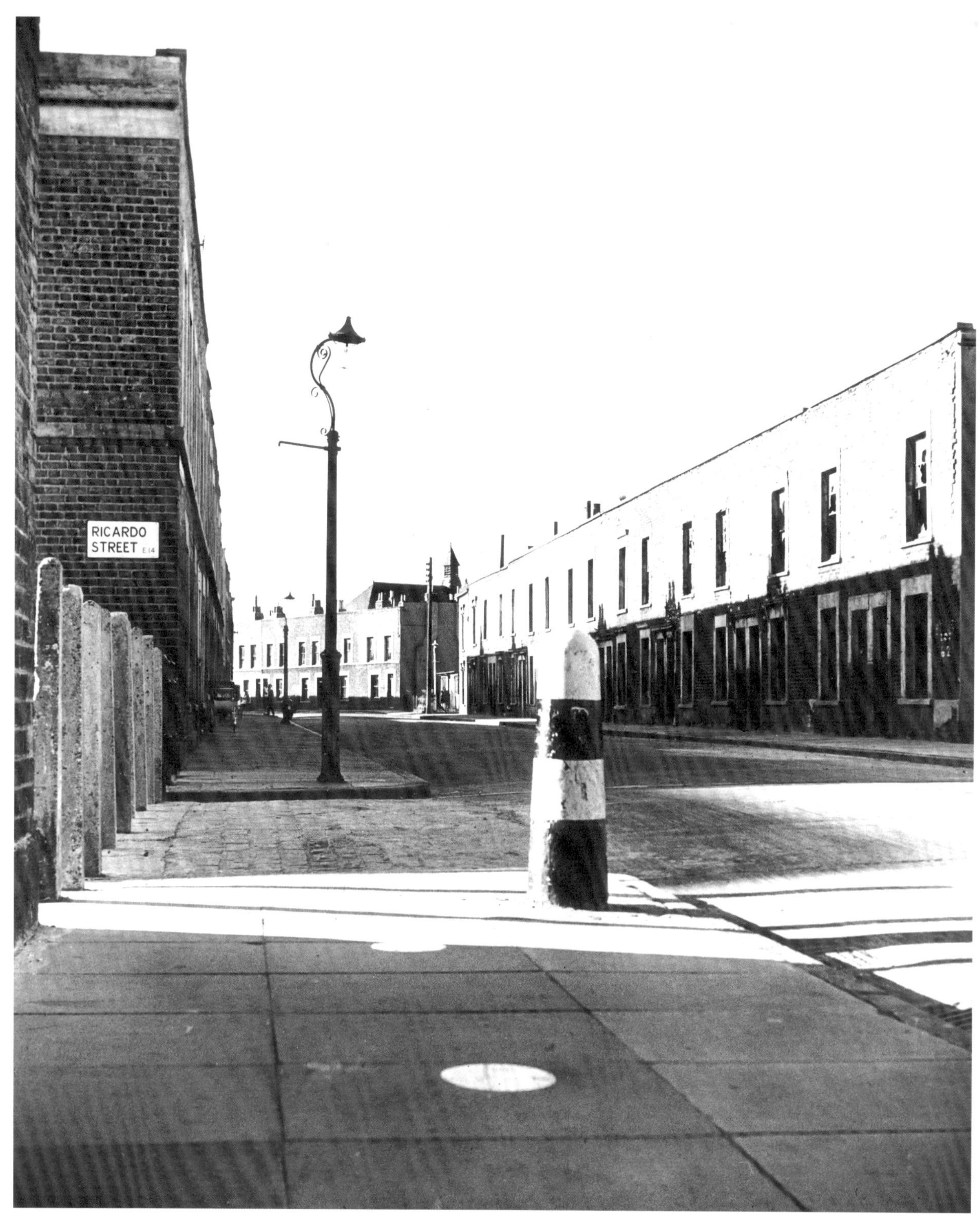
RICARDO
STREET E.14

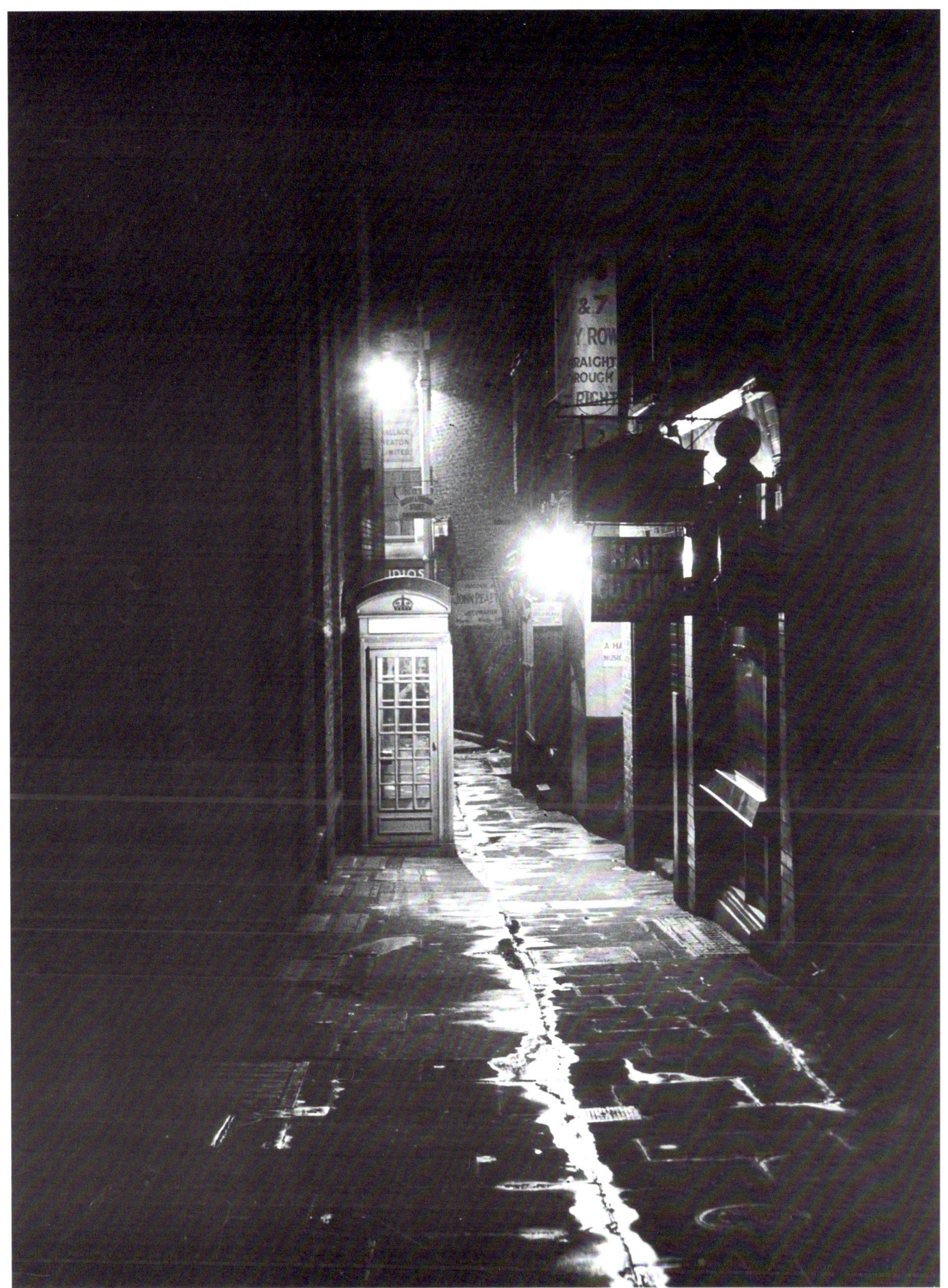

9

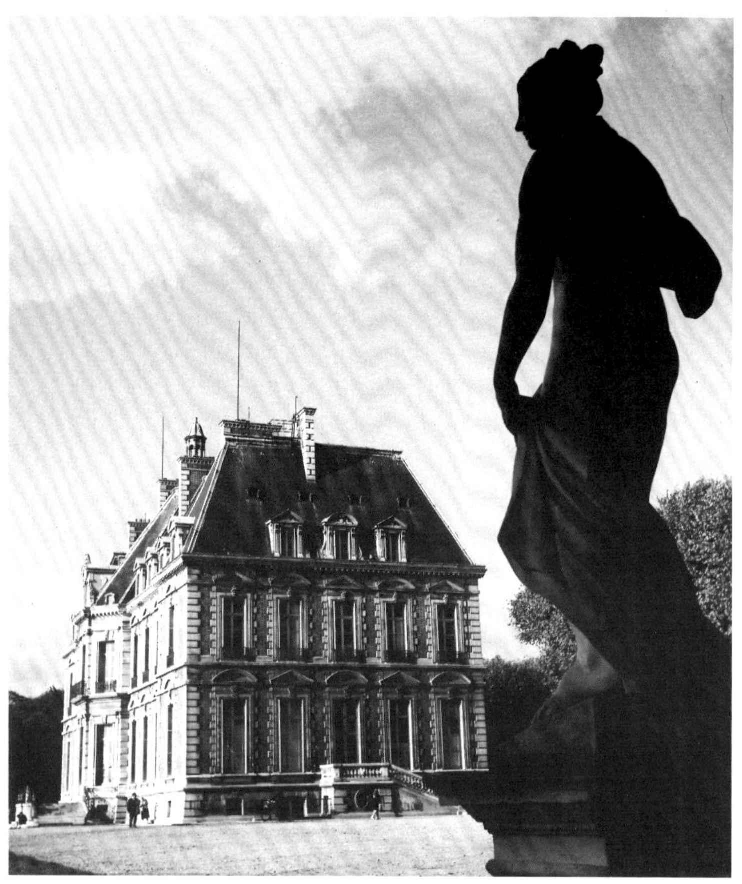

10

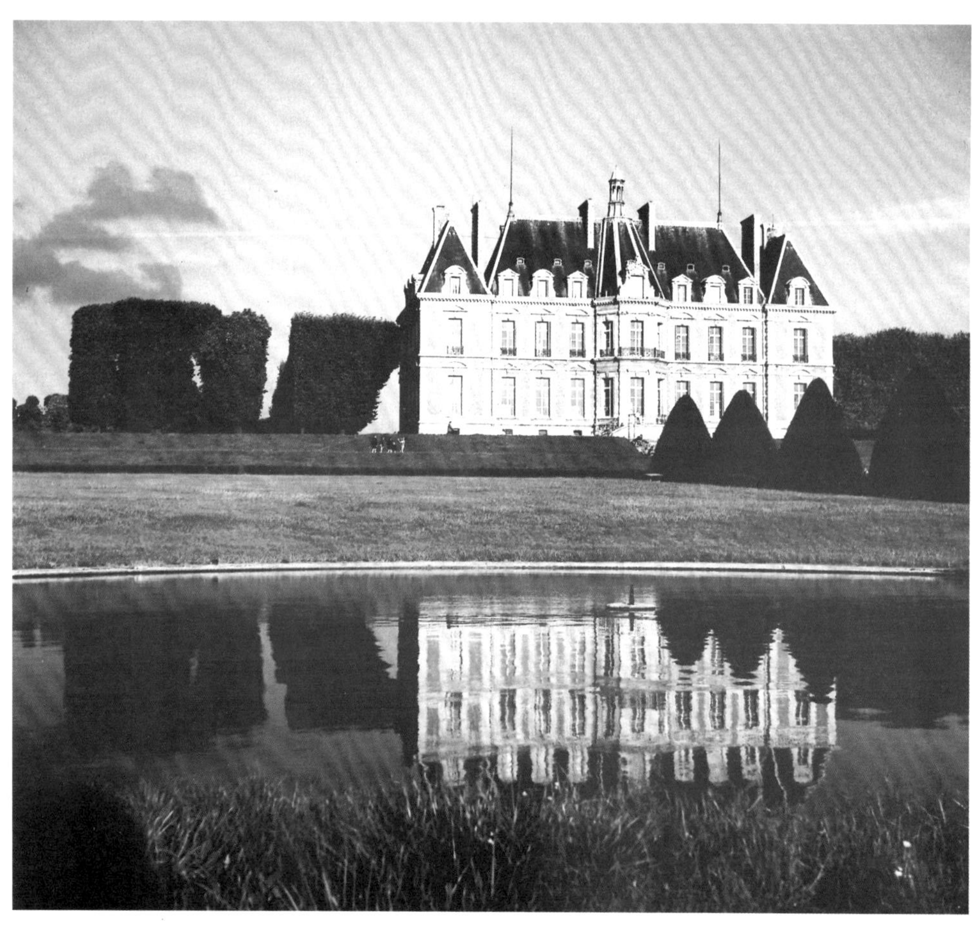

11

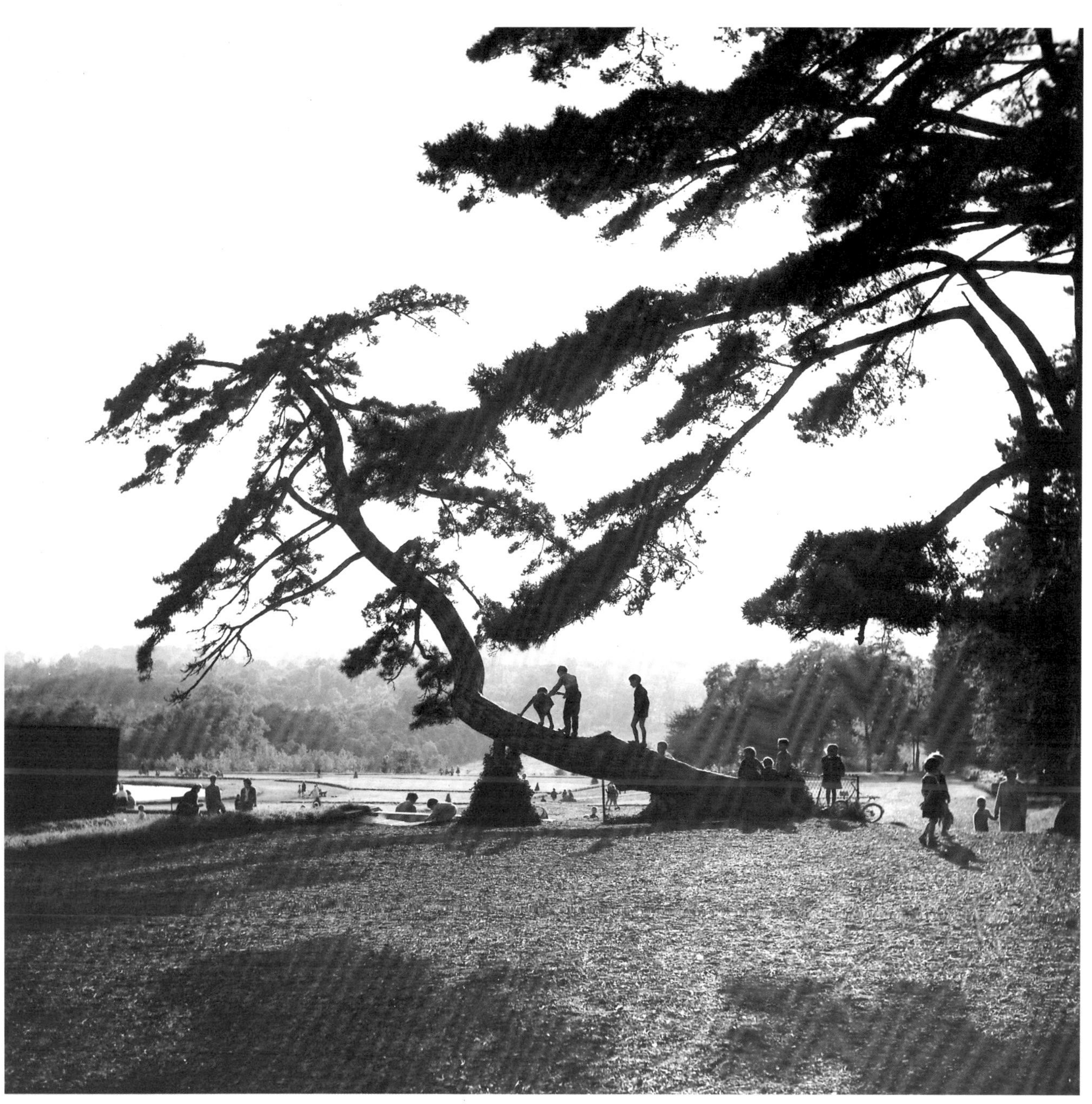

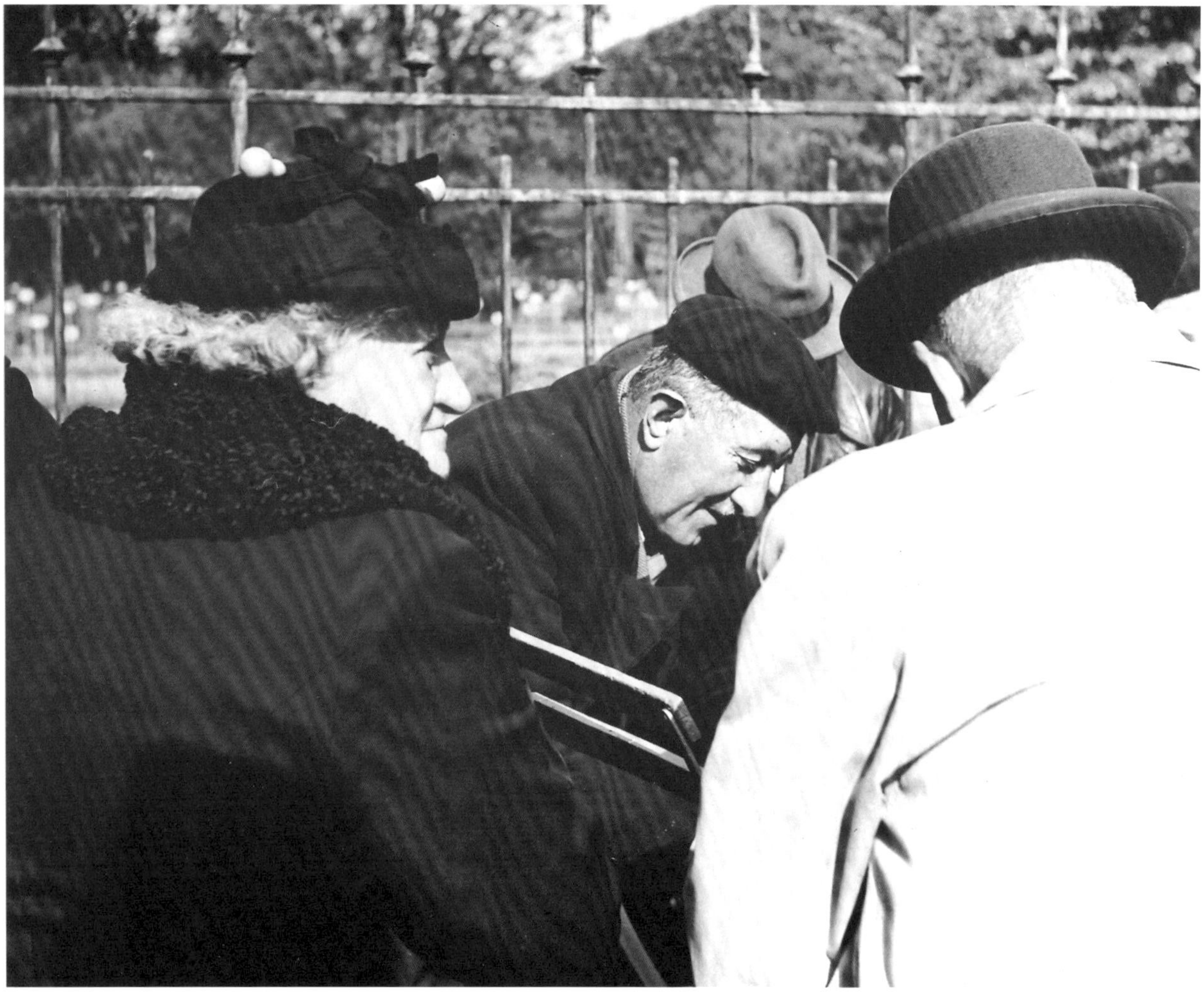

13

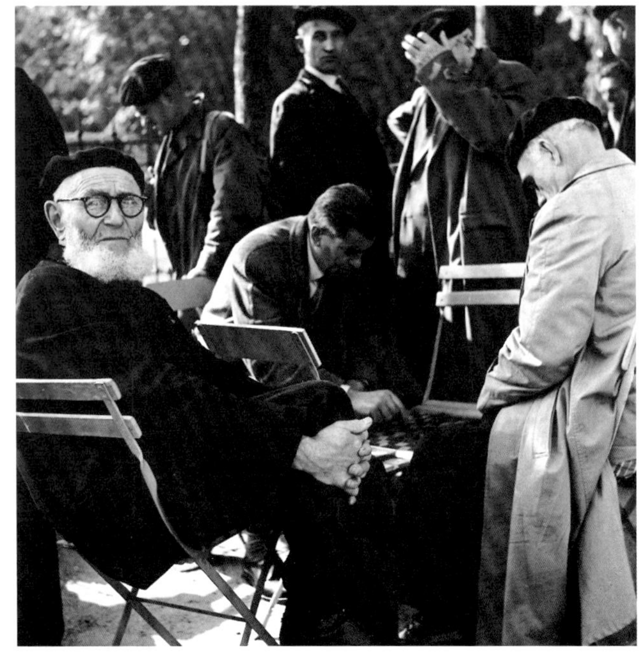

14

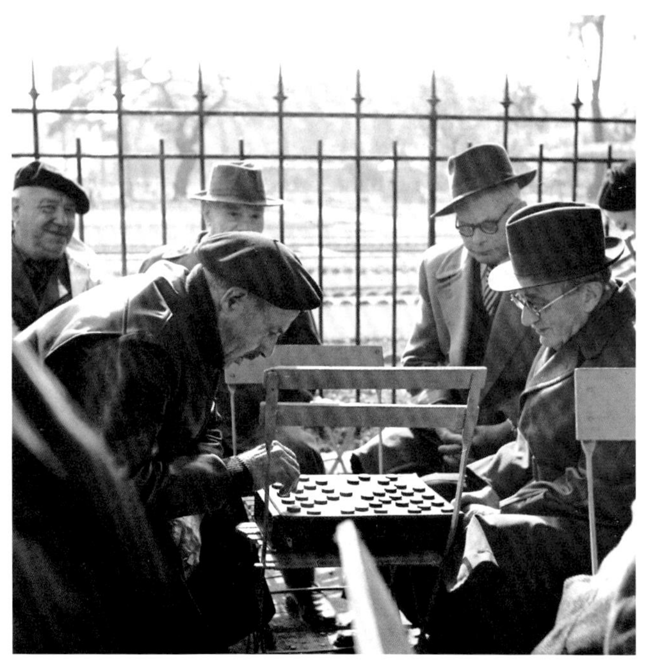

15

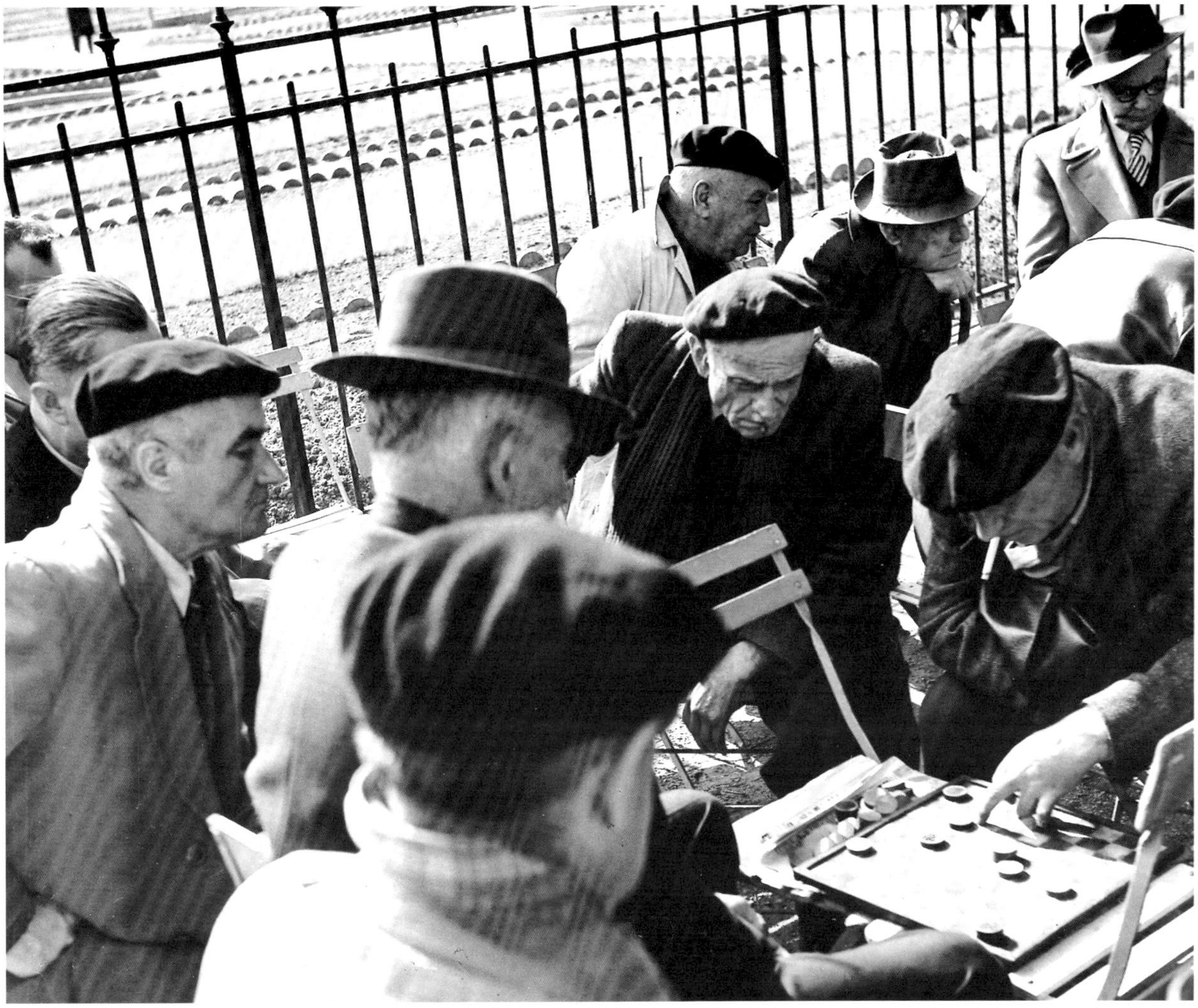

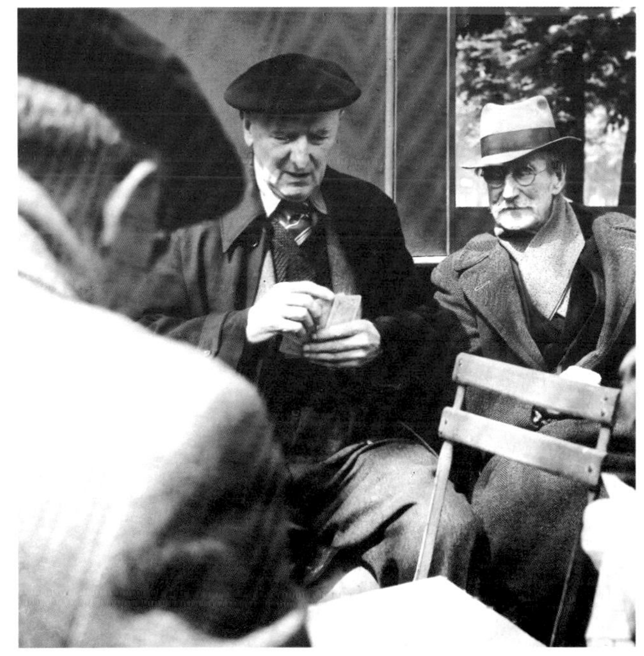

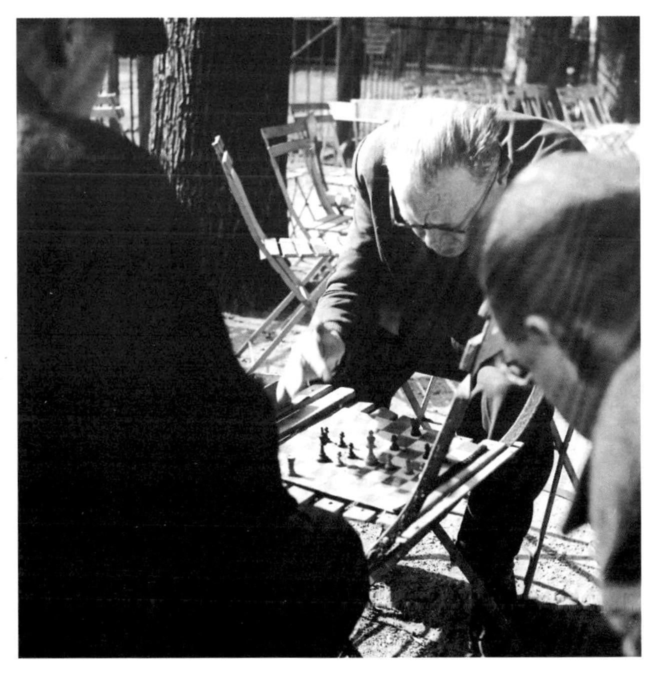

16

17

18

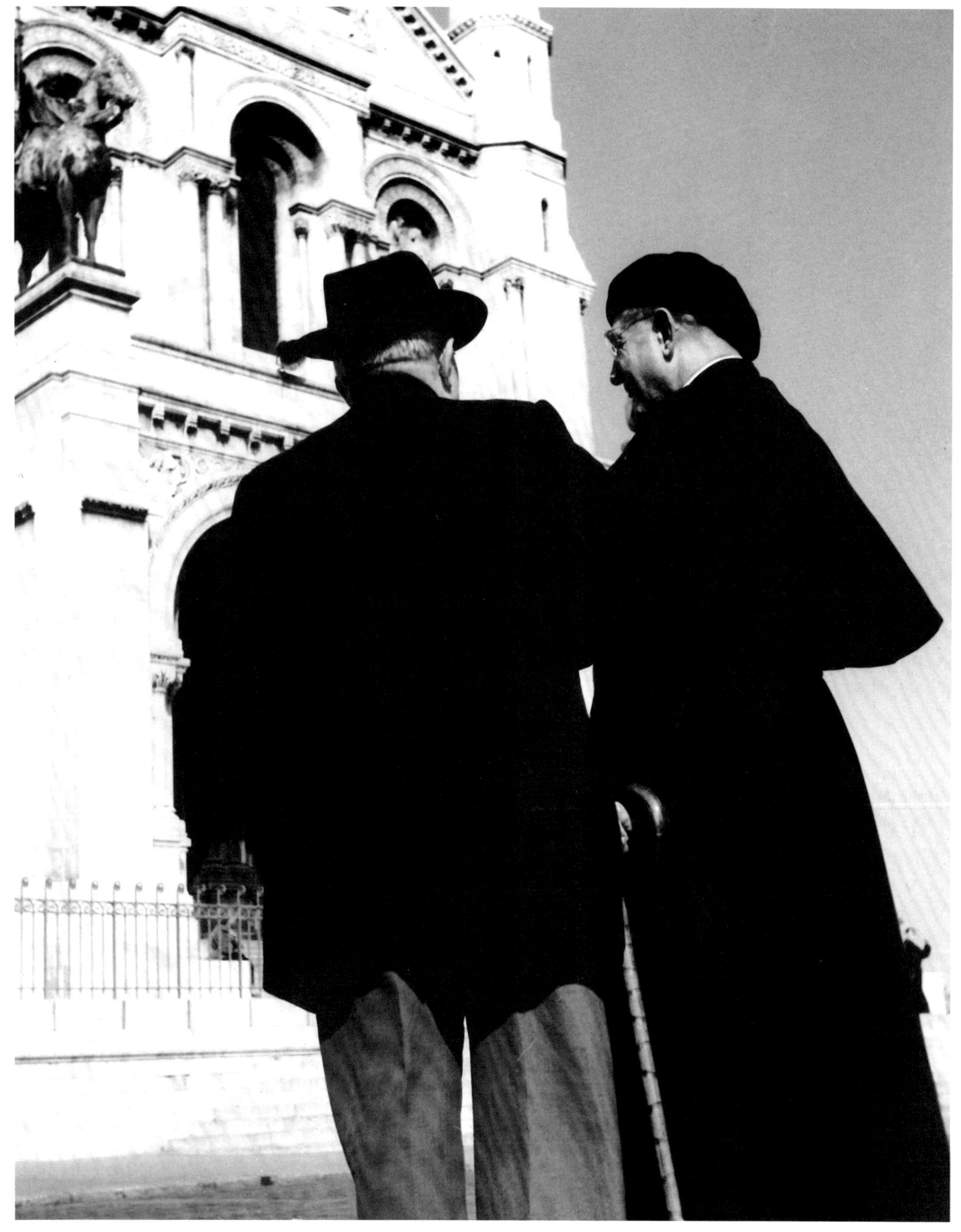

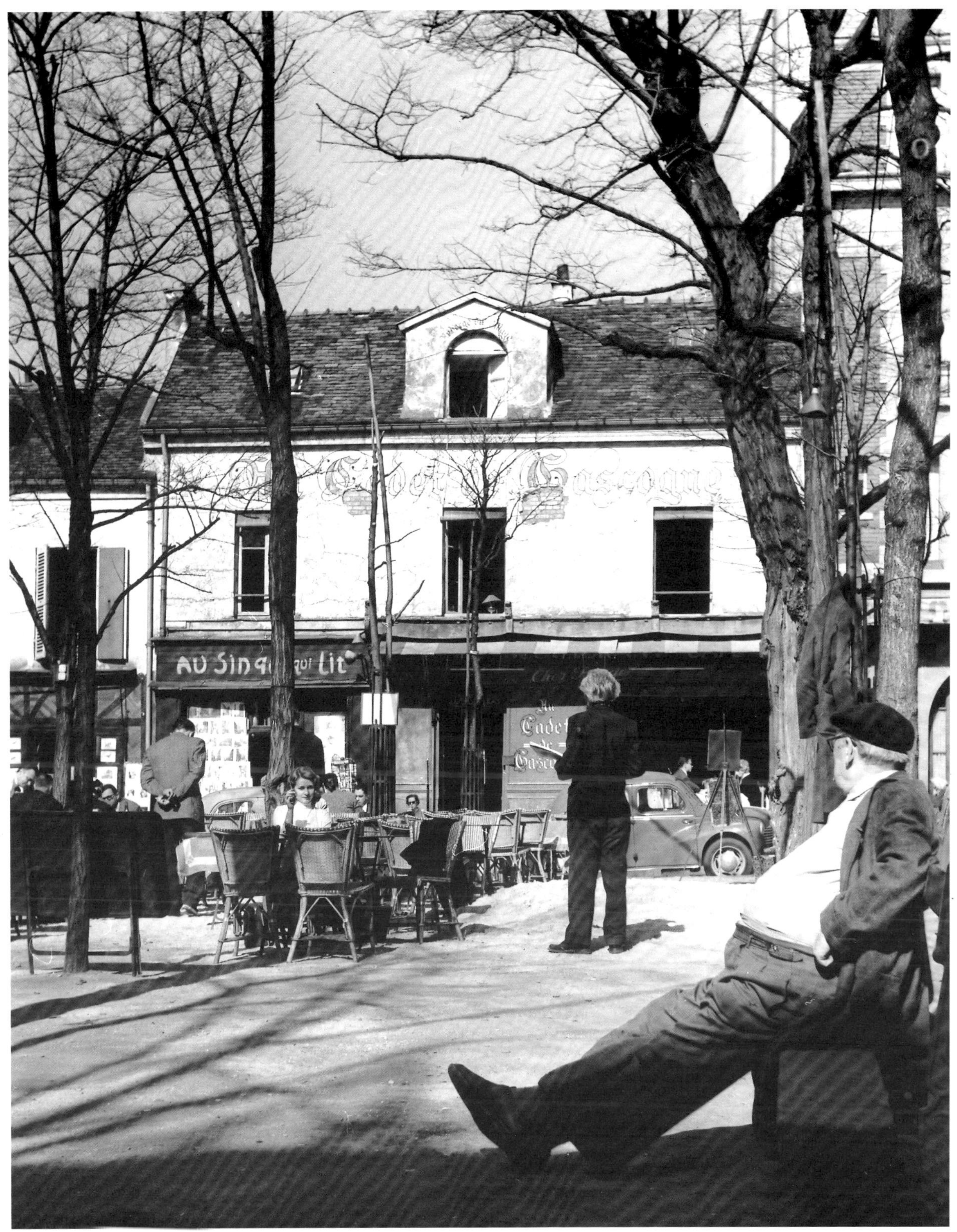

20

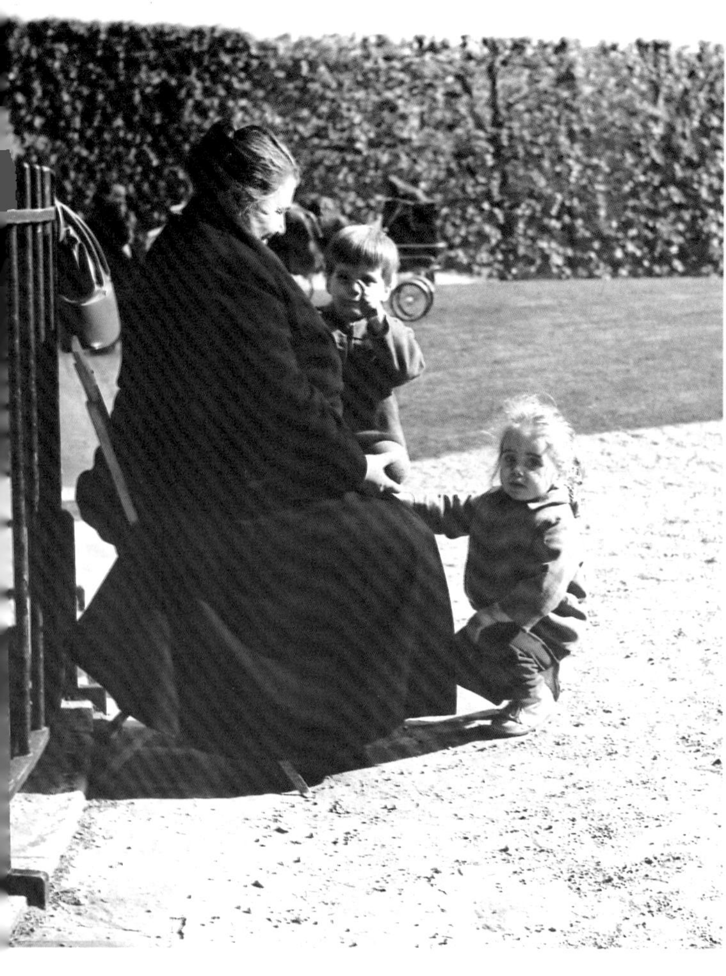

21

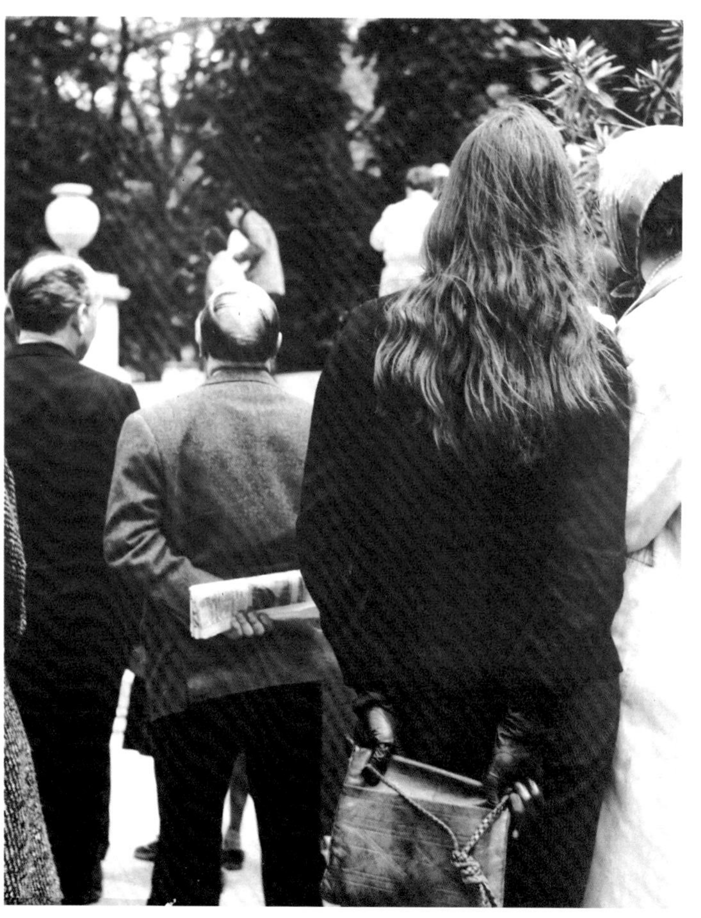

22

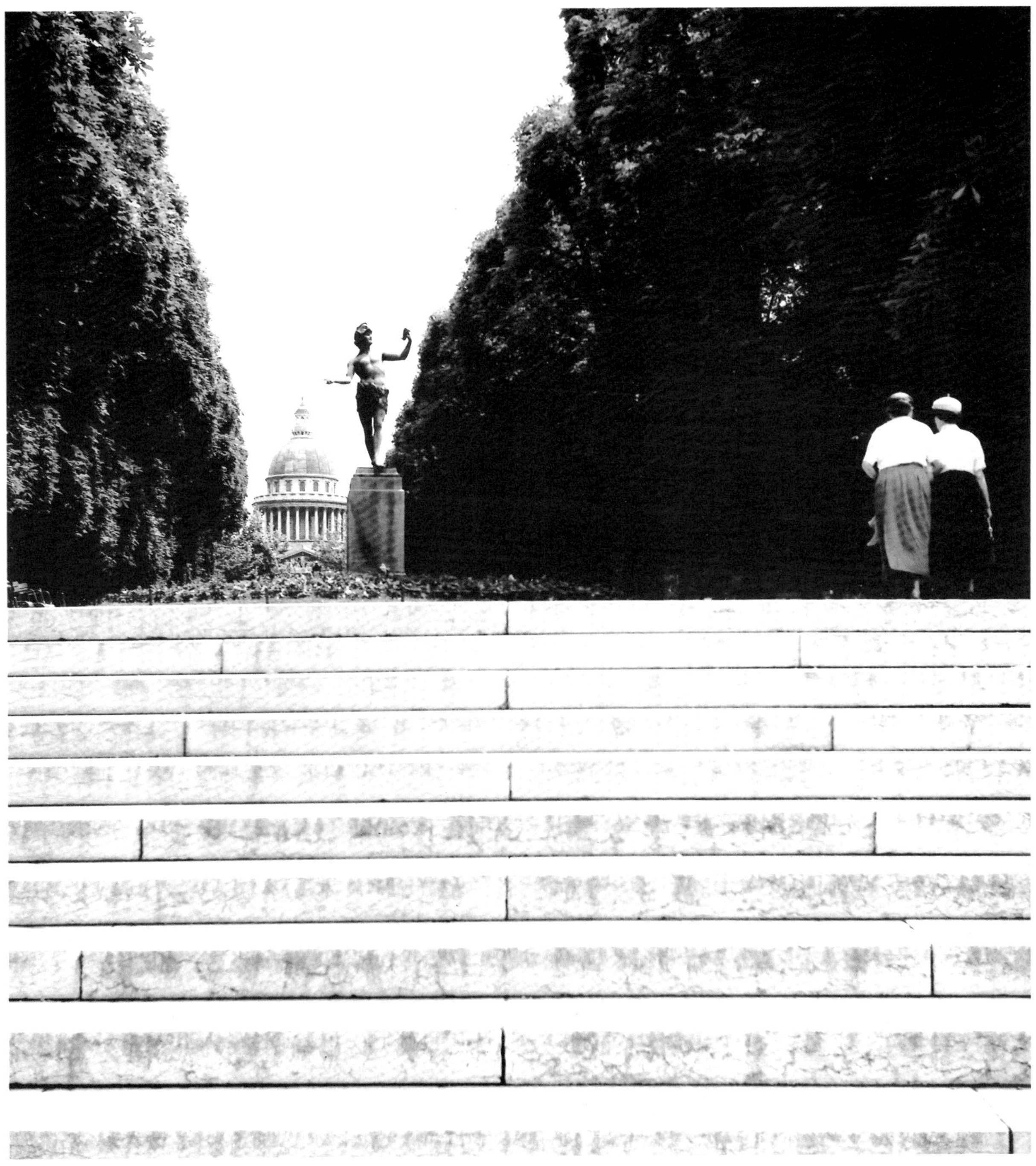

23

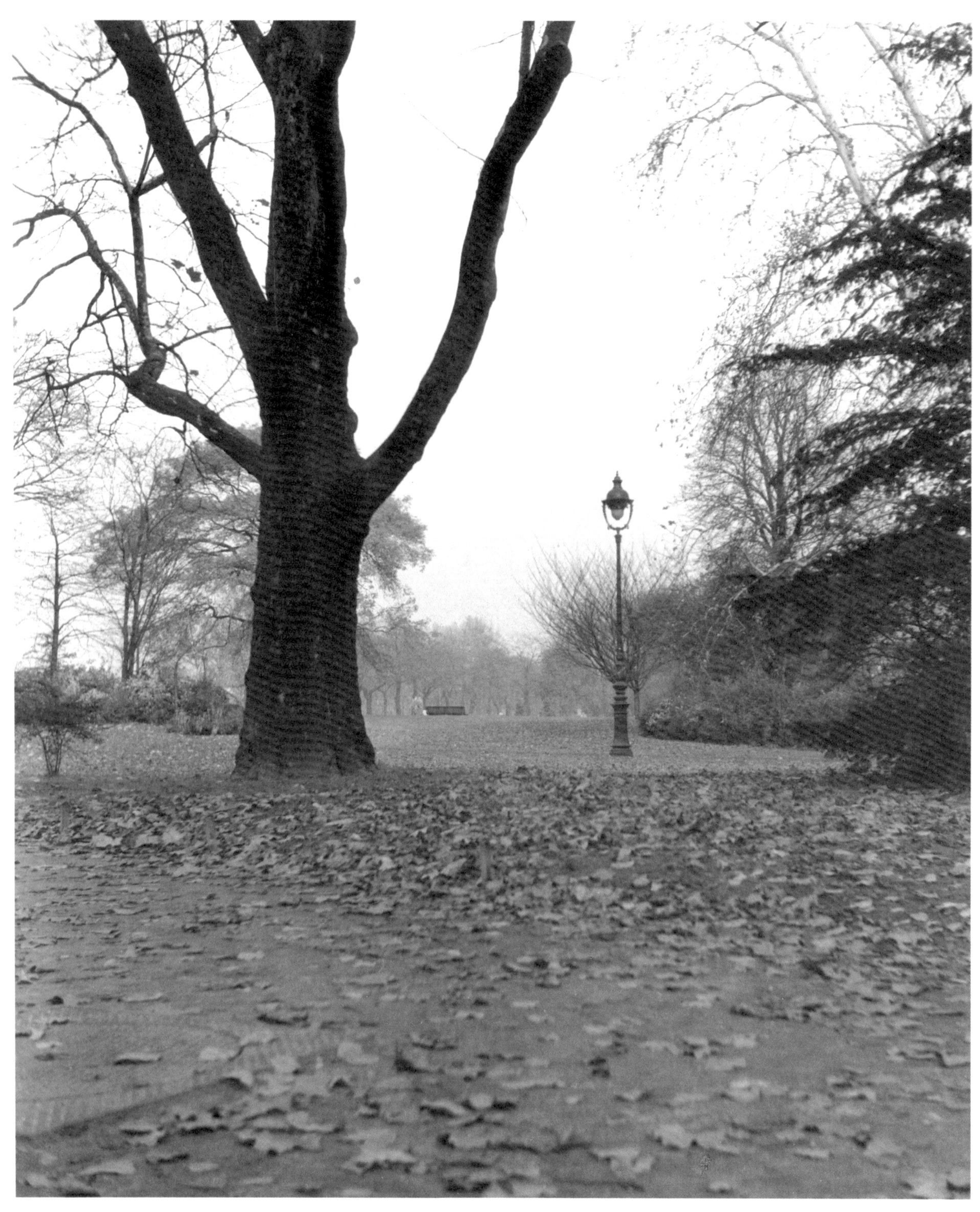

24

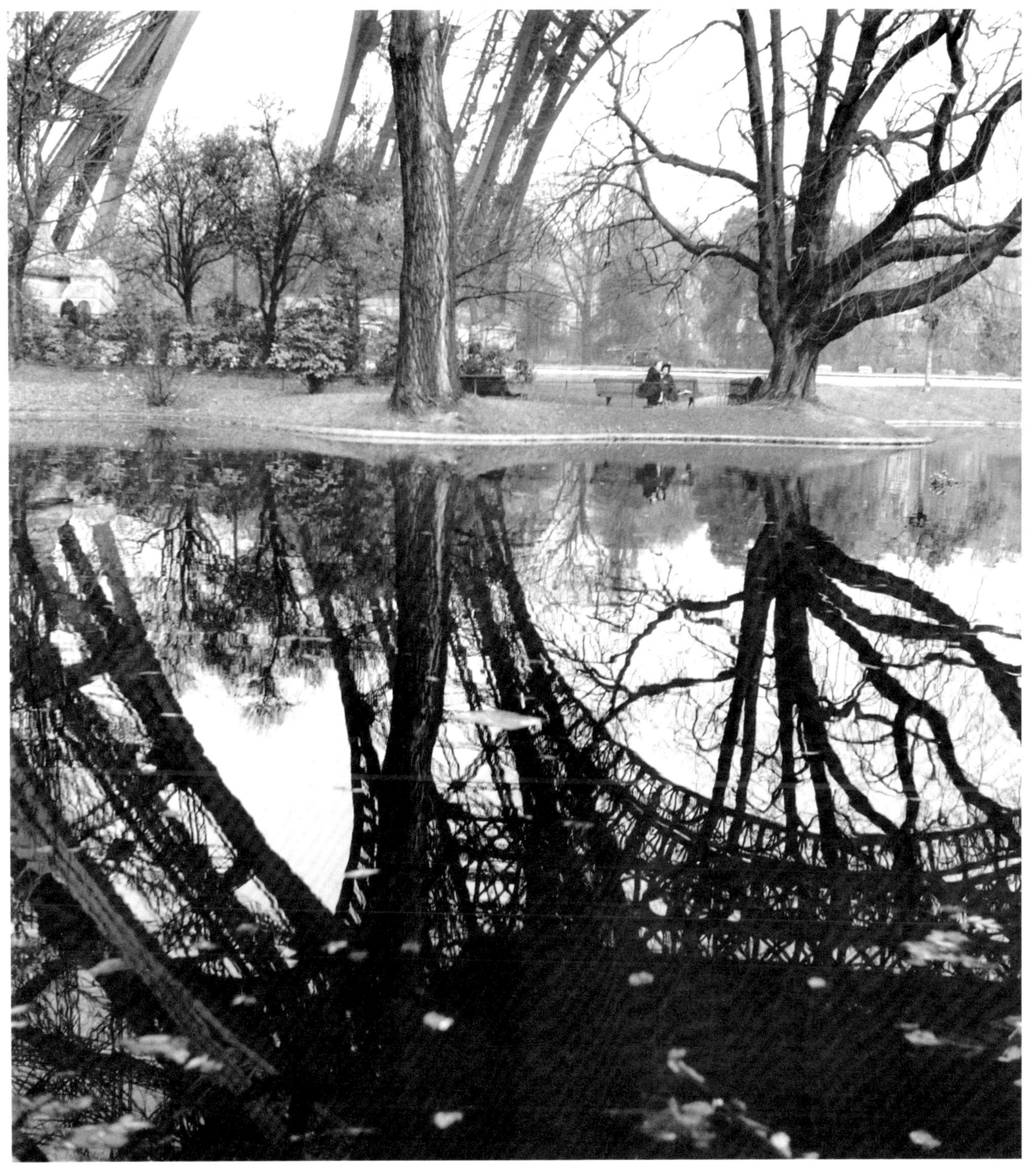

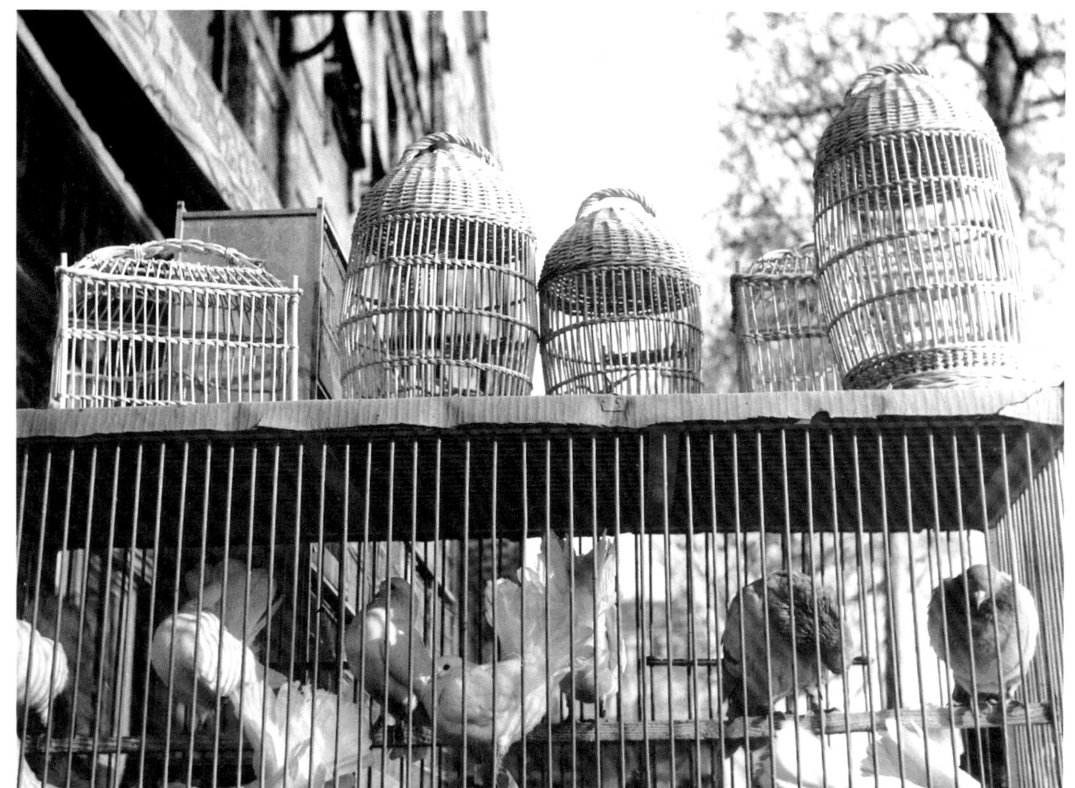

26

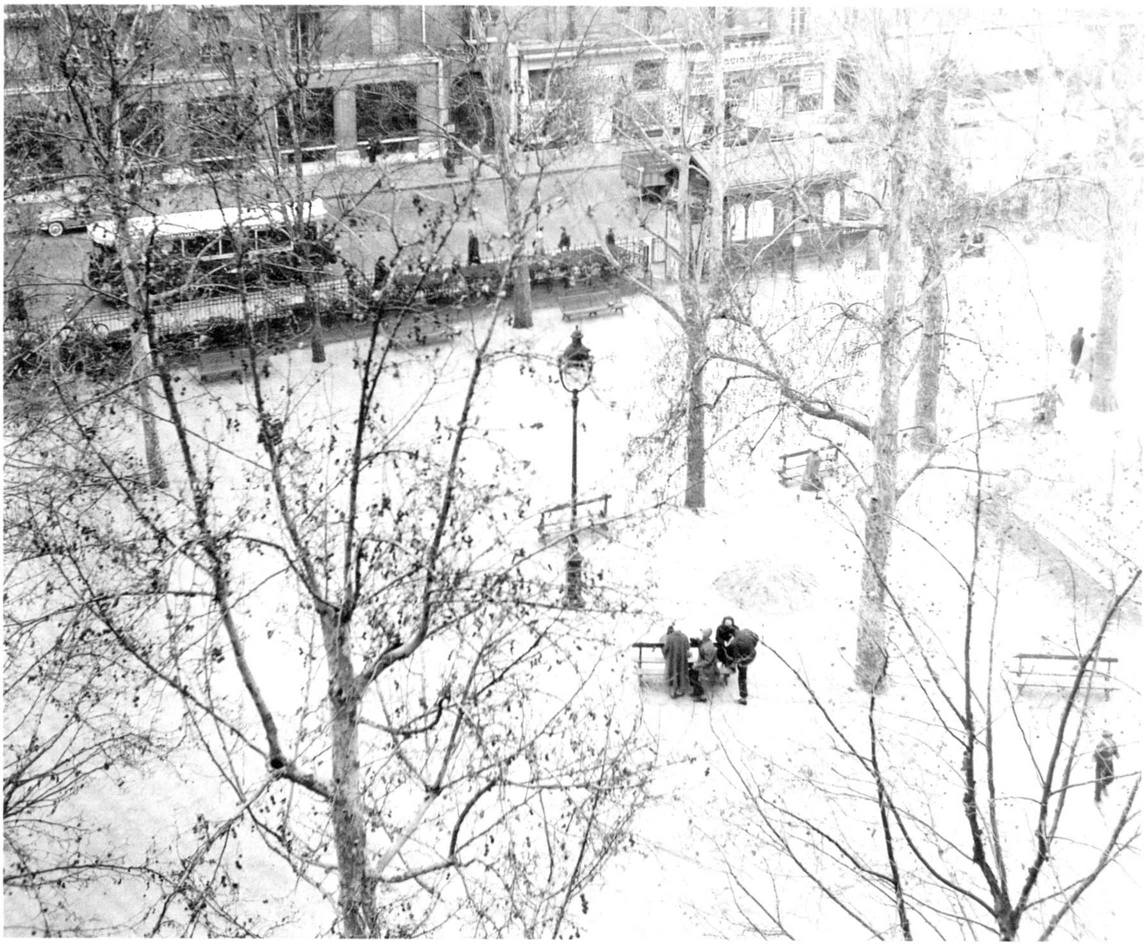

27

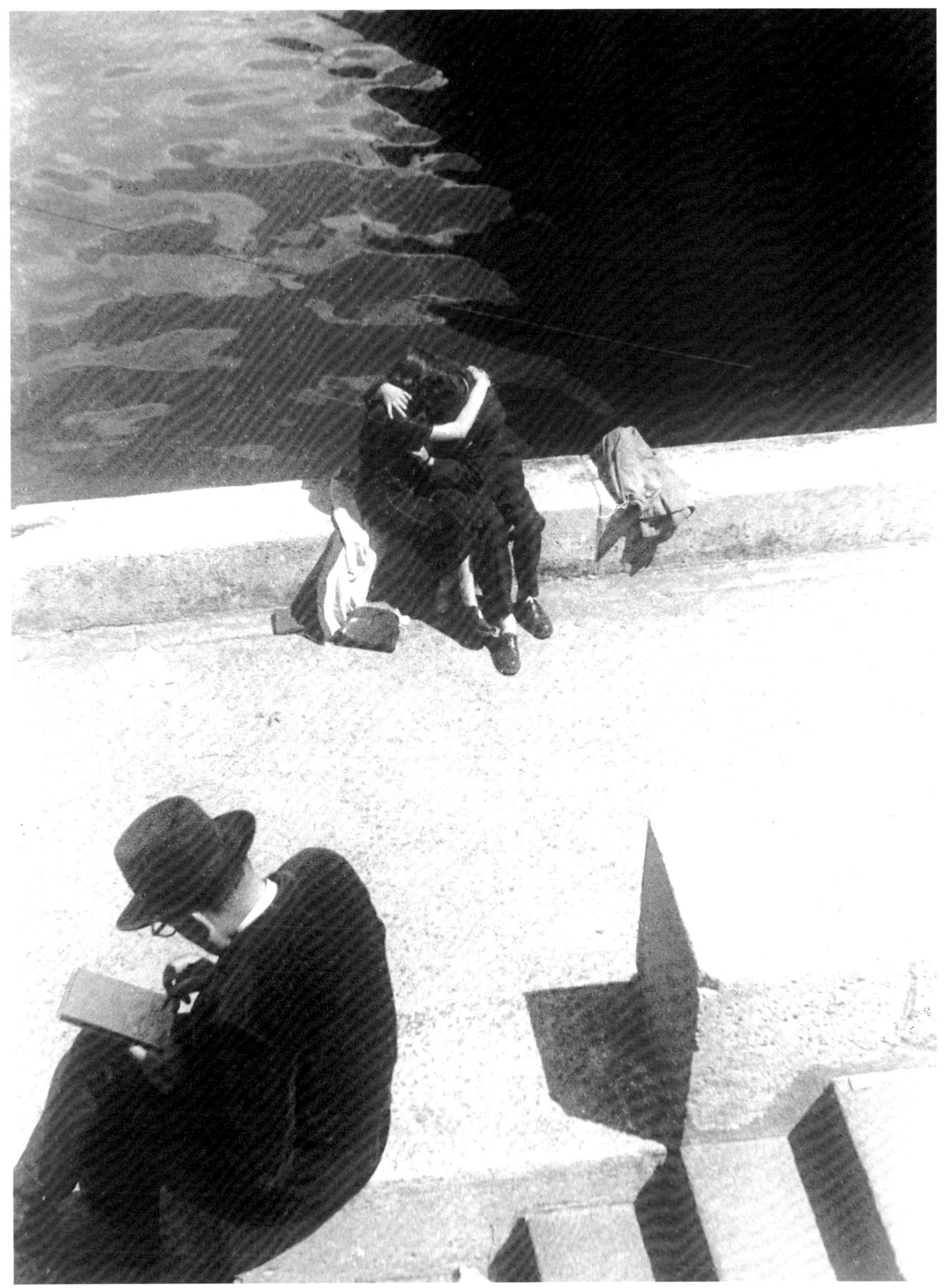

28

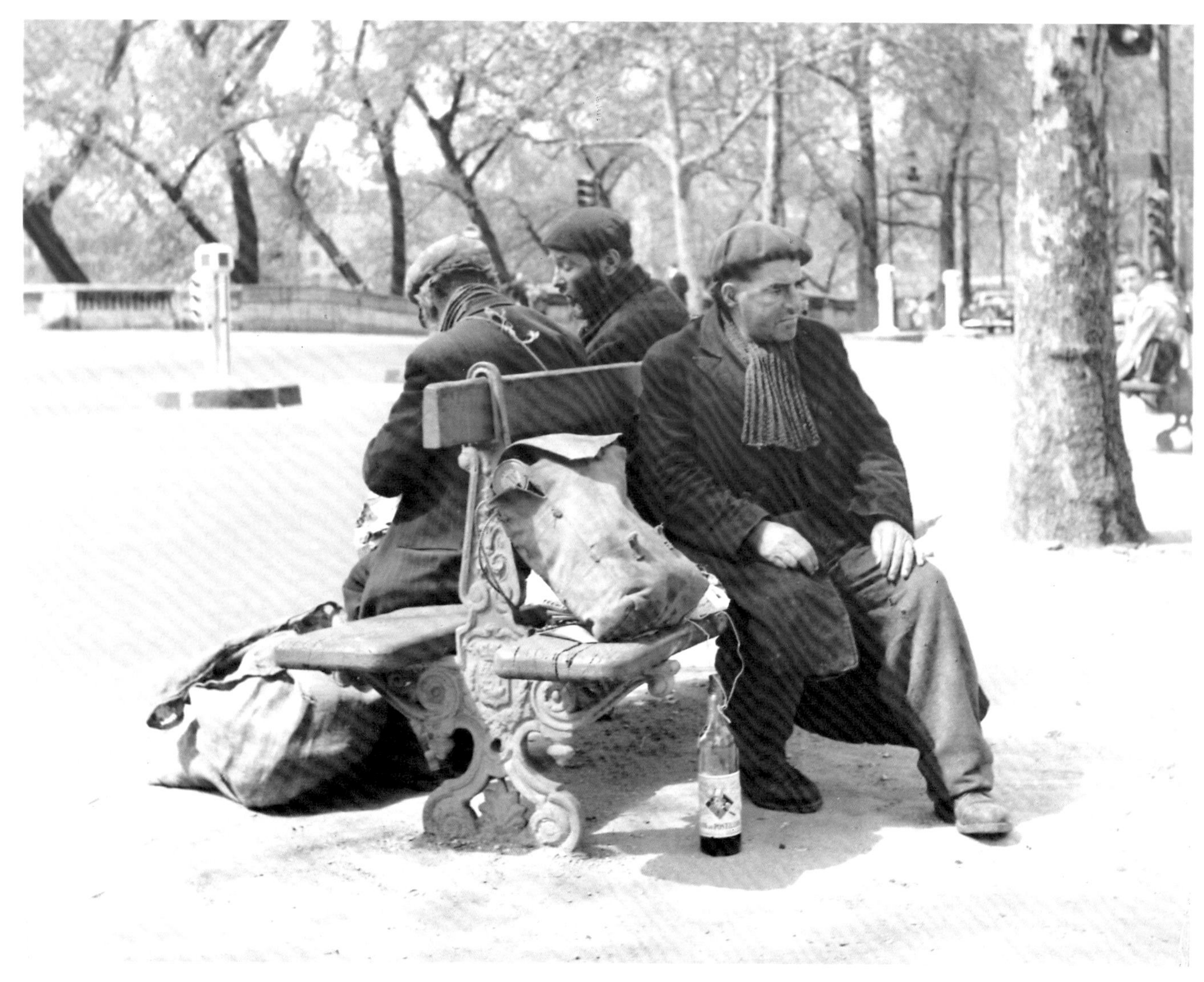

29

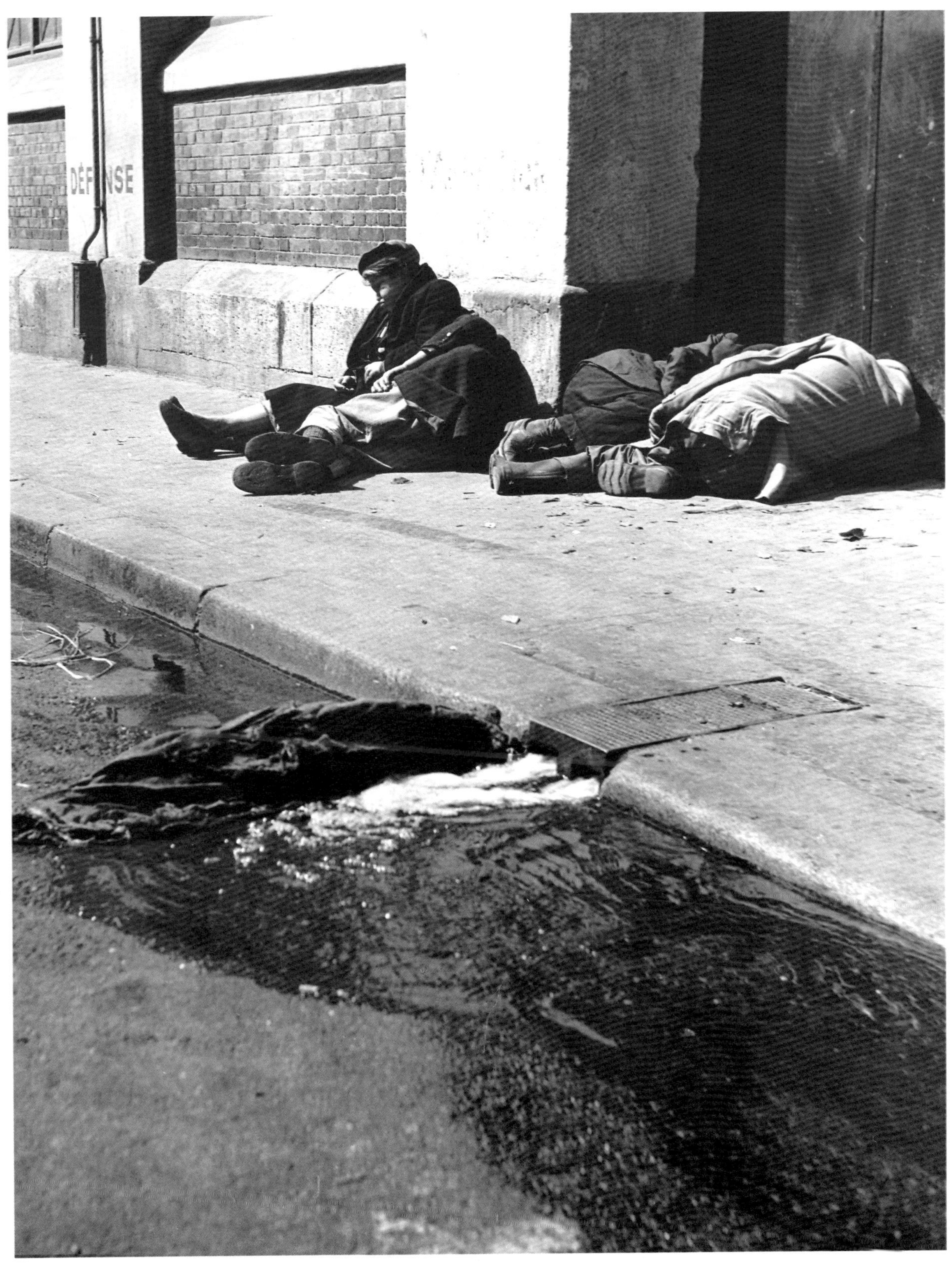

30

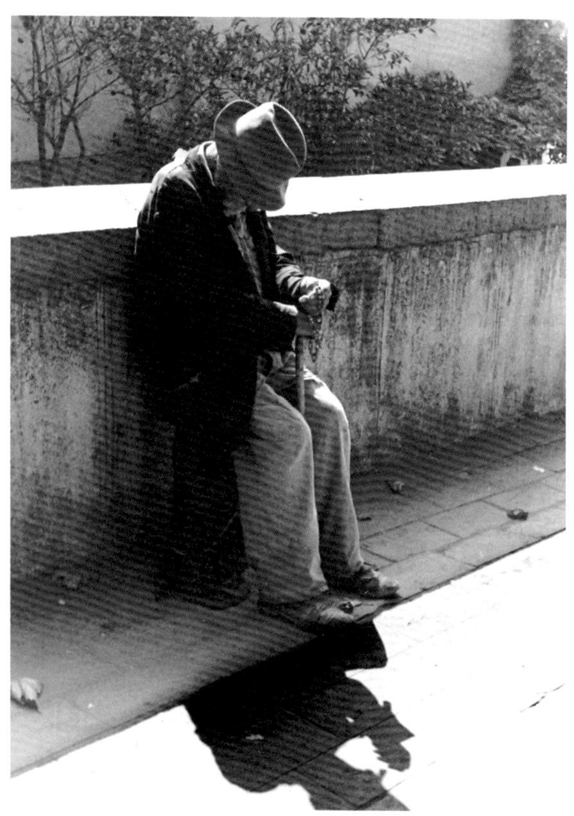

31

32

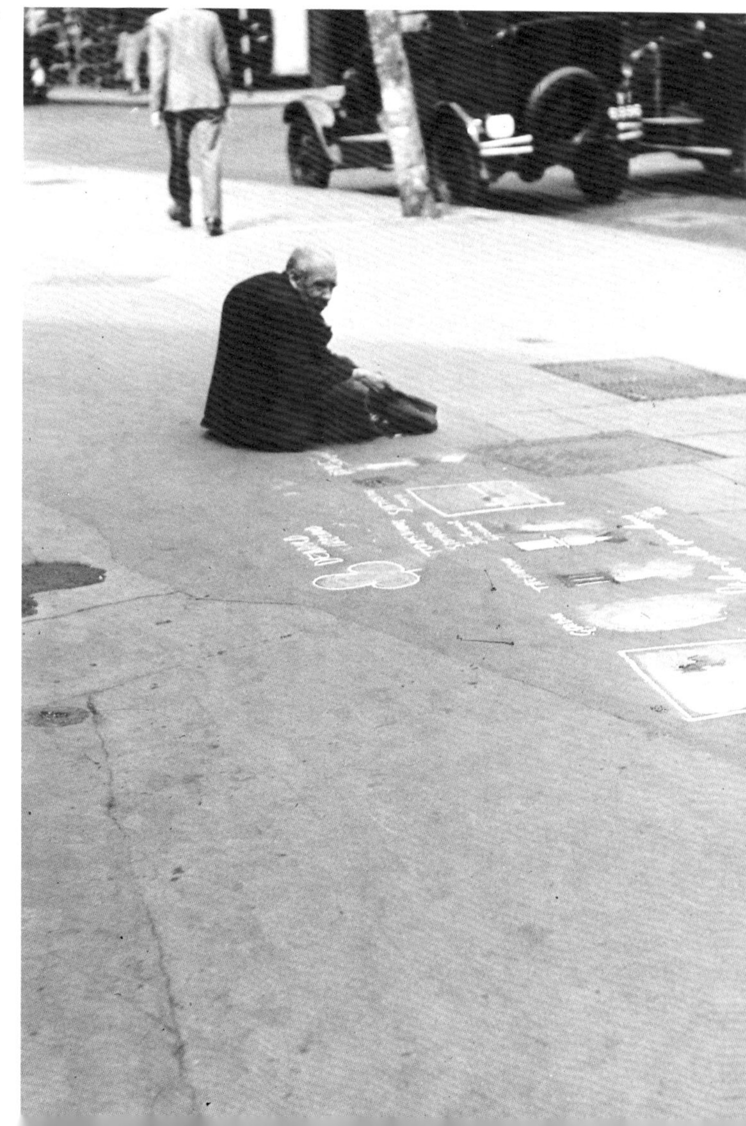

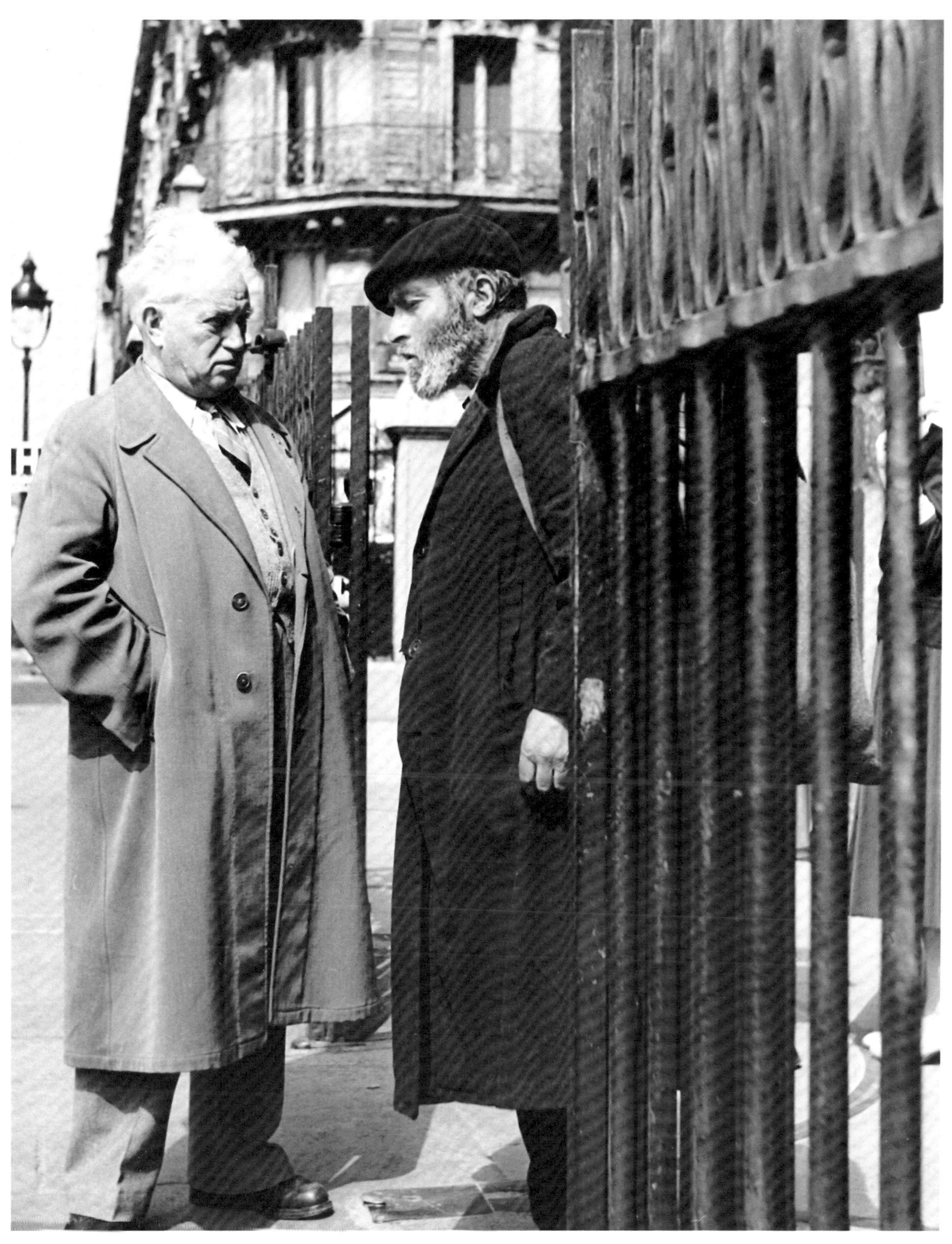

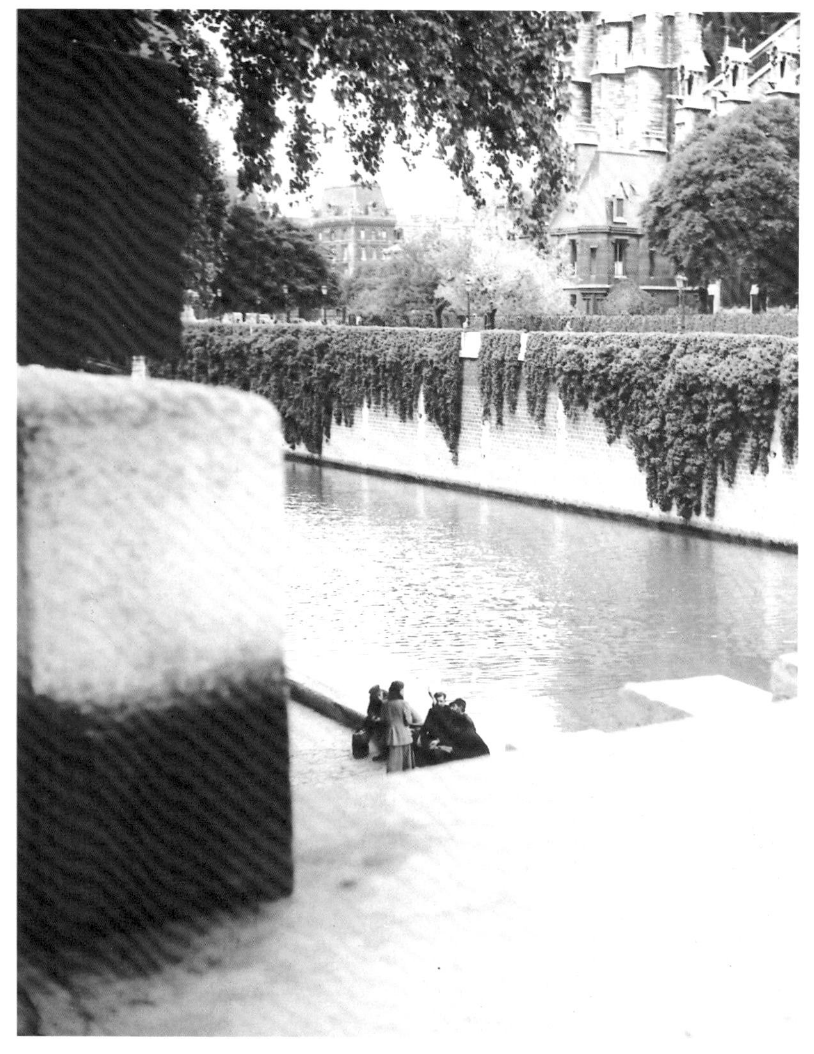

34

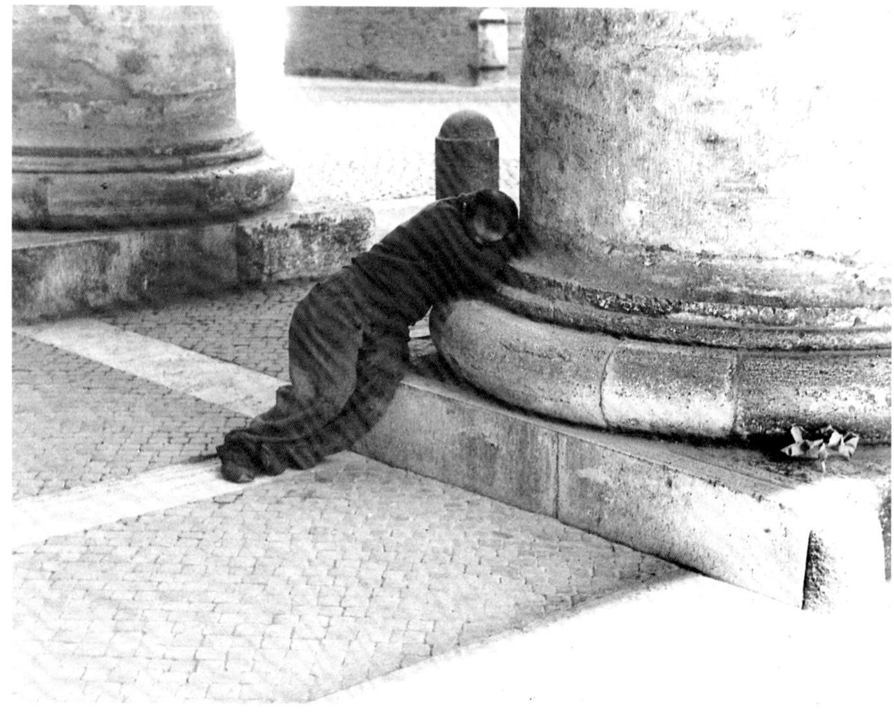

35

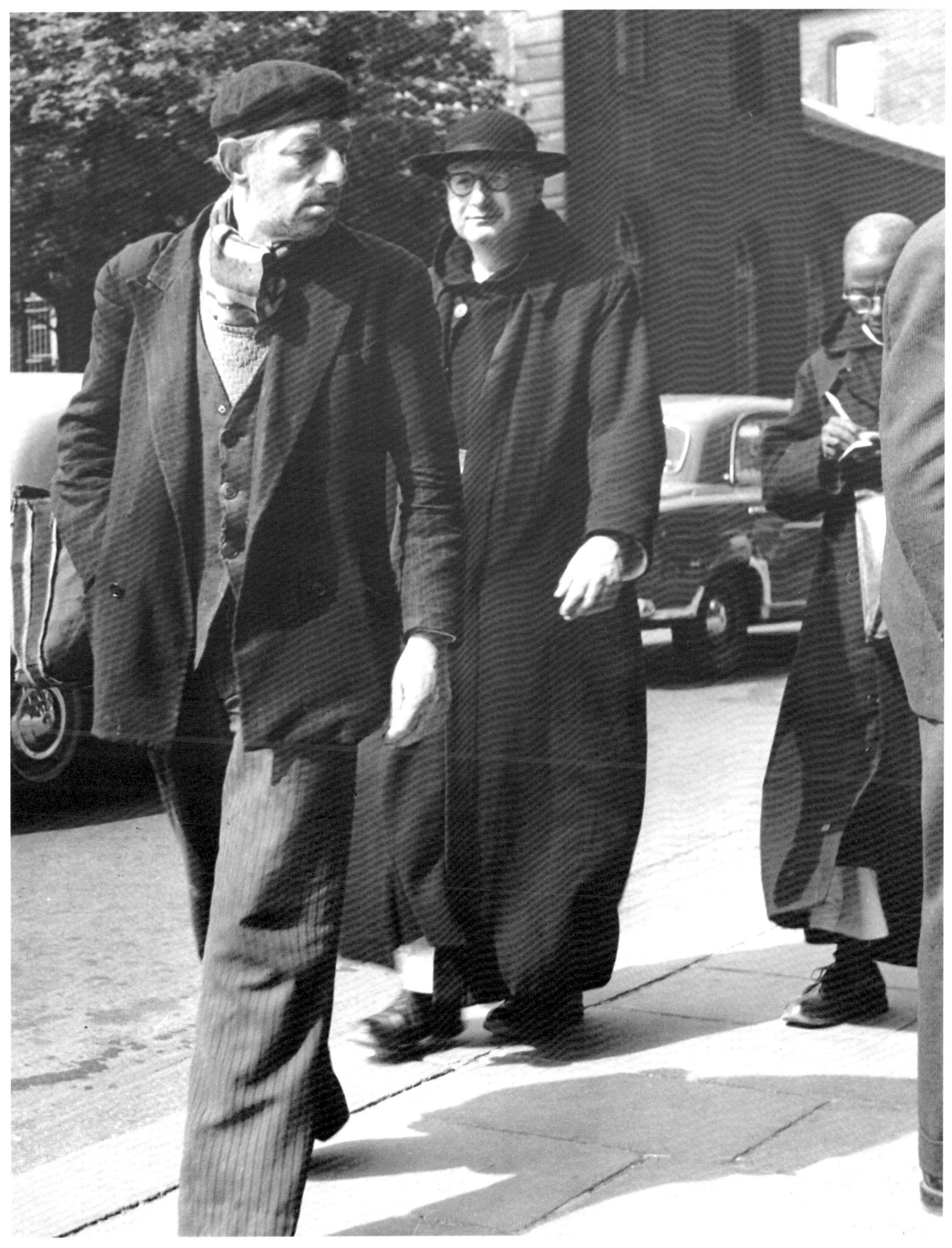

36

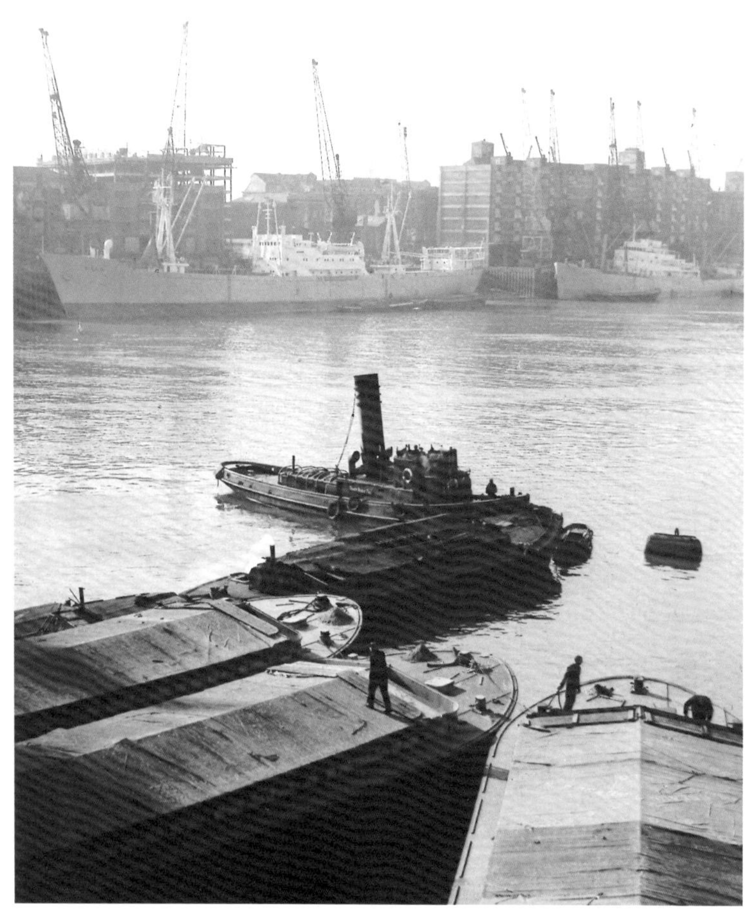

37

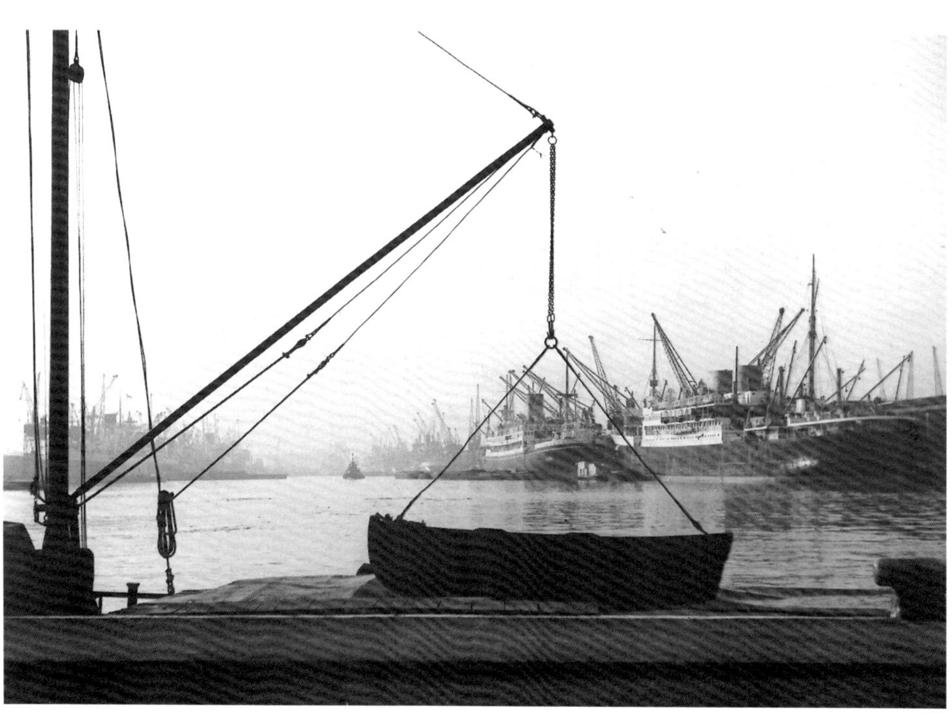

38

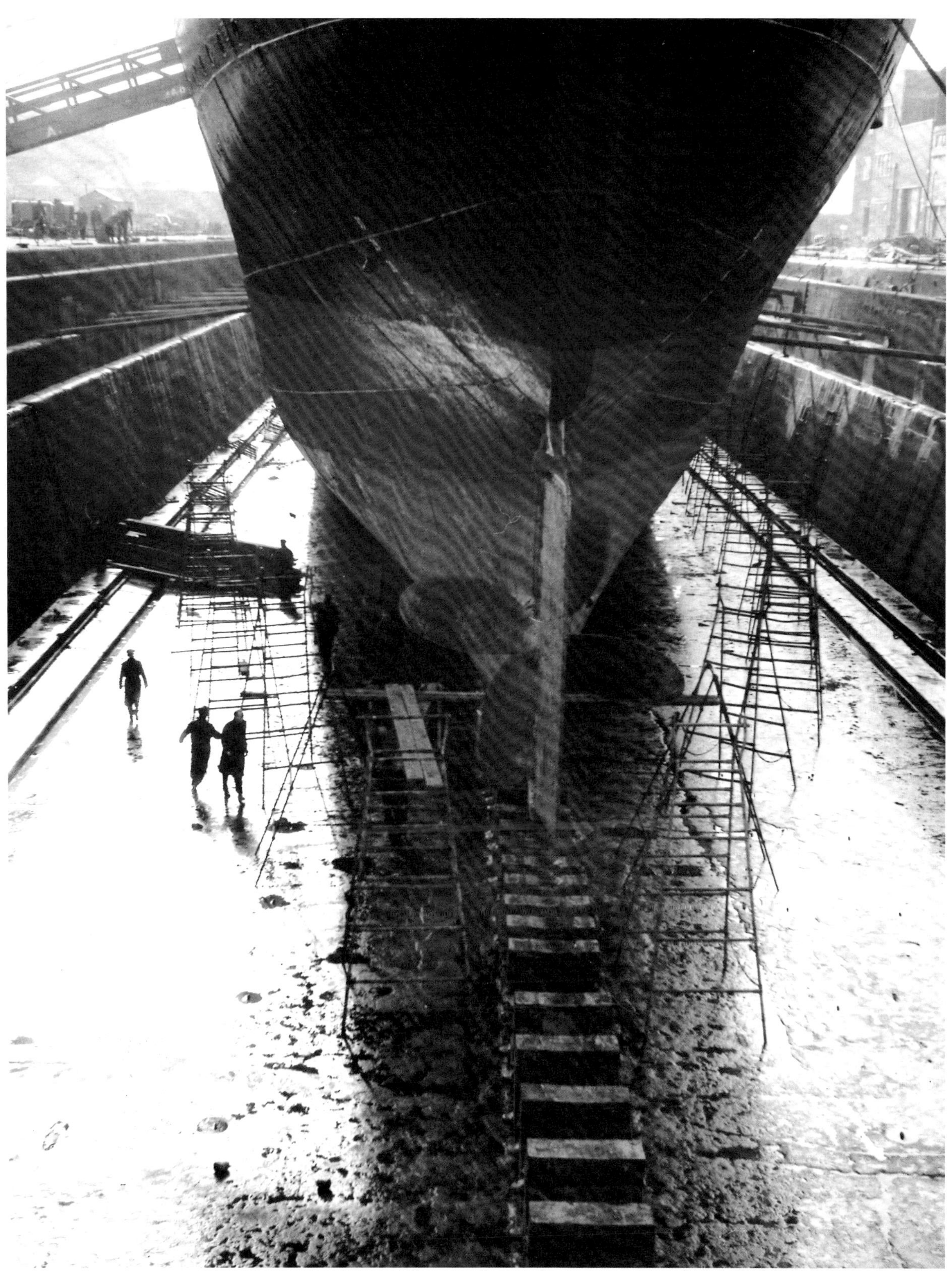

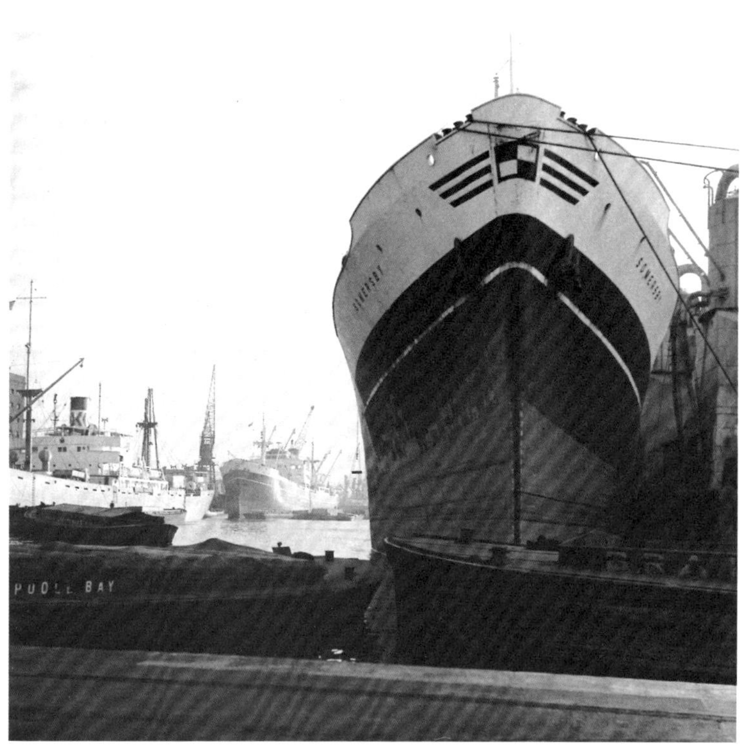

40

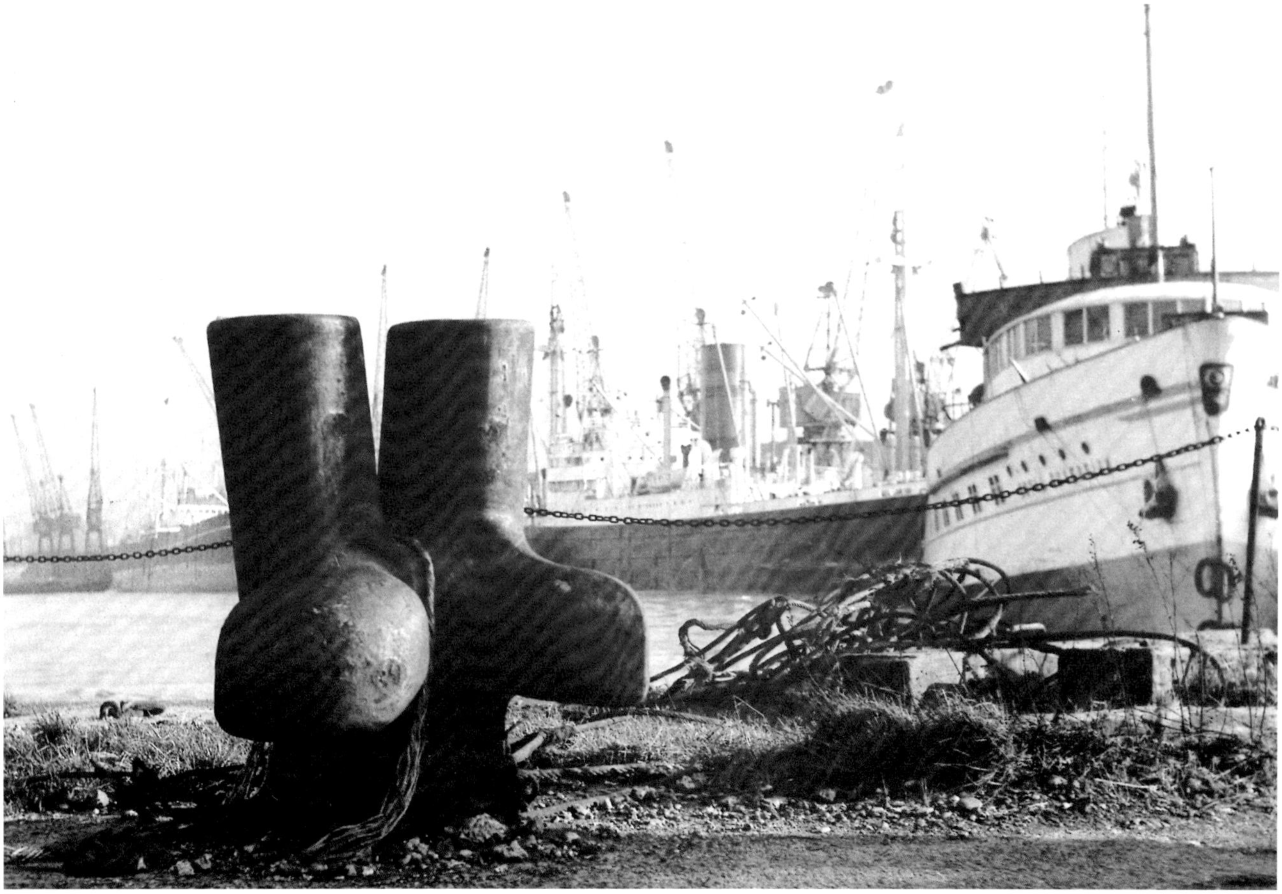

41

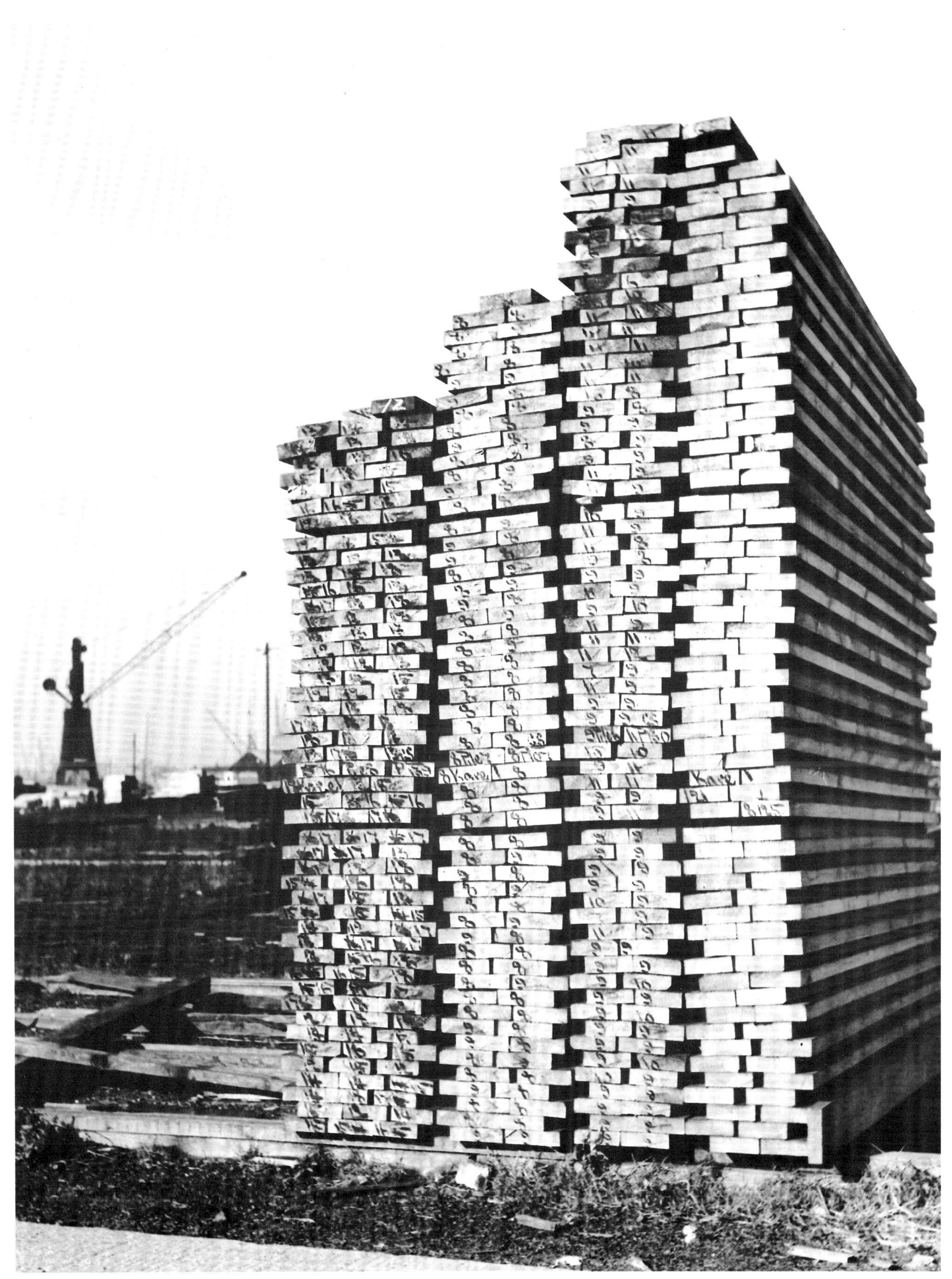

42

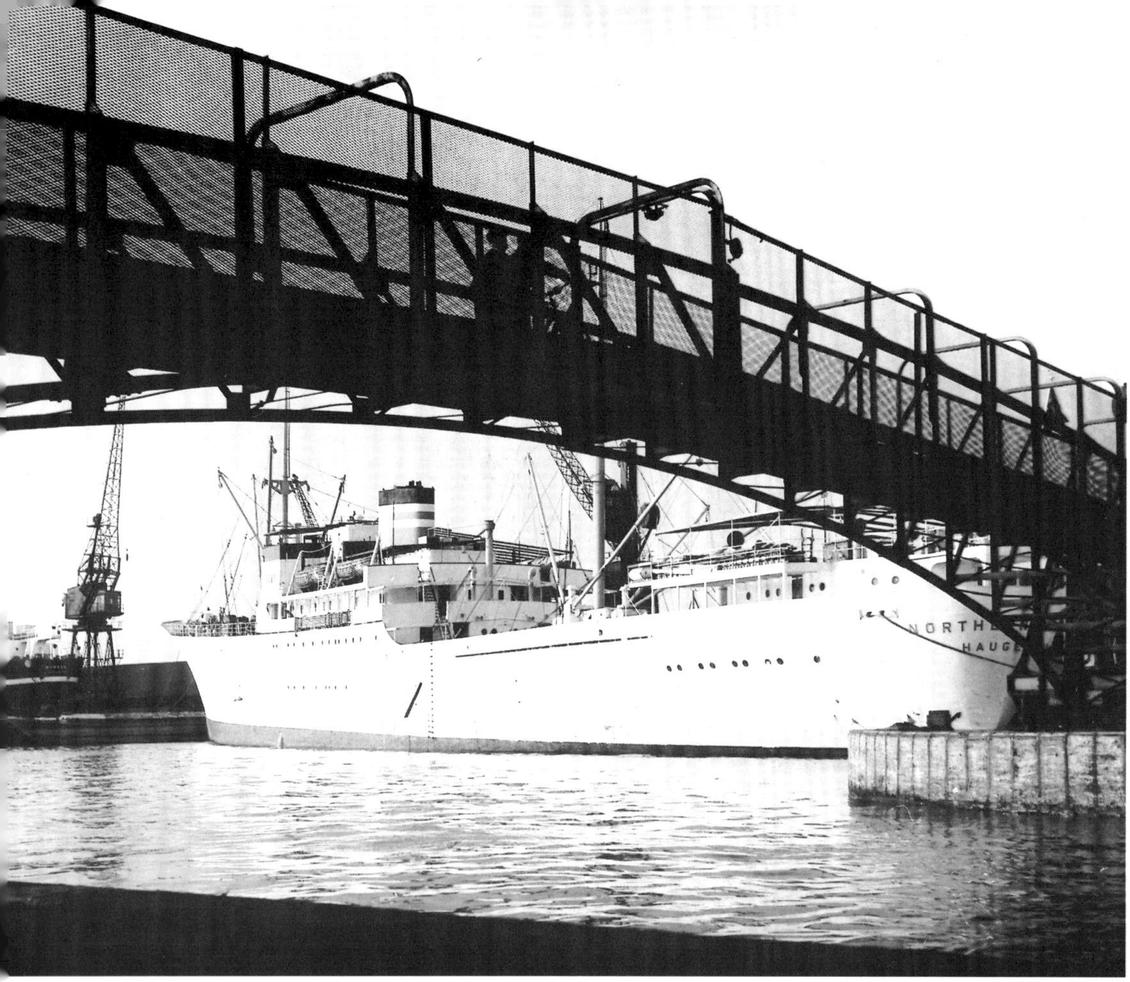

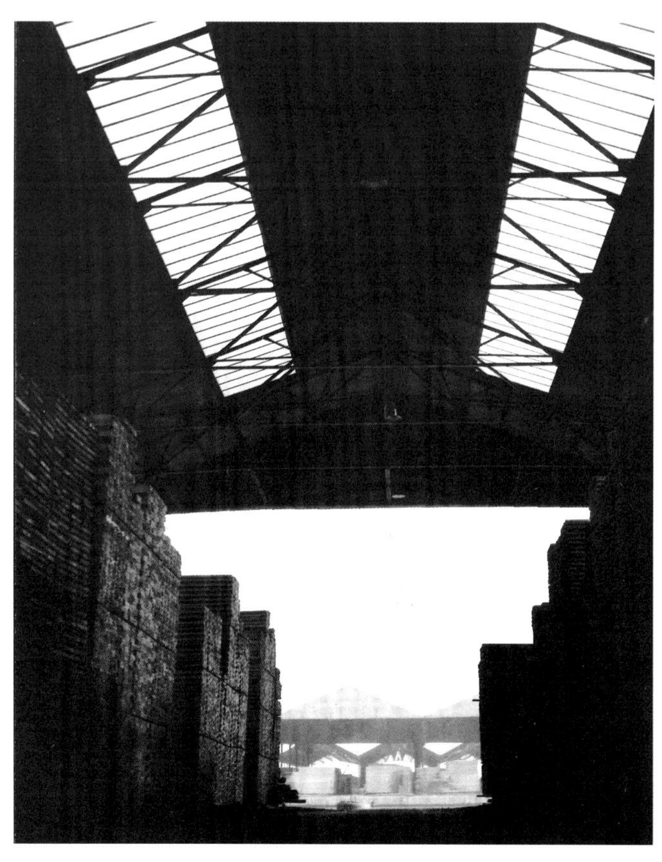

43

44

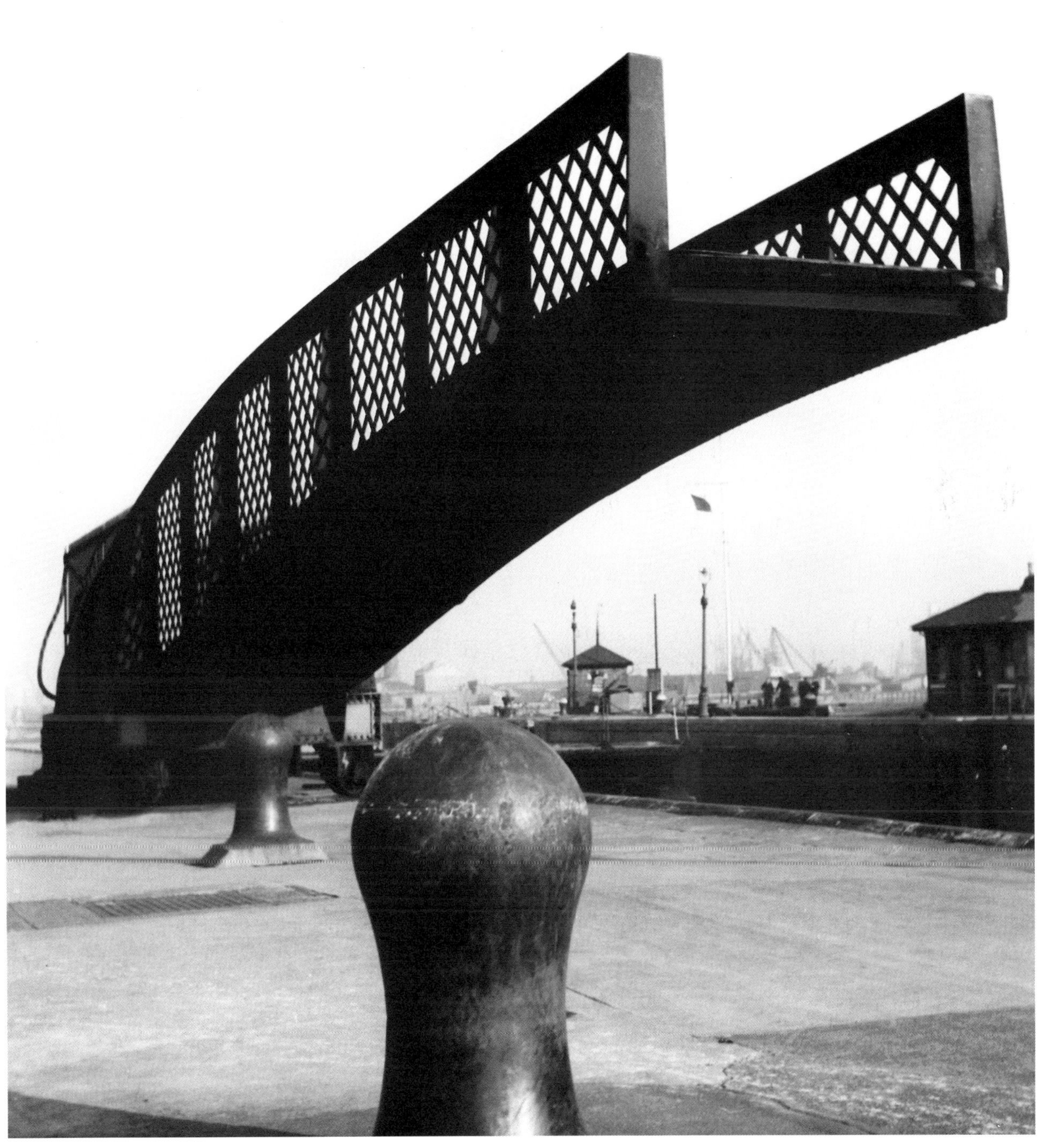

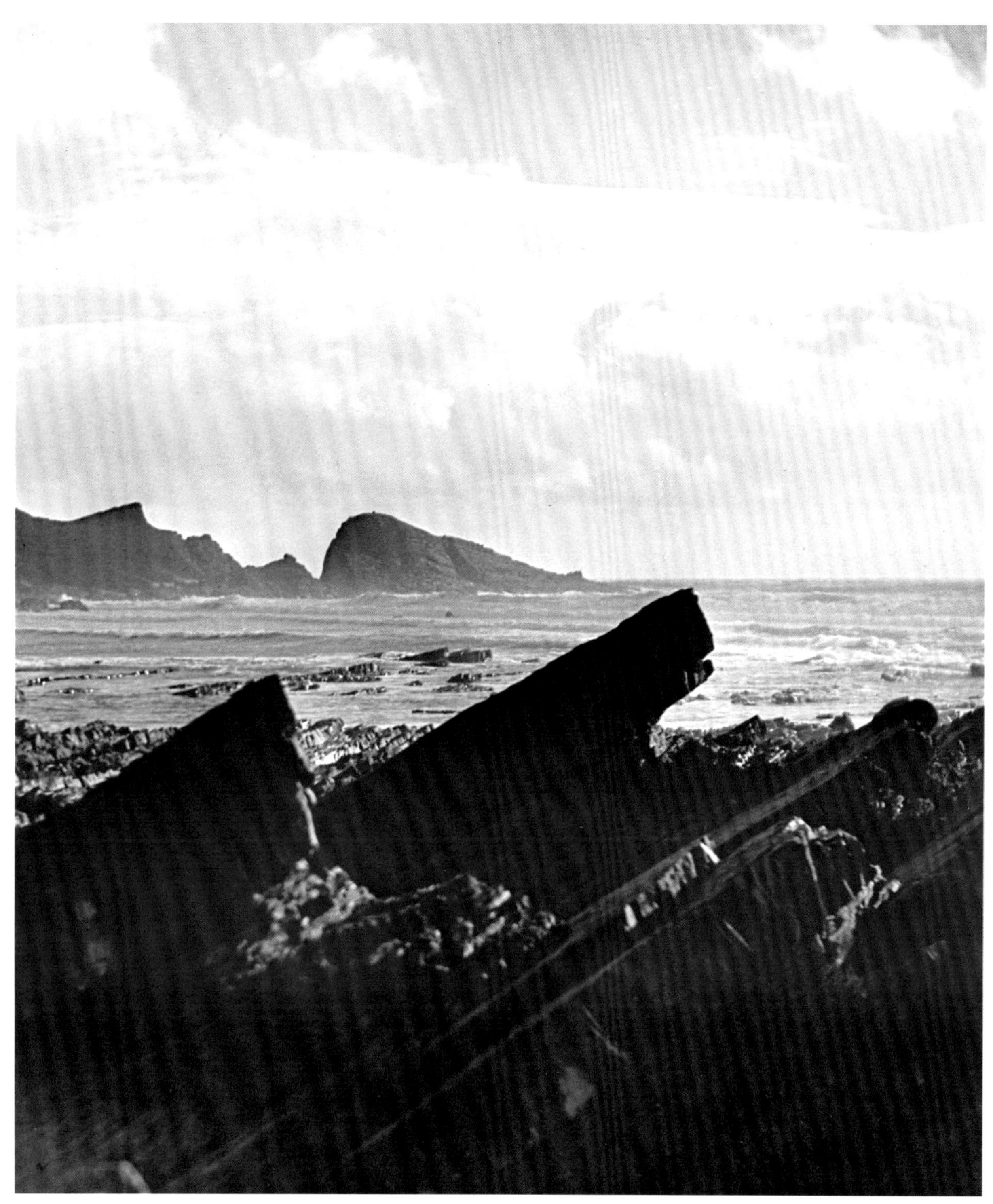

46

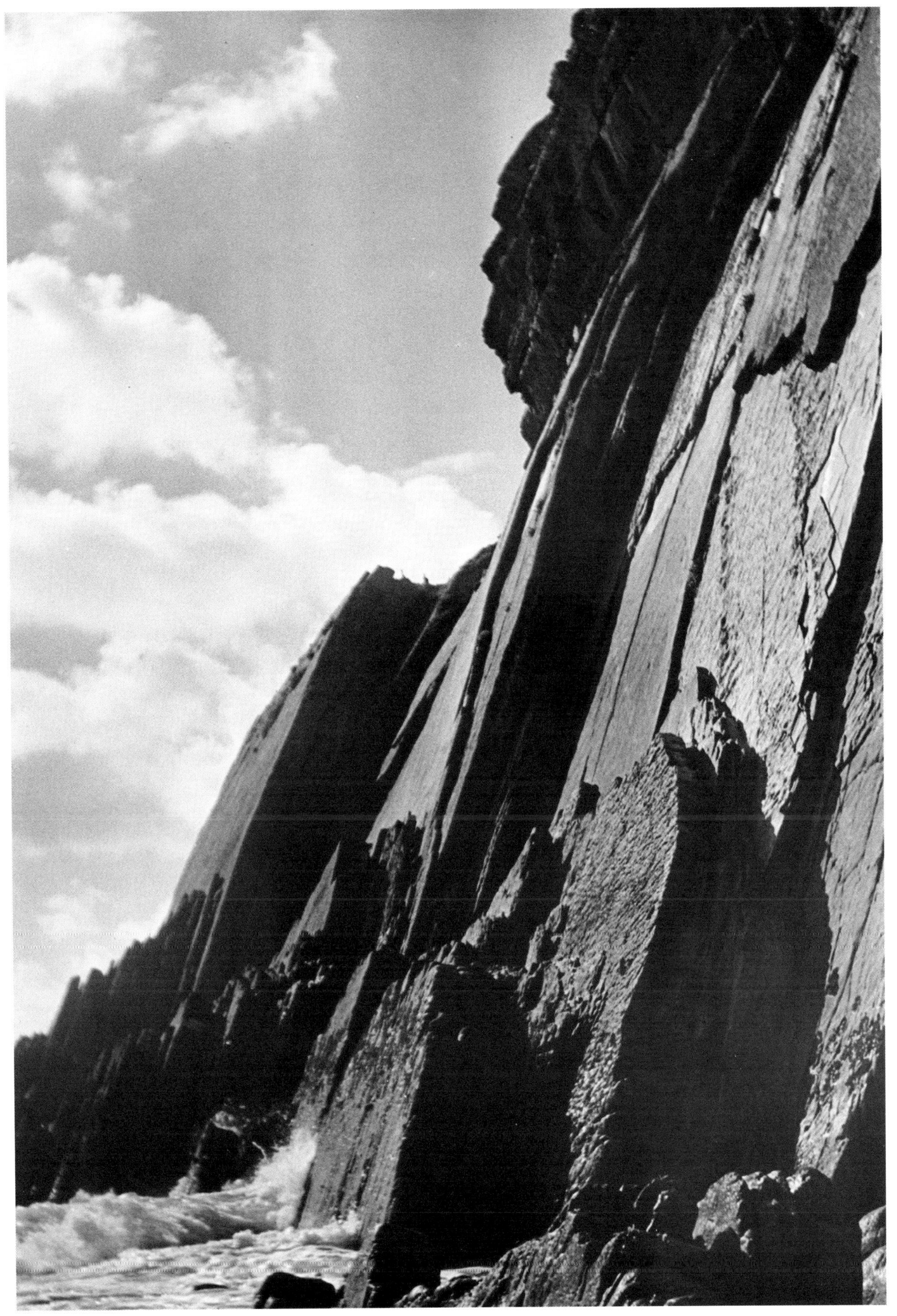

47

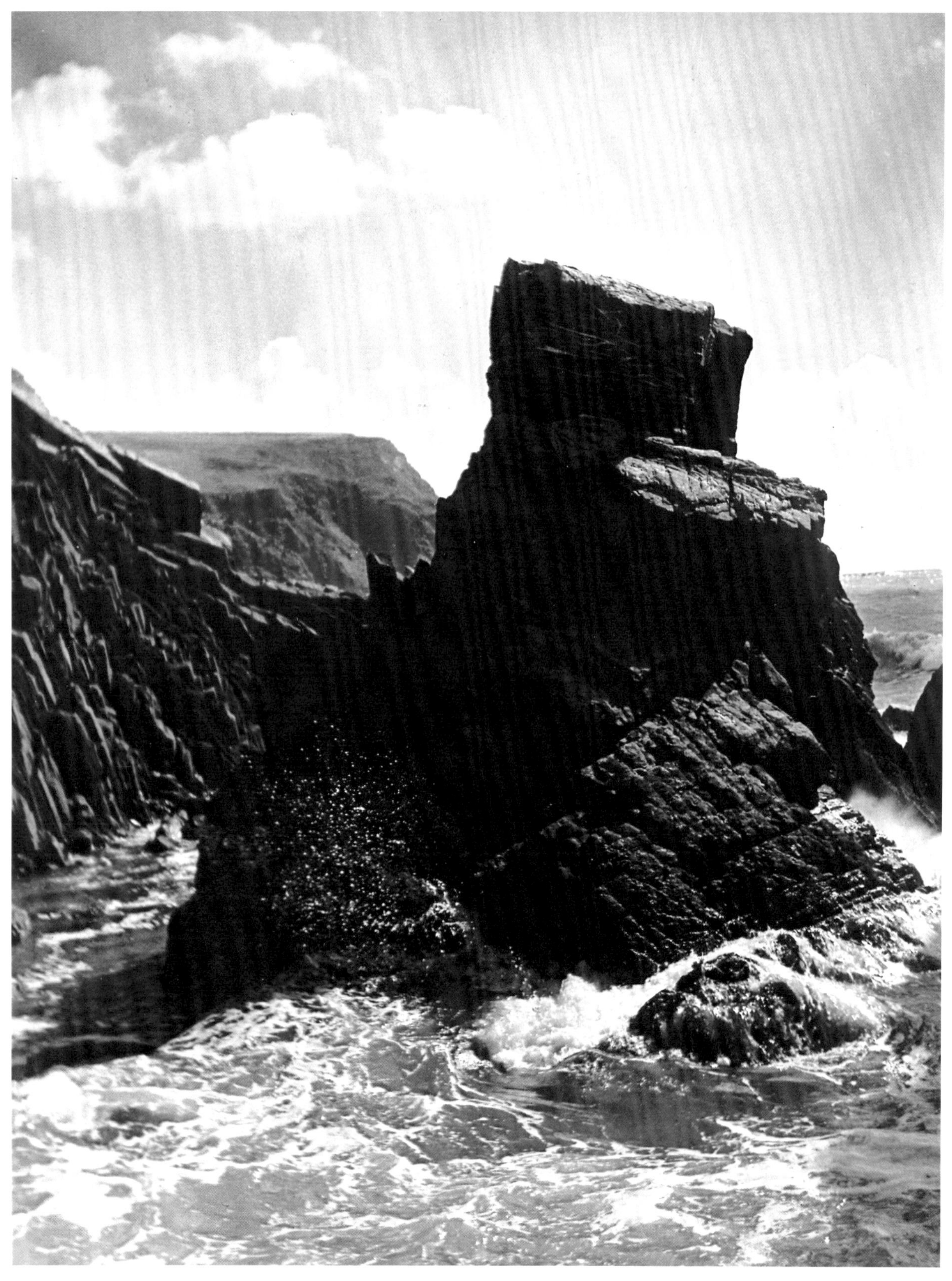

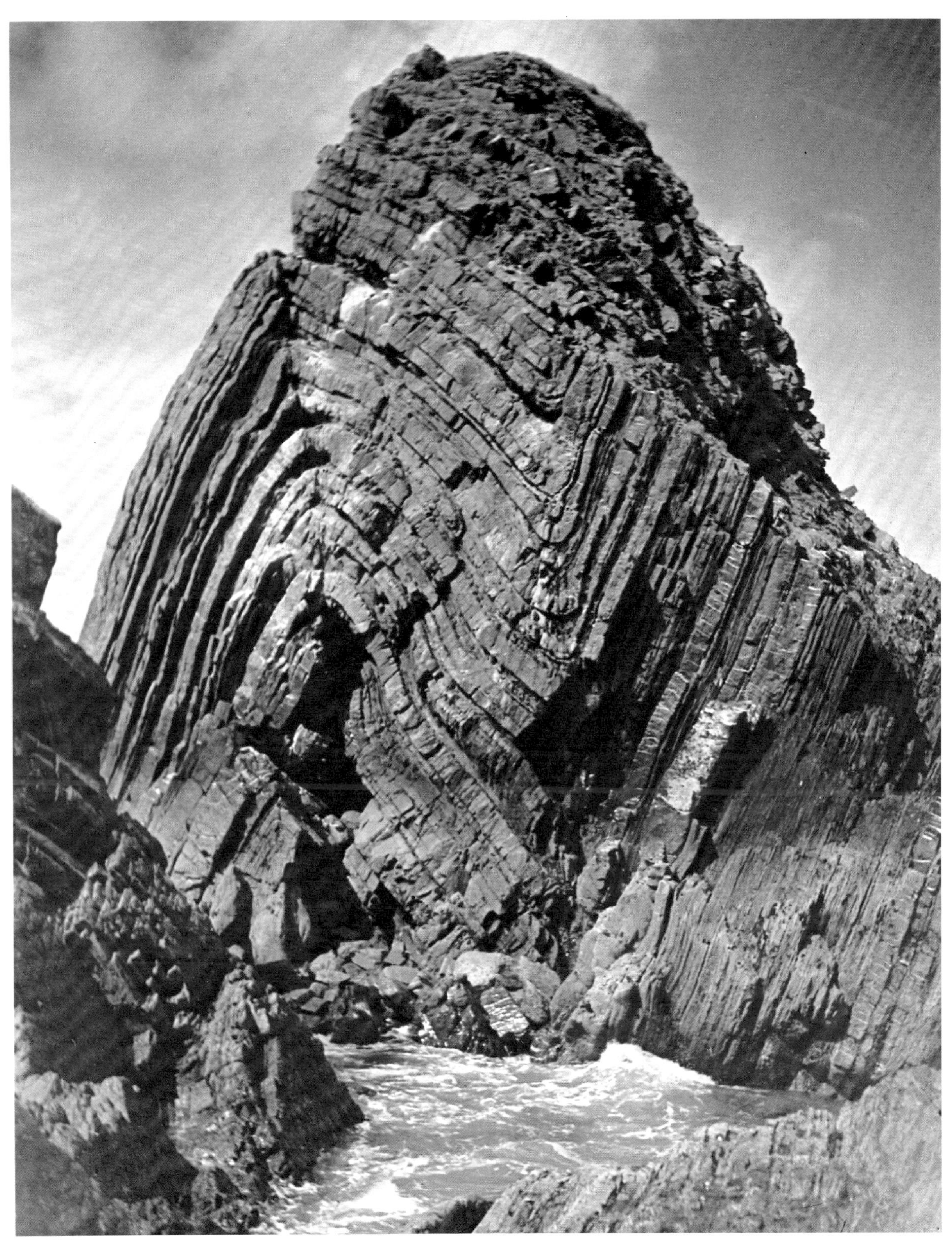

49

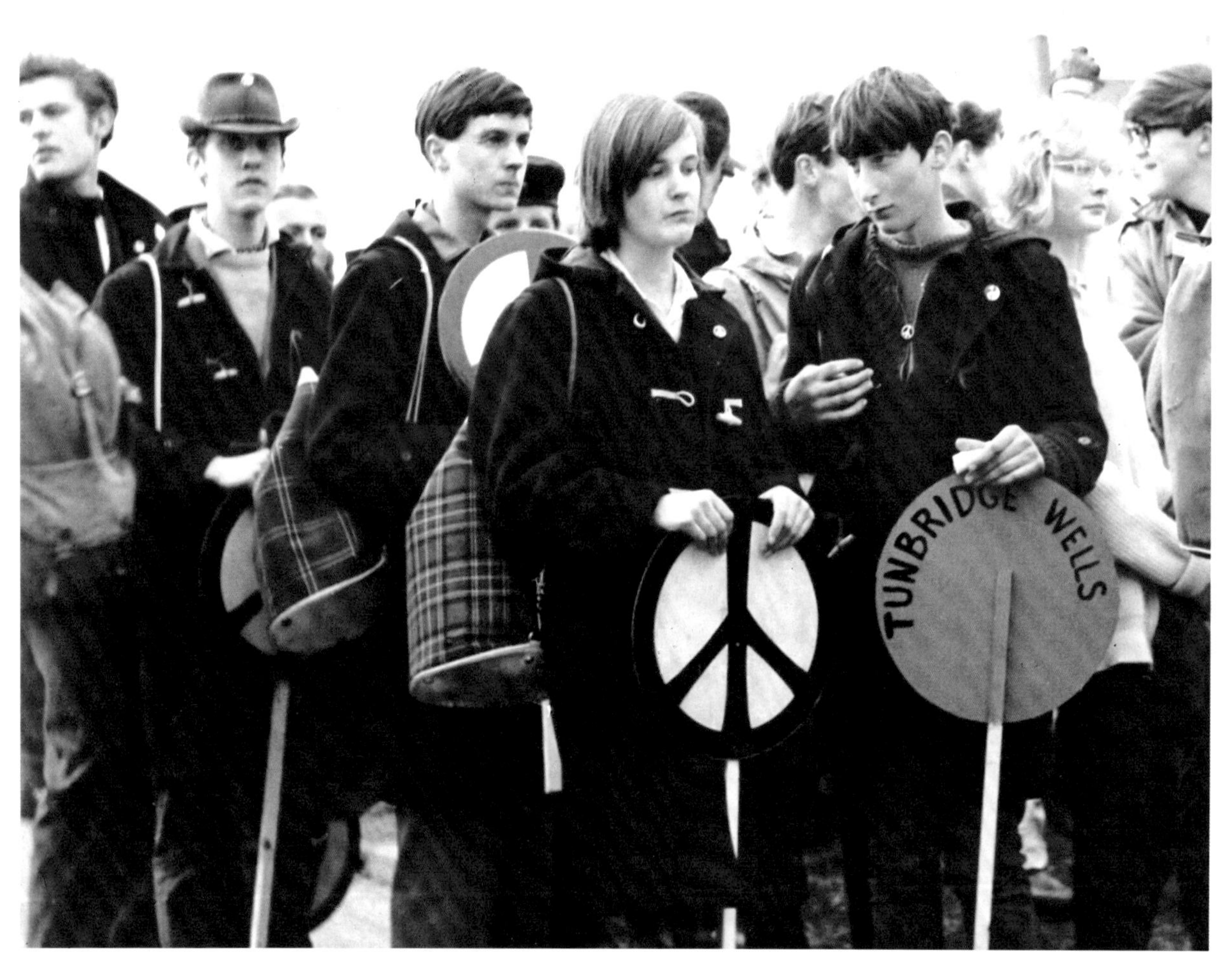

50

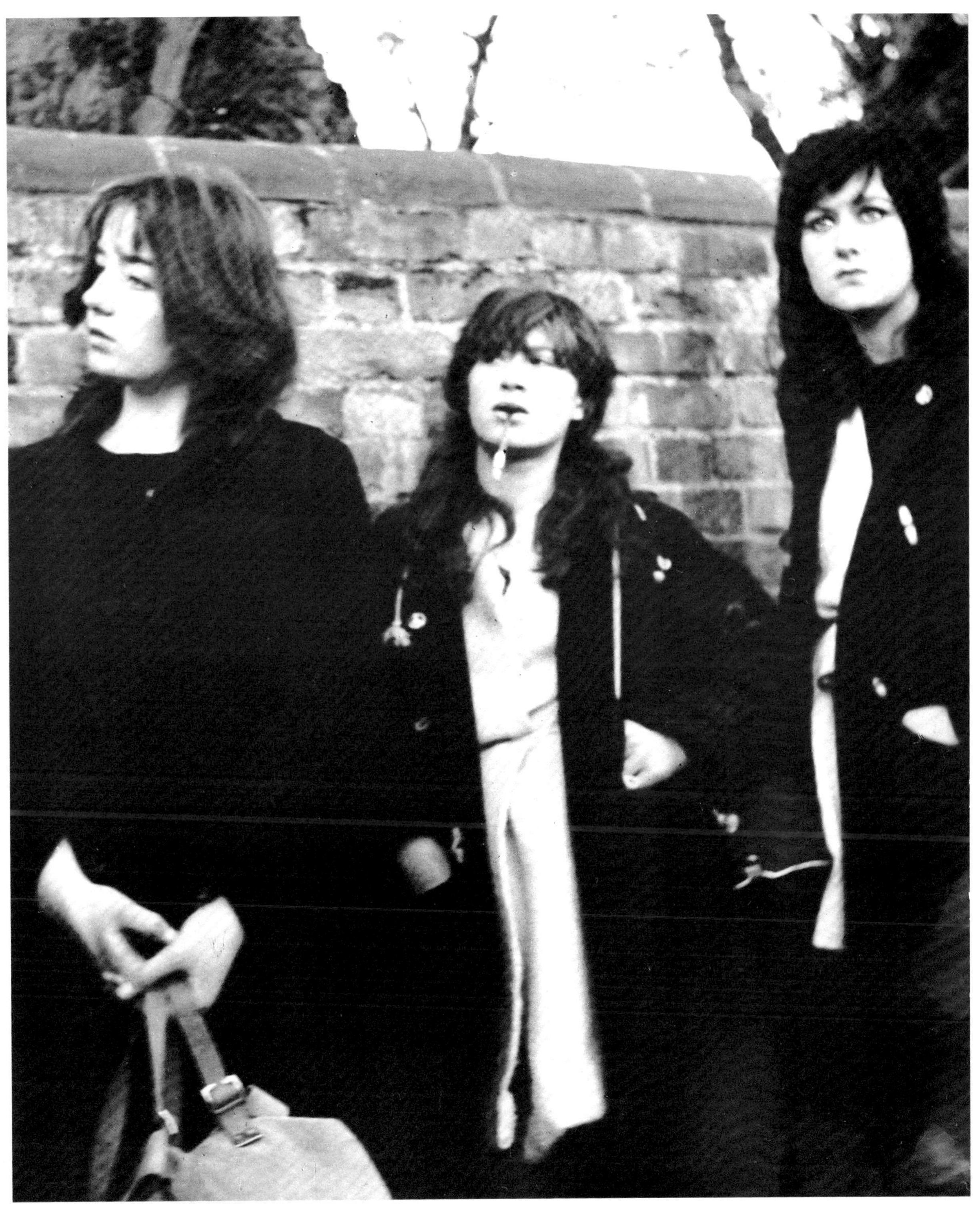

51

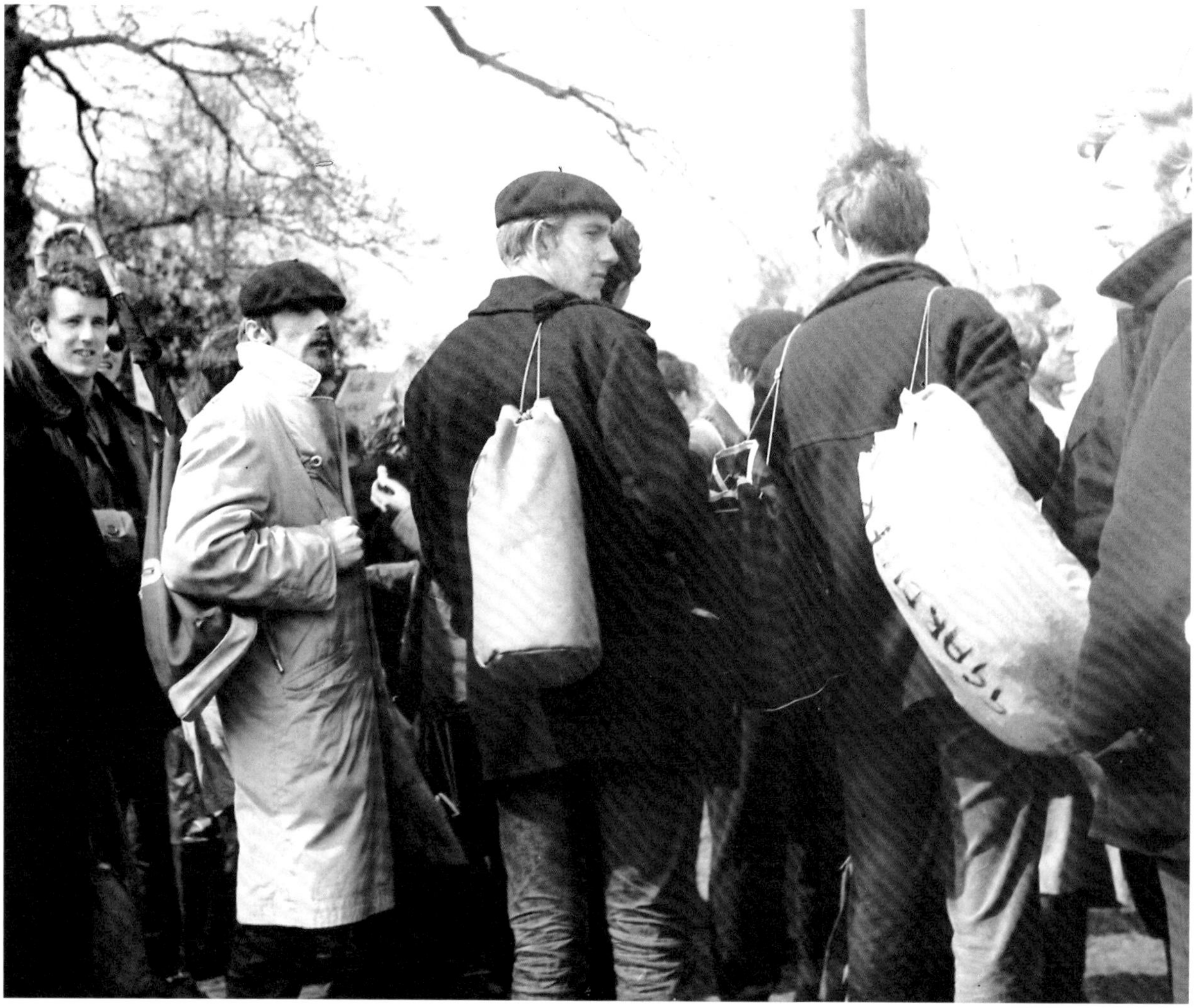

52

53

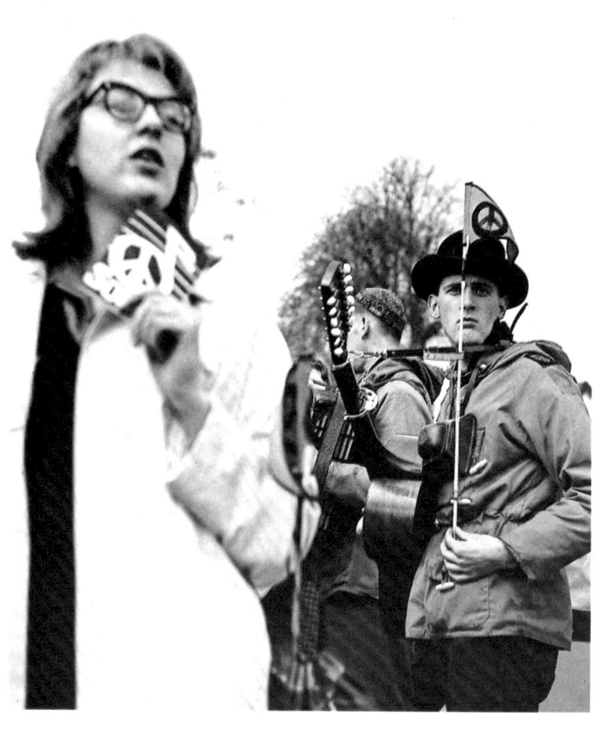

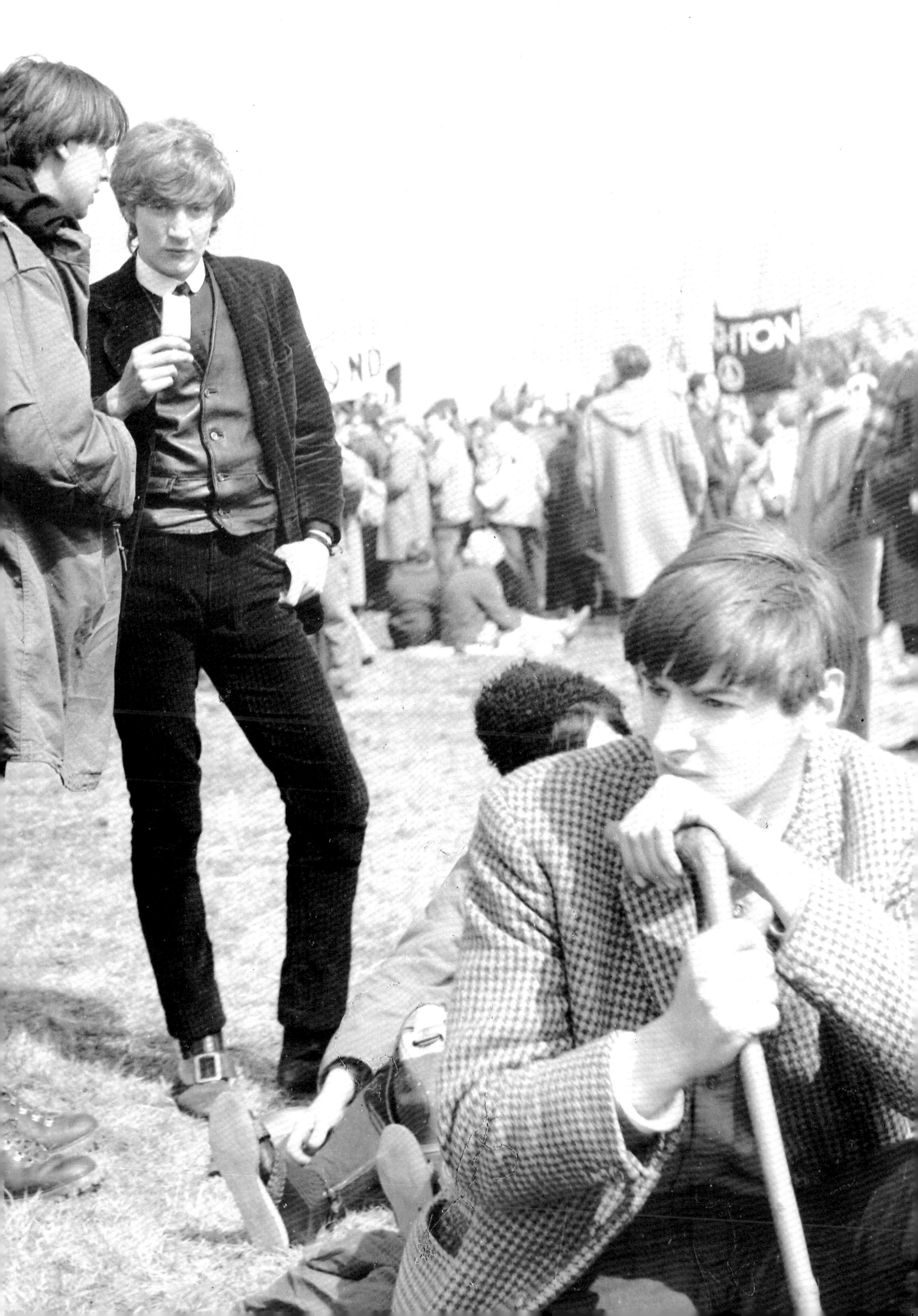

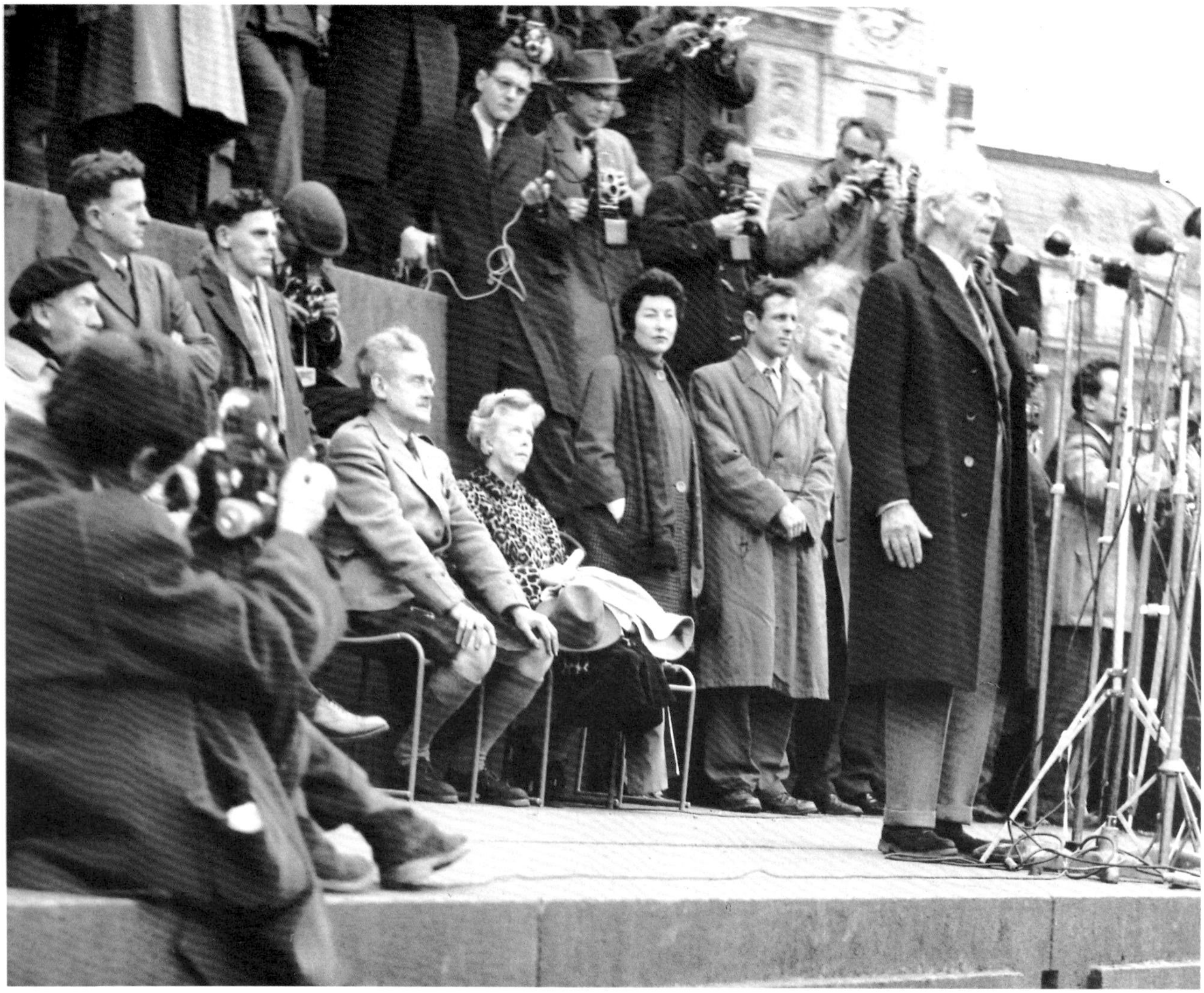

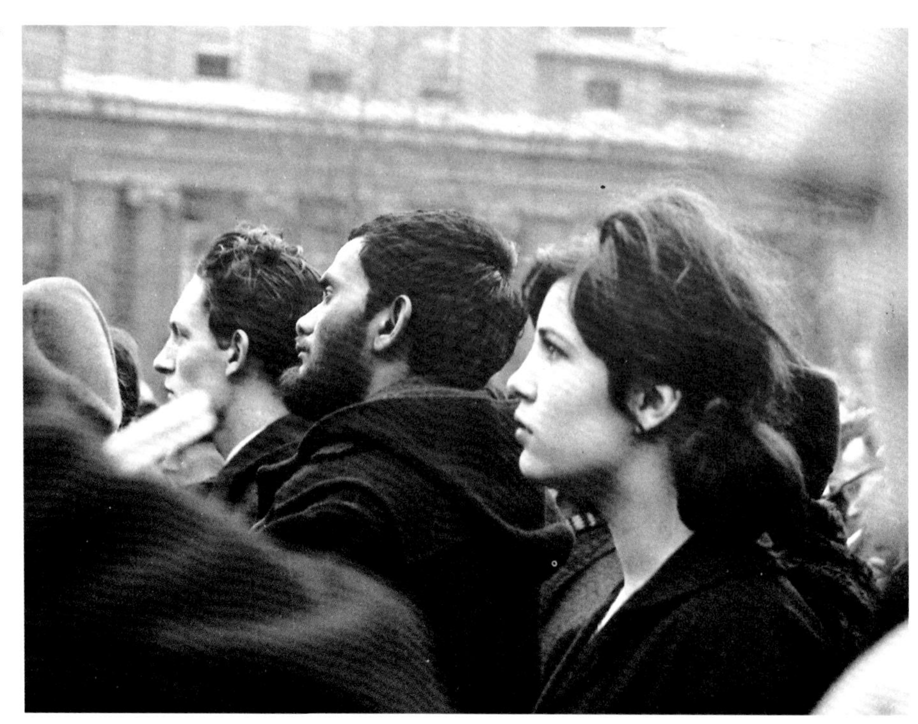

55

56

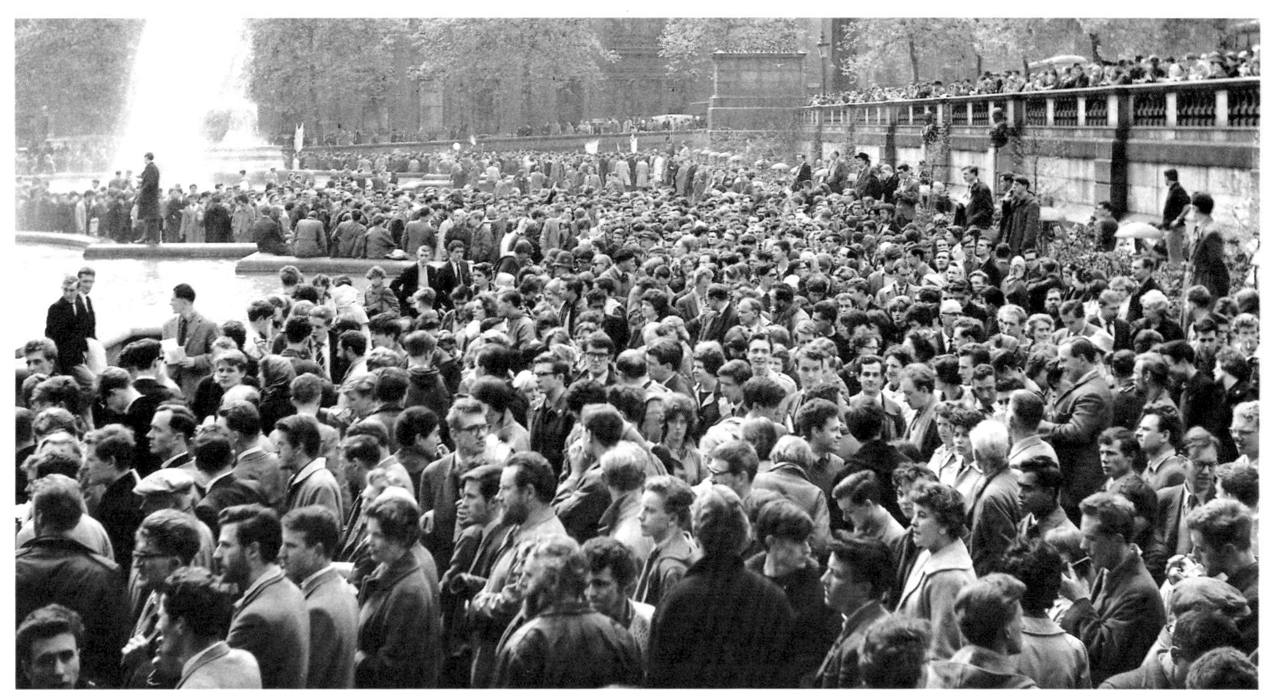

57

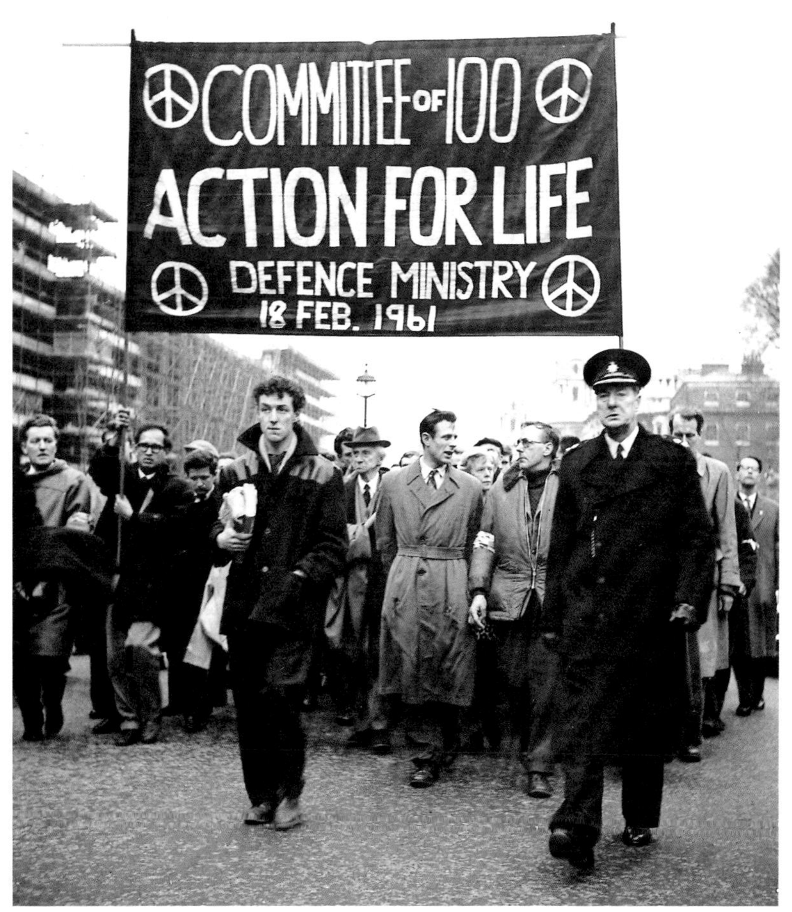

COMMITTEE OF 100
ACTION FOR LIFE
DEFENCE MINISTRY
18 FEB. 1961

58

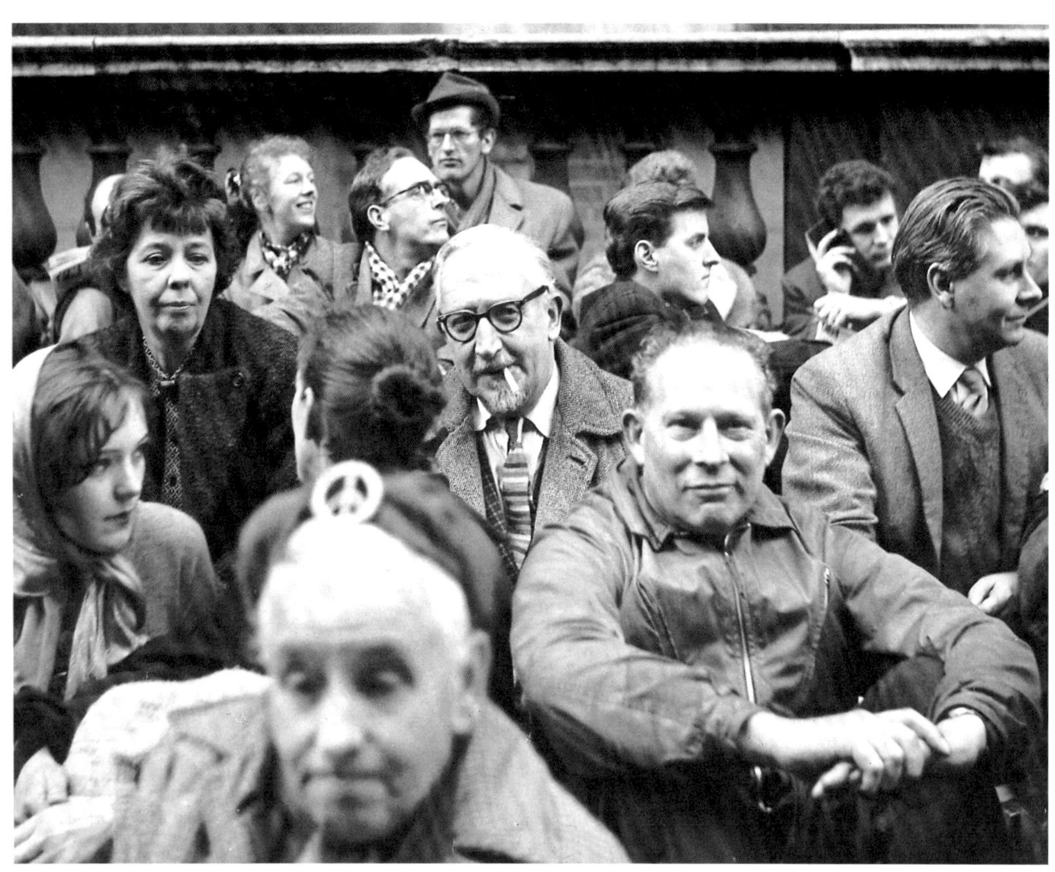

59

60

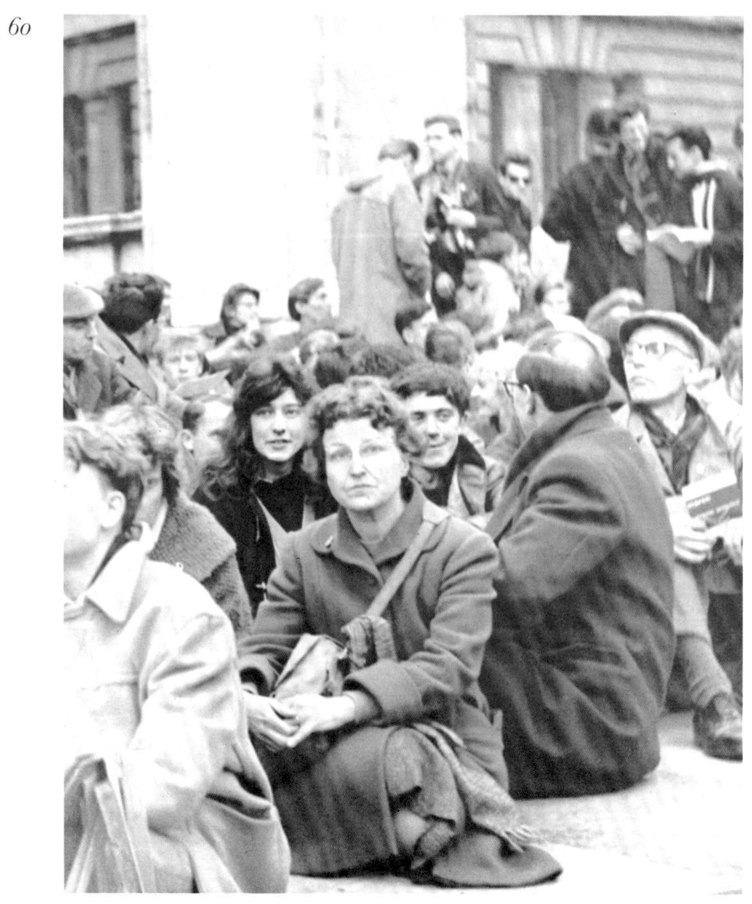

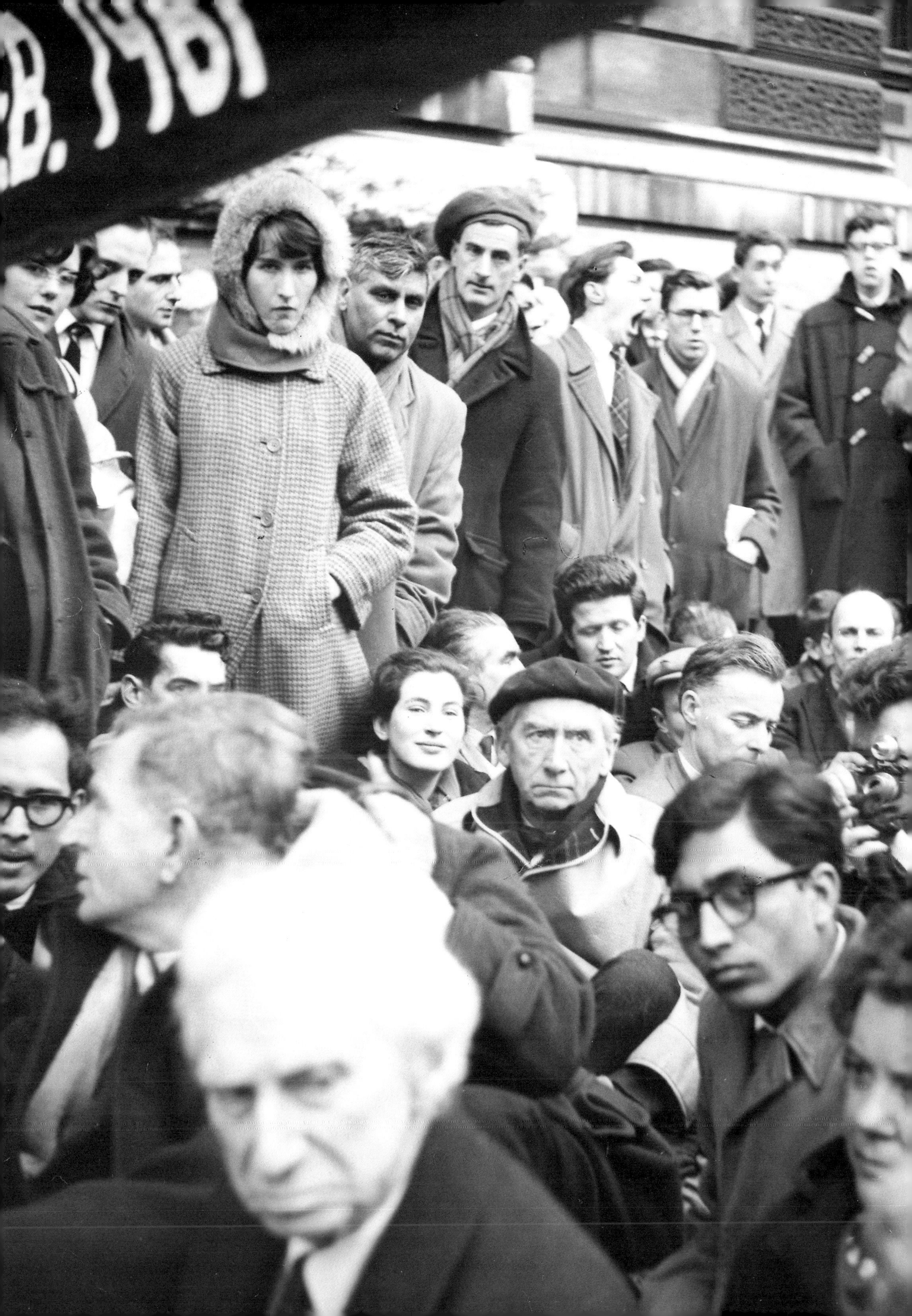
EB. 1961

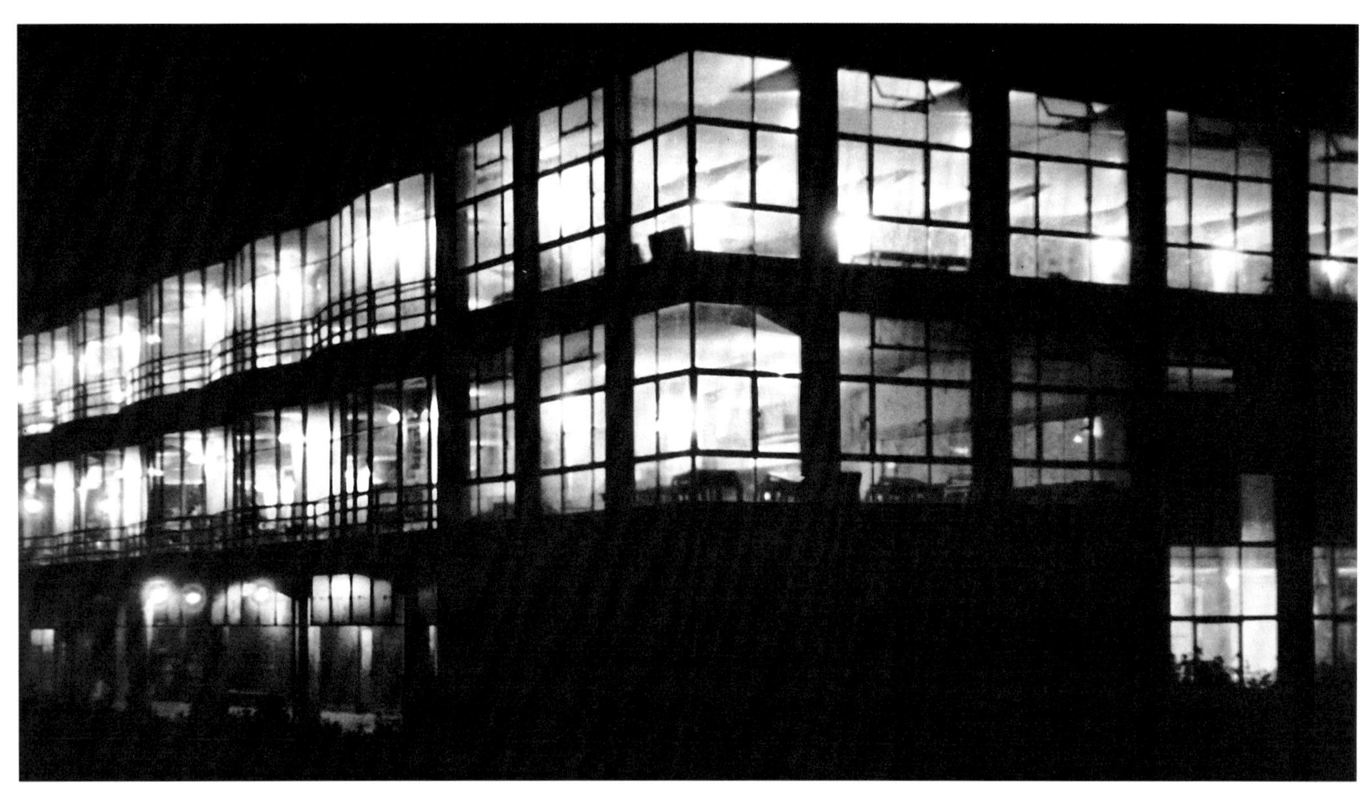

62

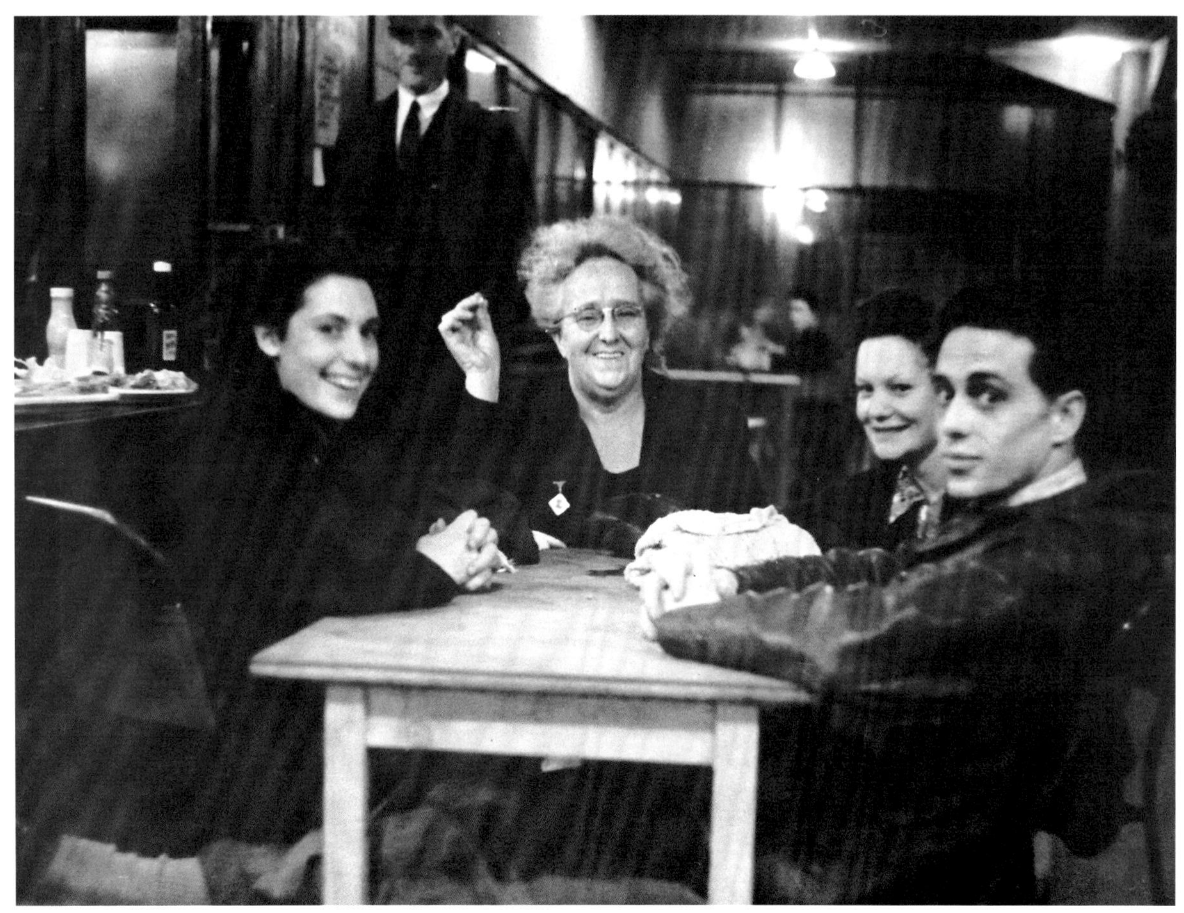

63

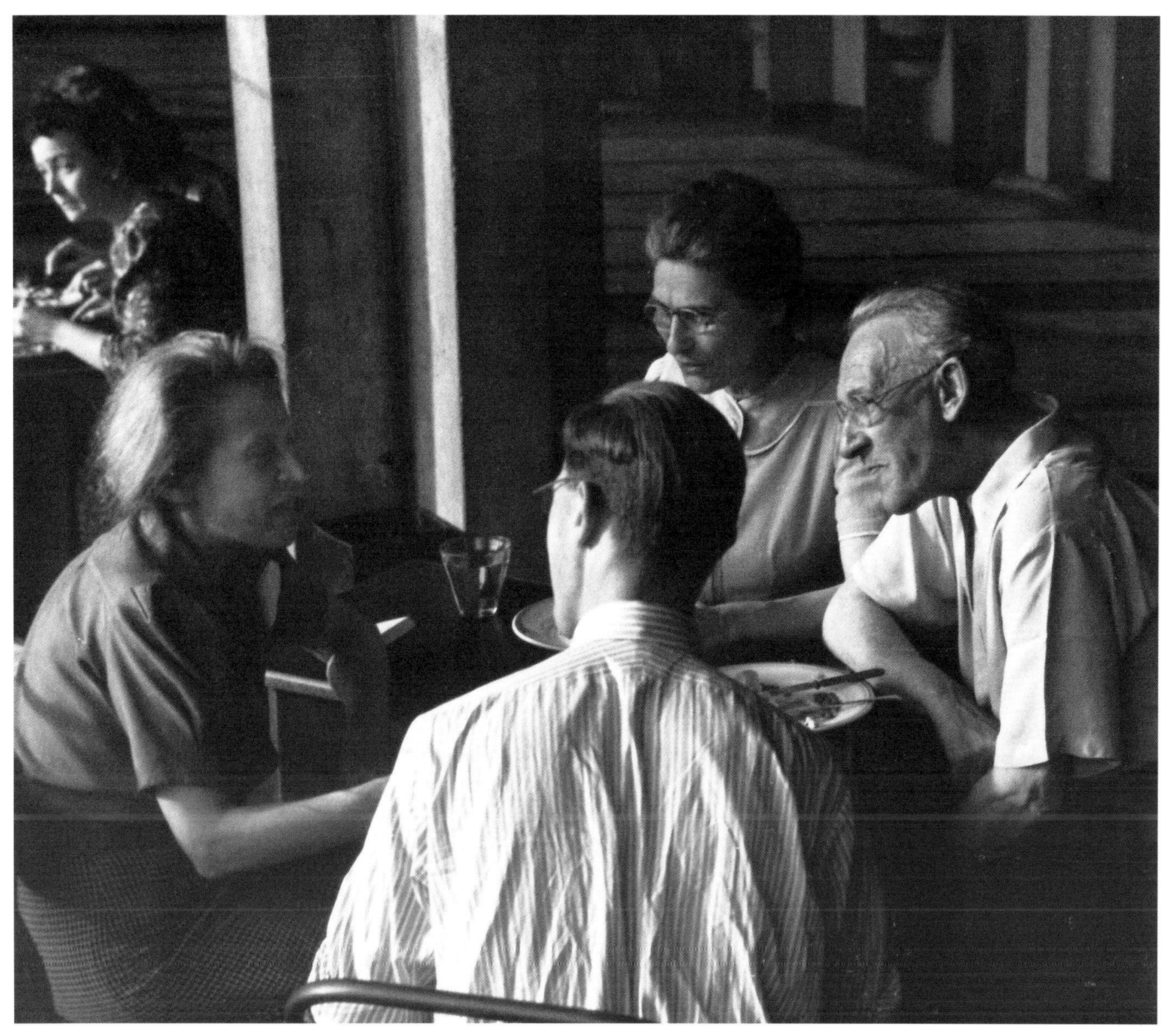

64

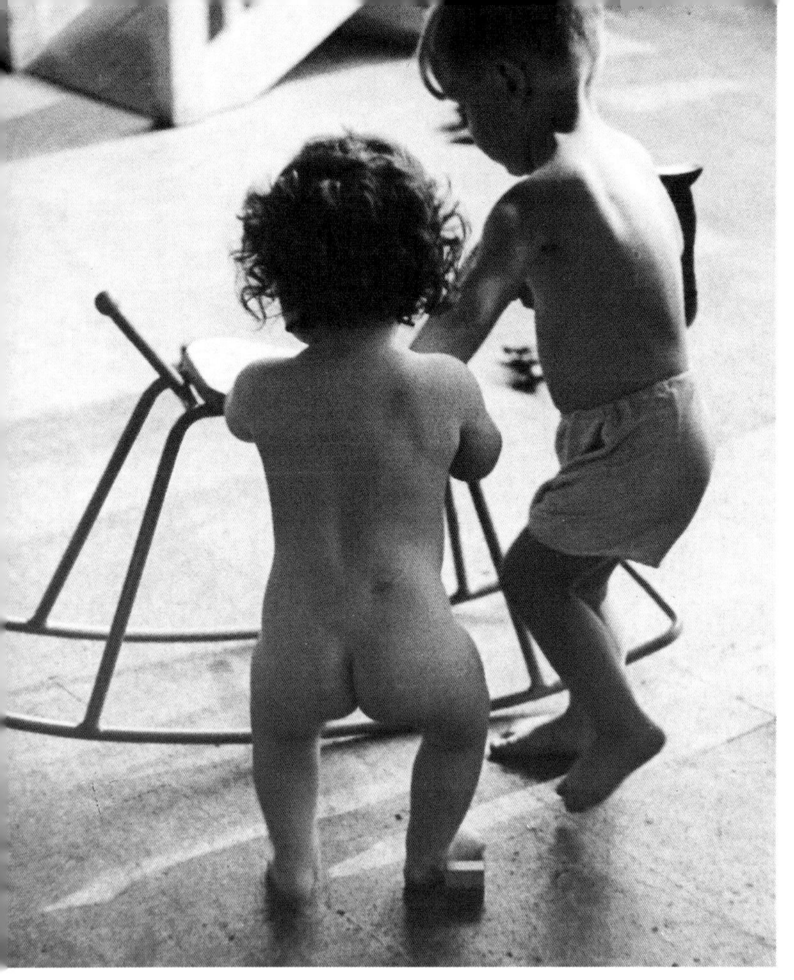

65

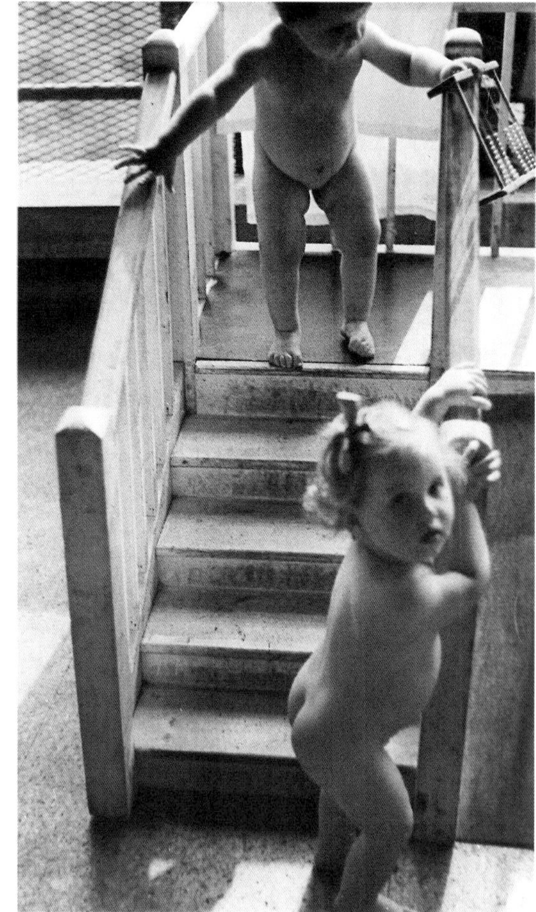

66

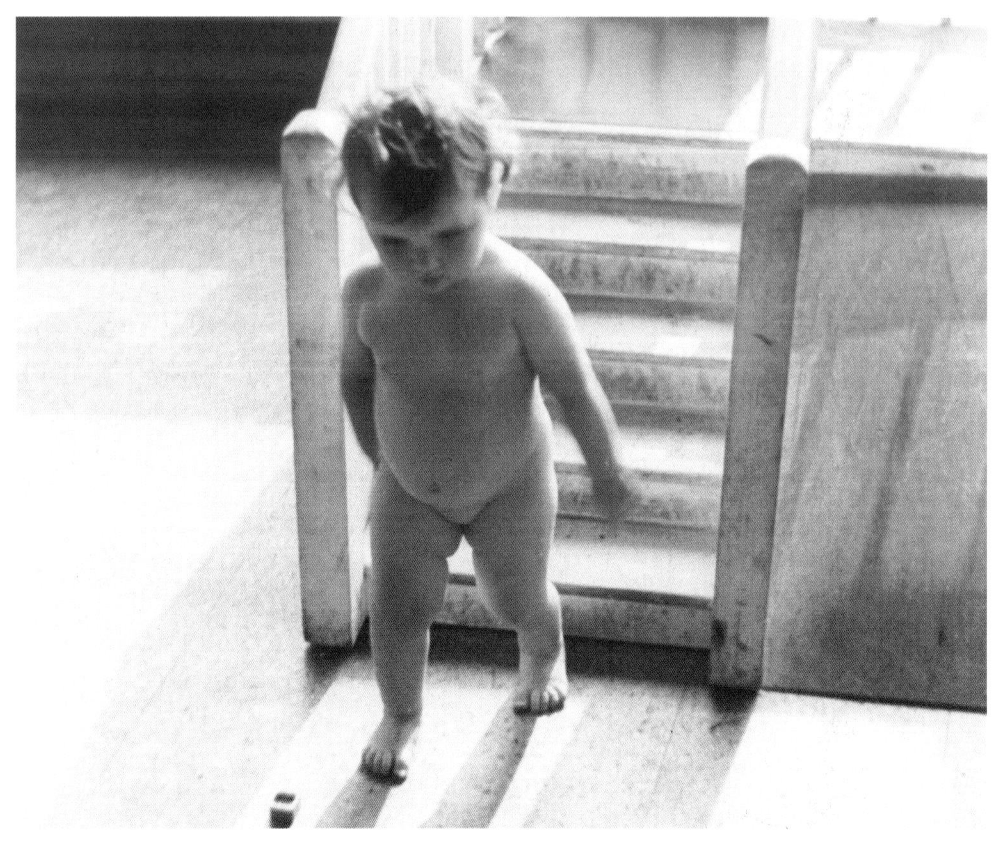

67

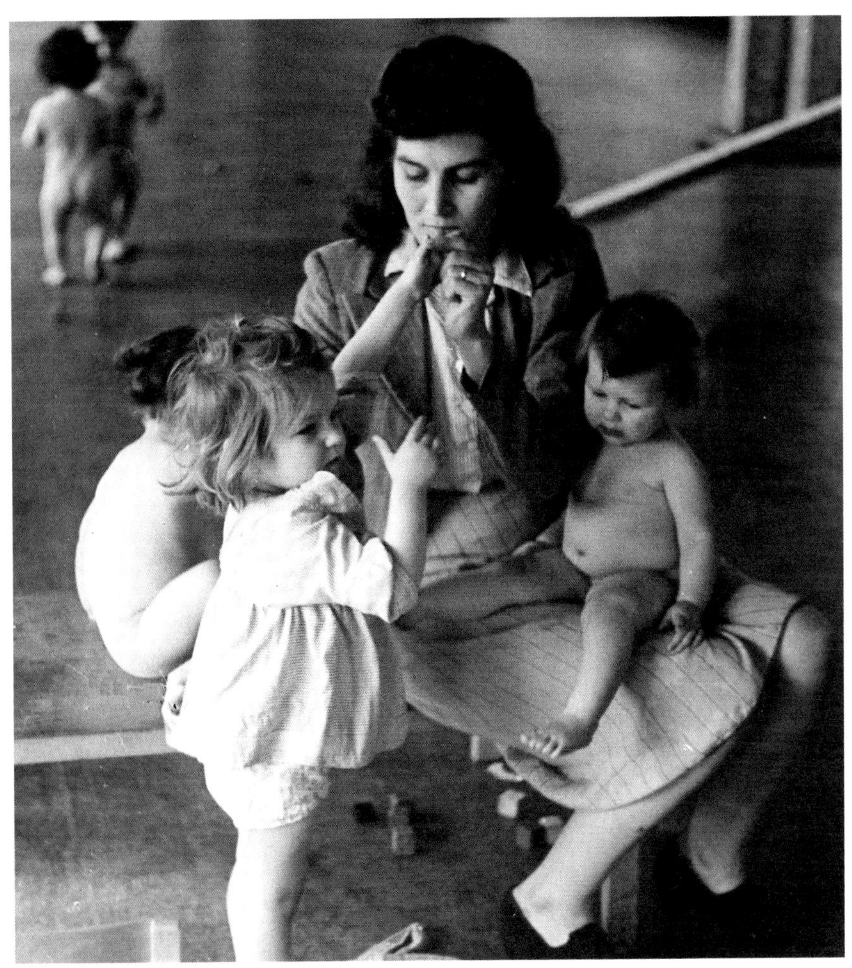

68

69

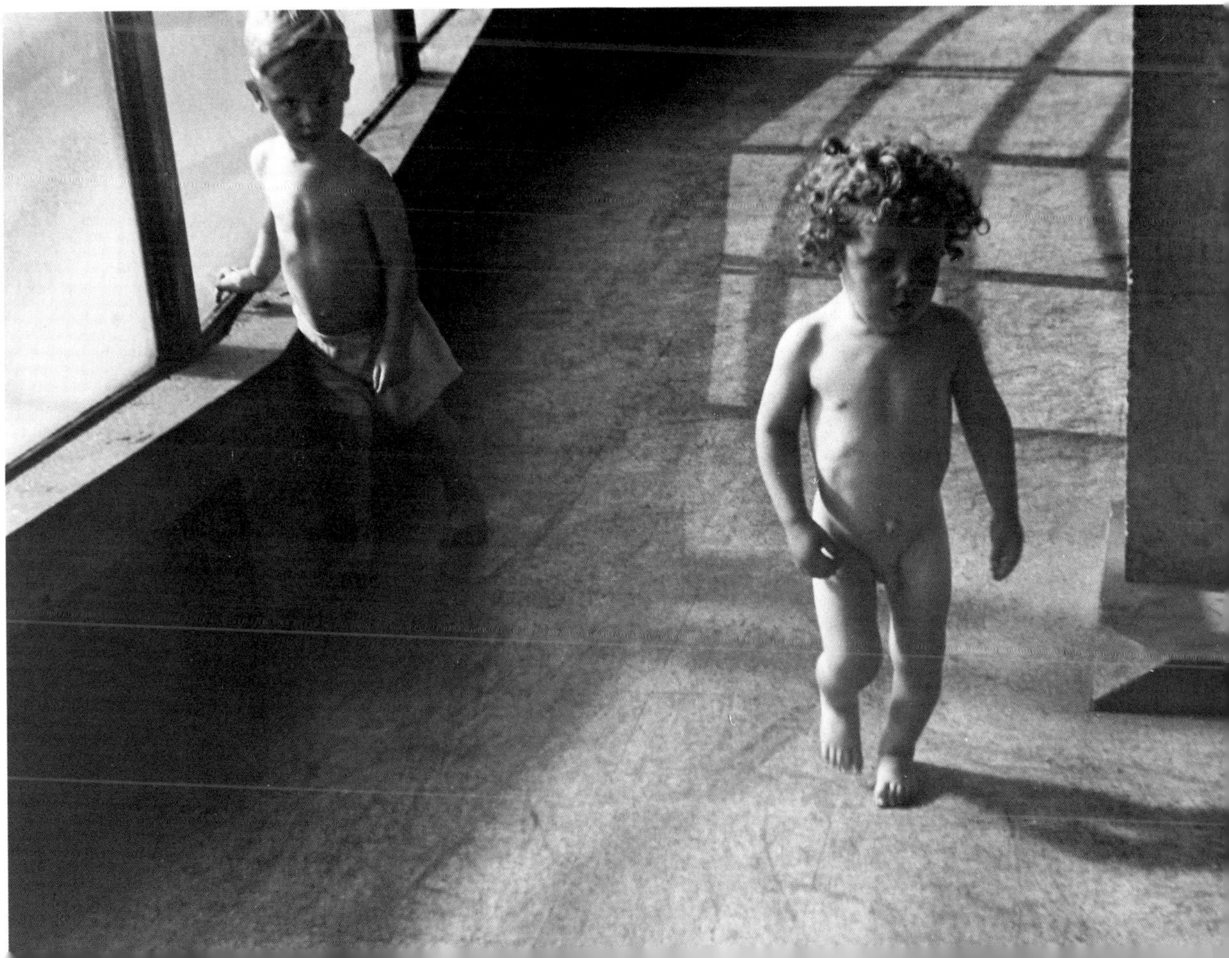

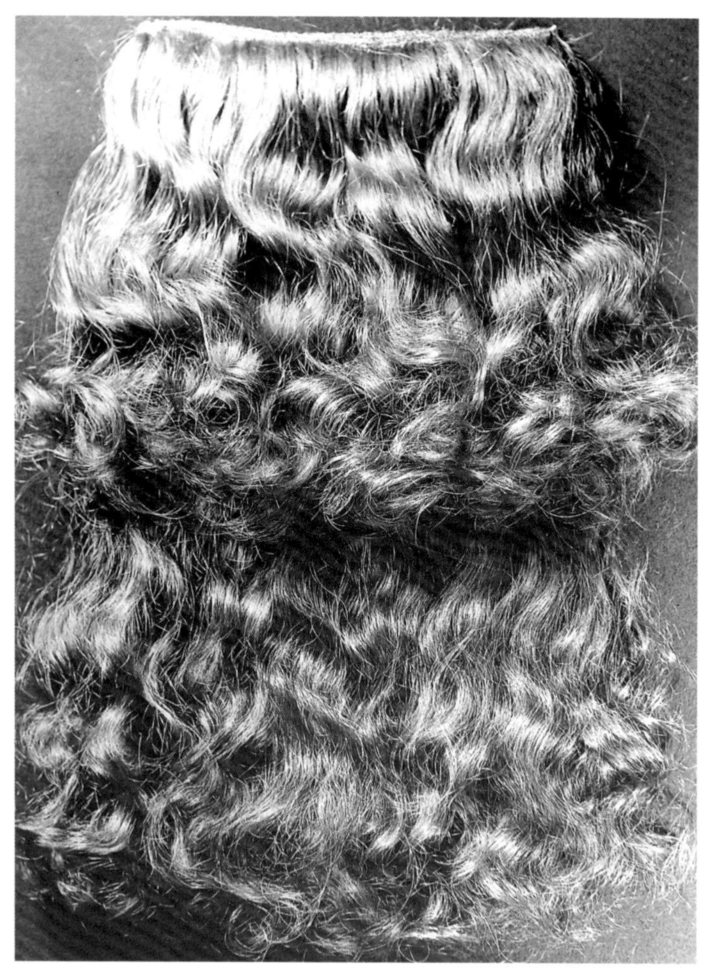

70

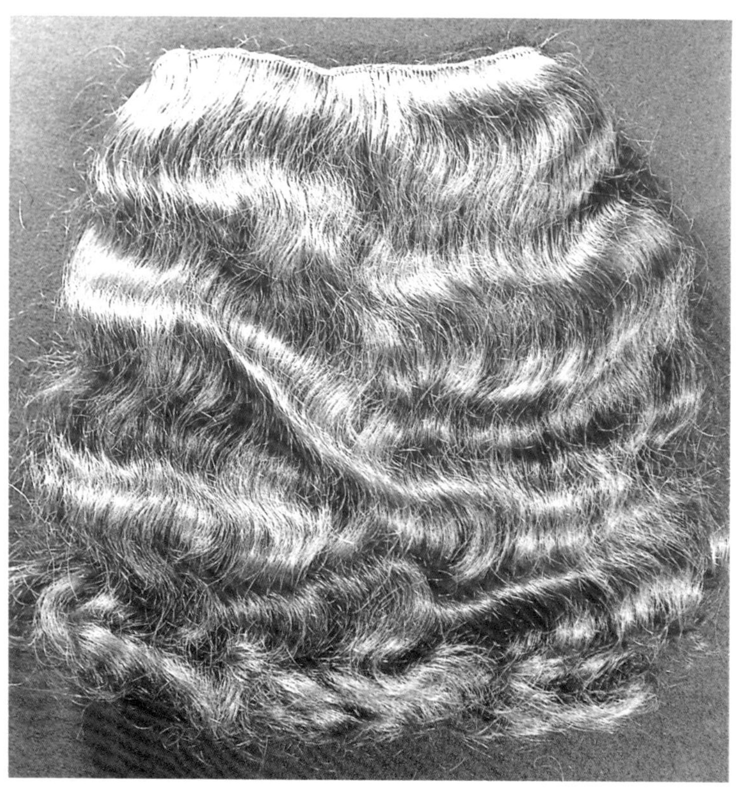

71

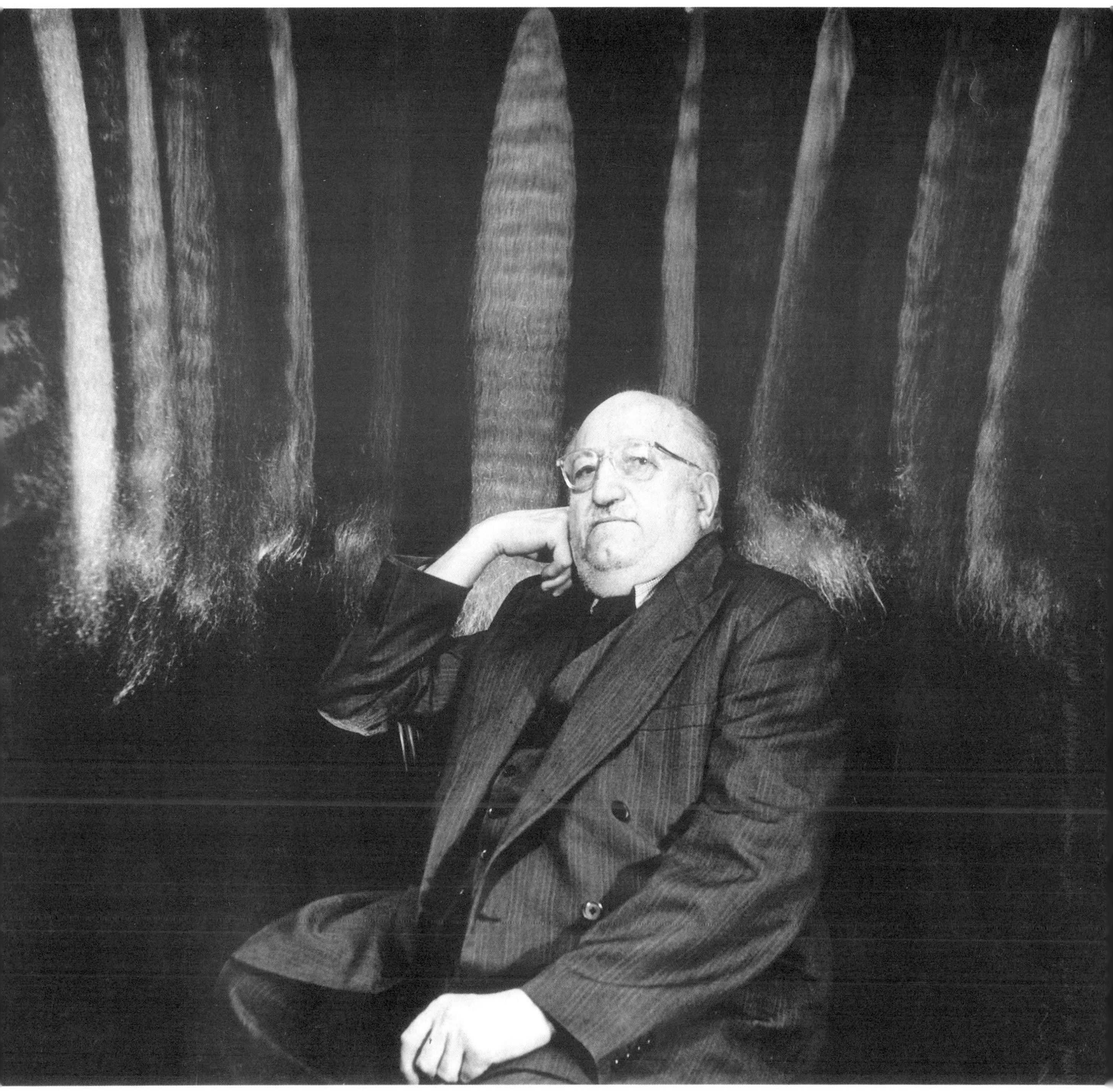

72

A.WINGROVE & SON
A.WINGRO...
GILLS FARM
GROWERS.
Gills Farm,
A.WINGROVE & SON
Longfield 2180
DARENTH, KENT.

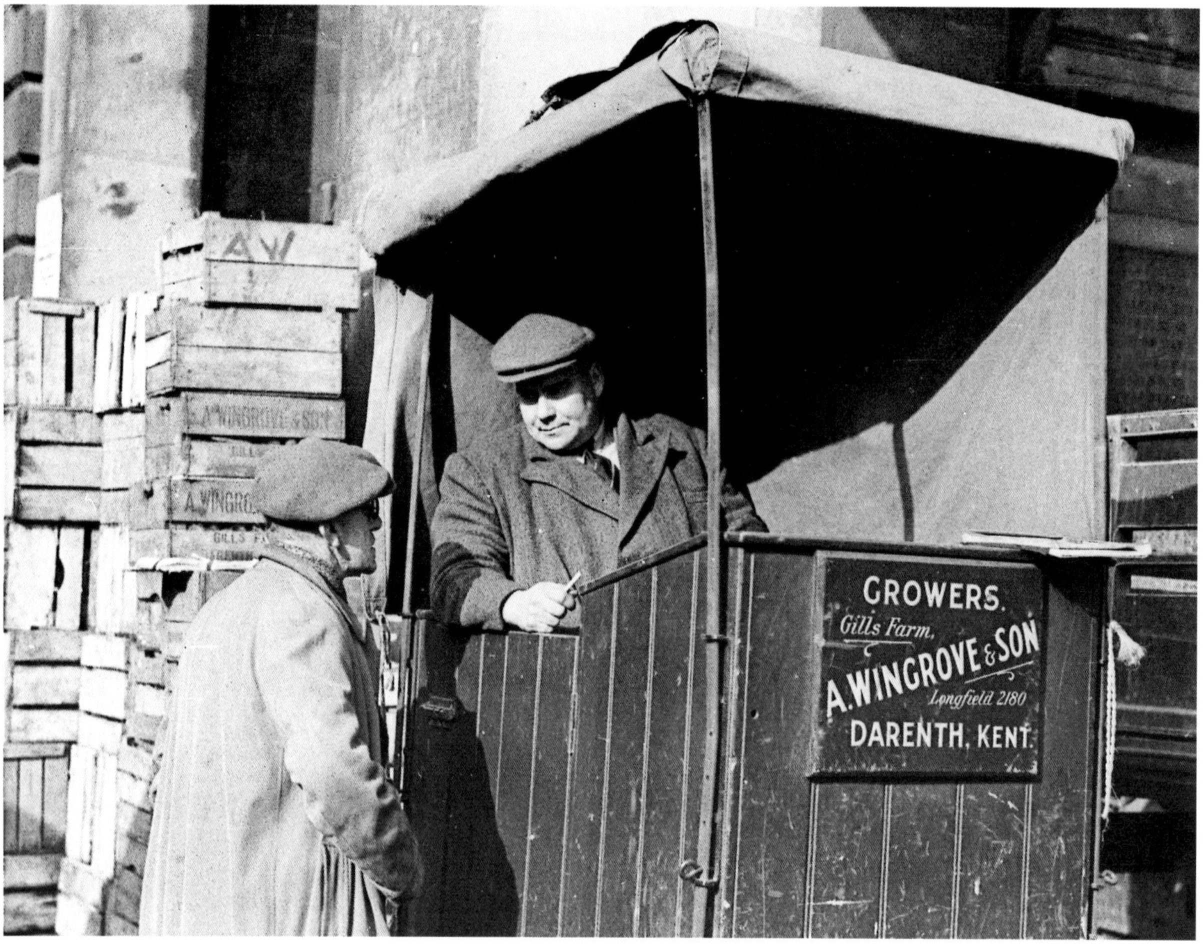

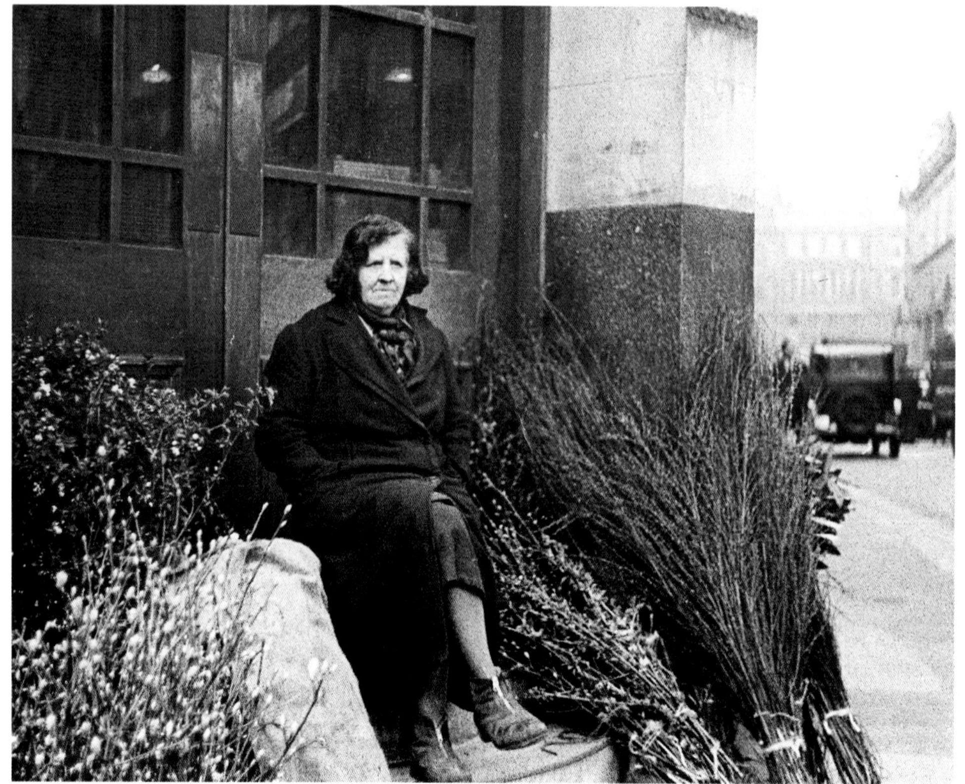

73

74

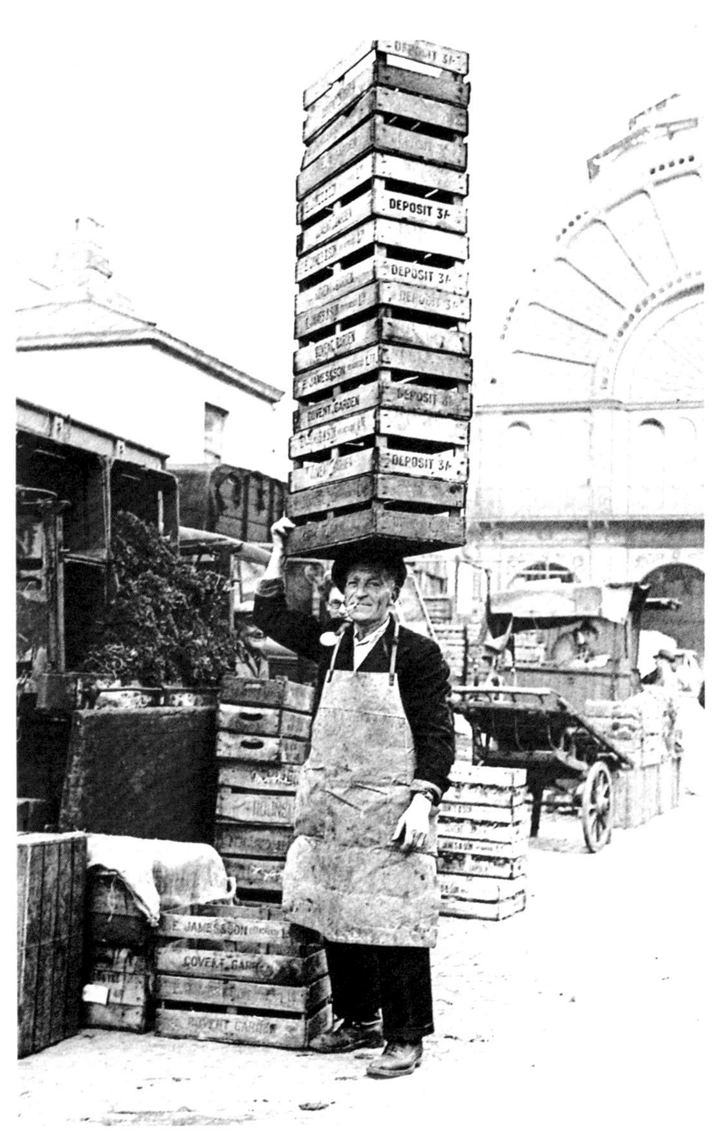

75

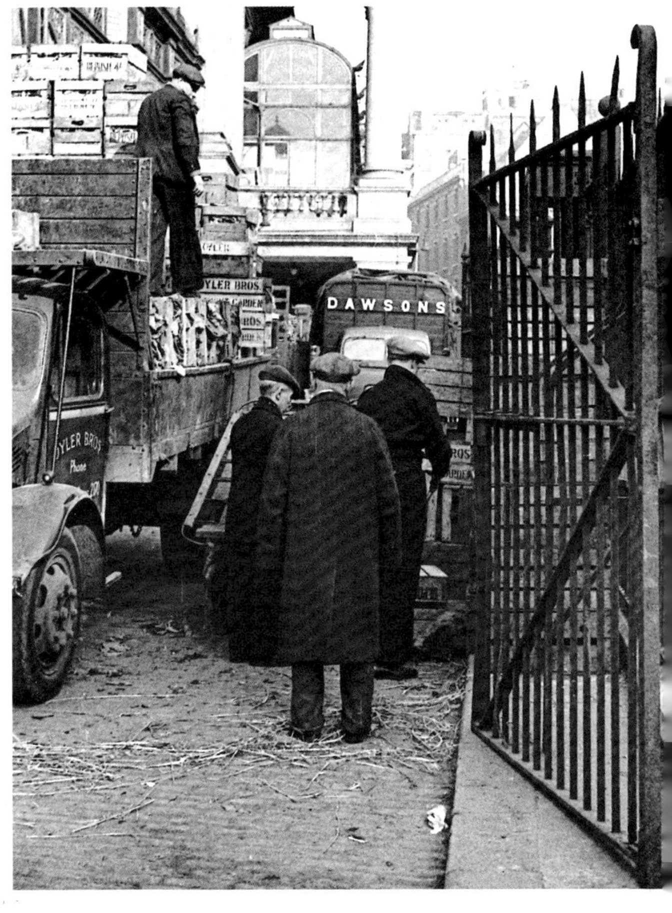

76

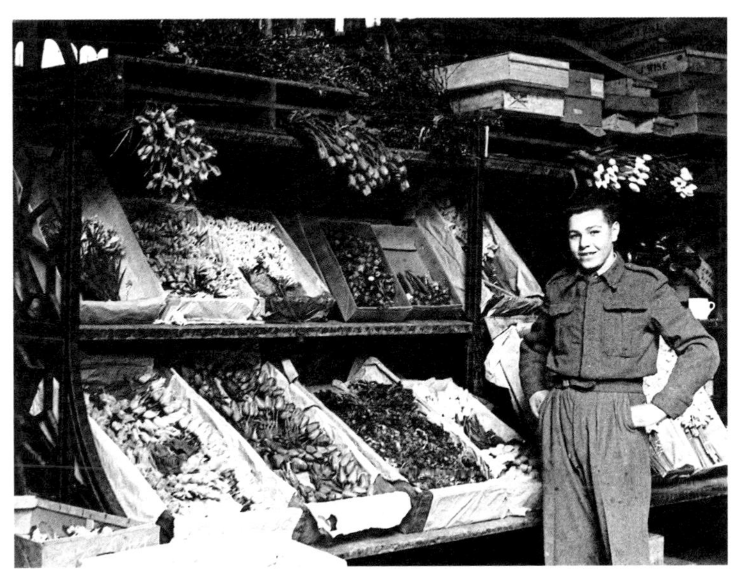

77

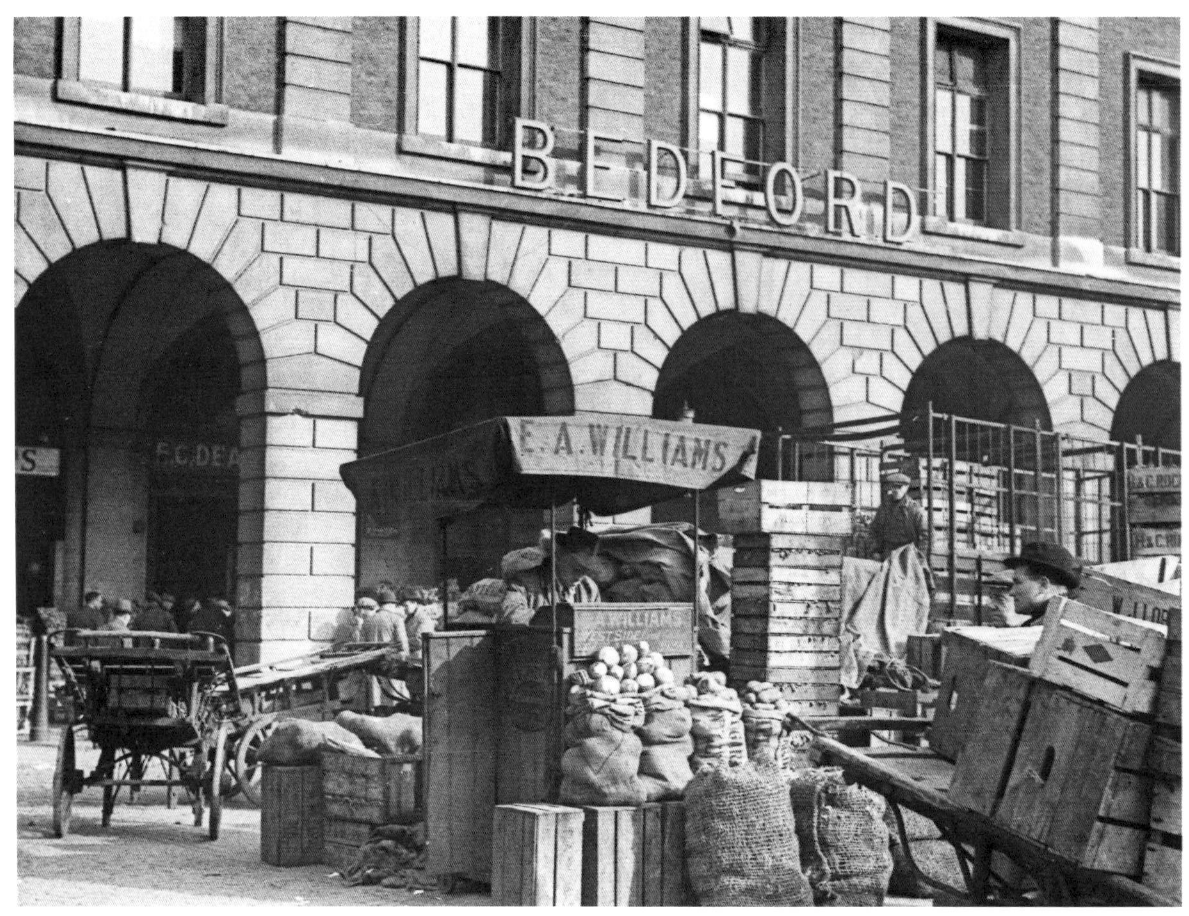

78

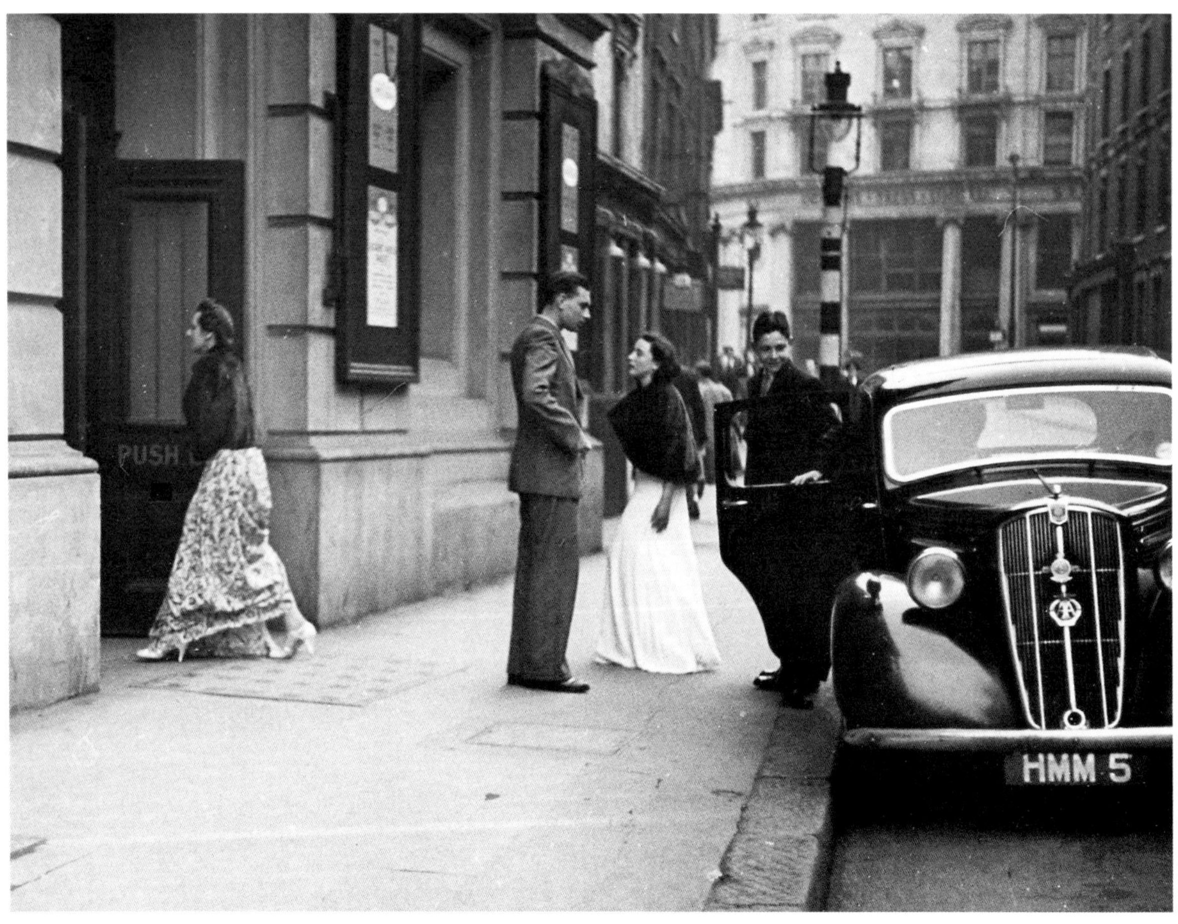

79

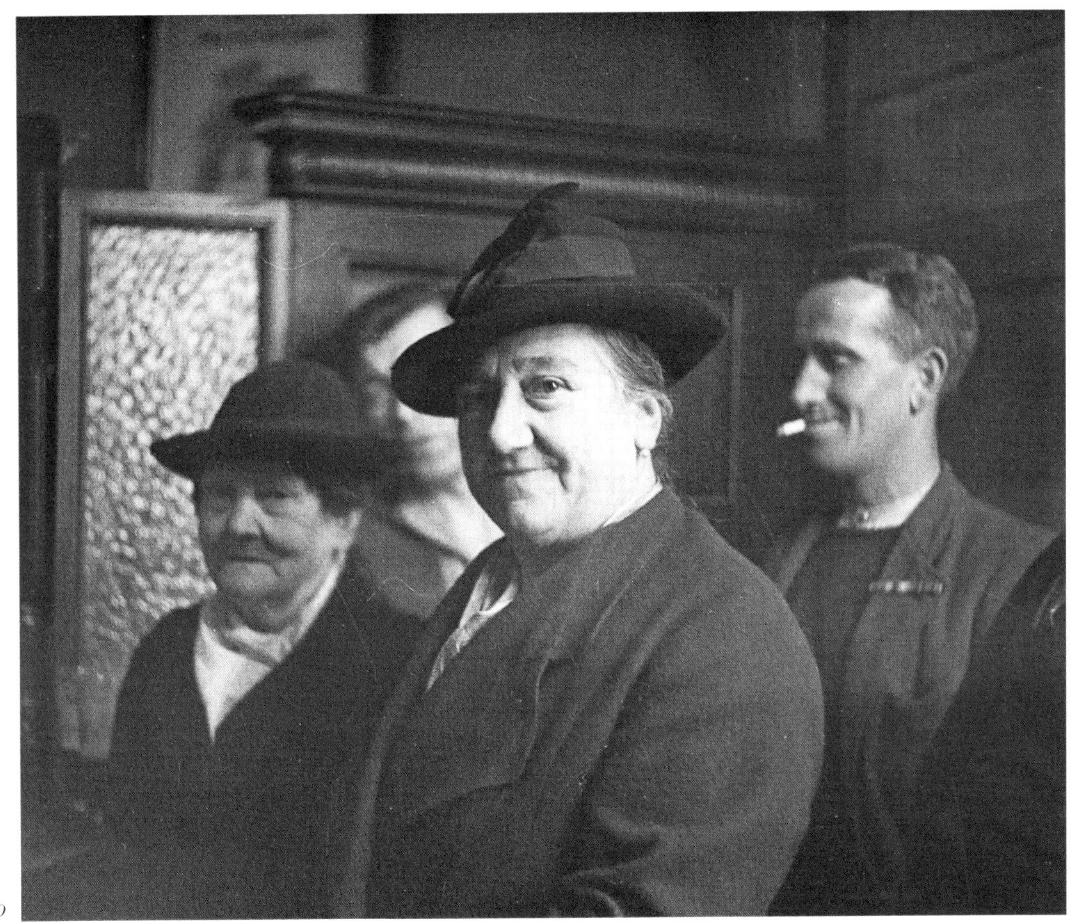

80

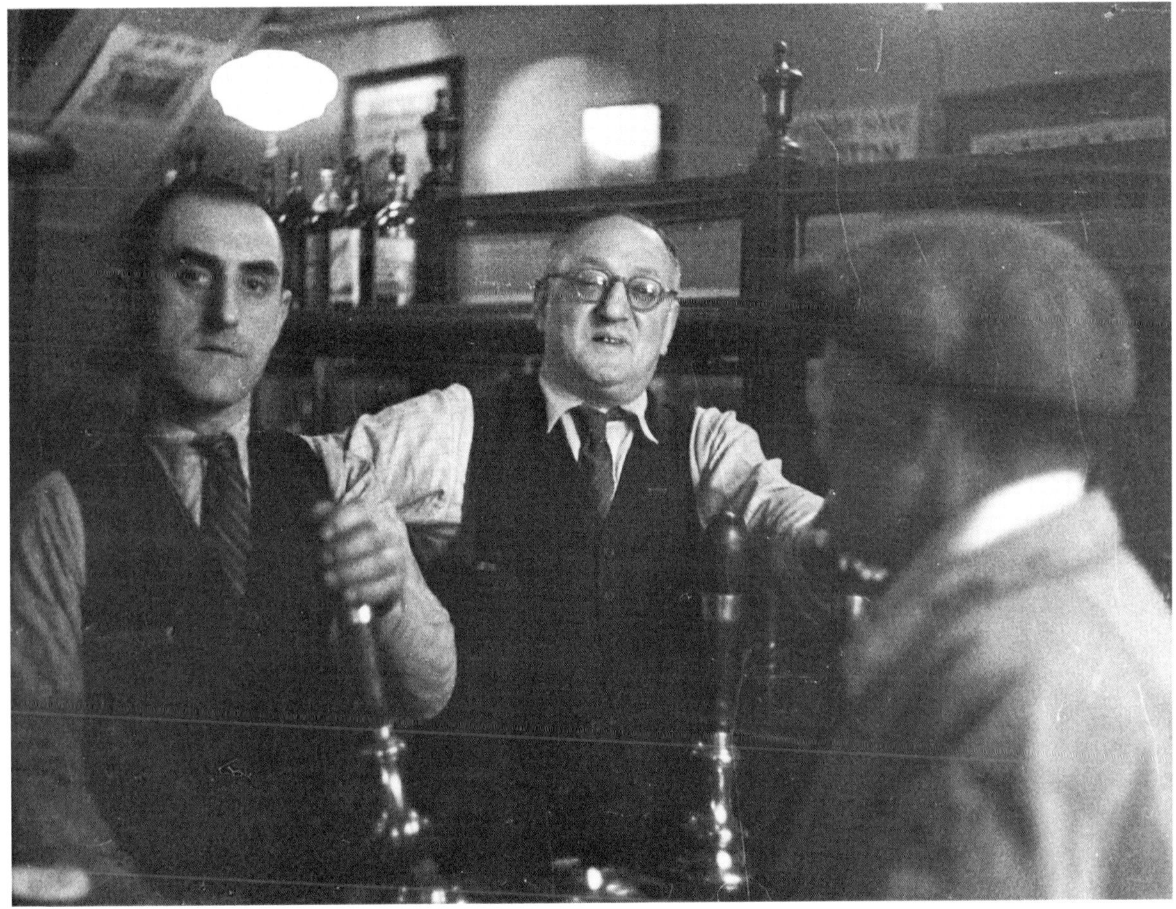

81

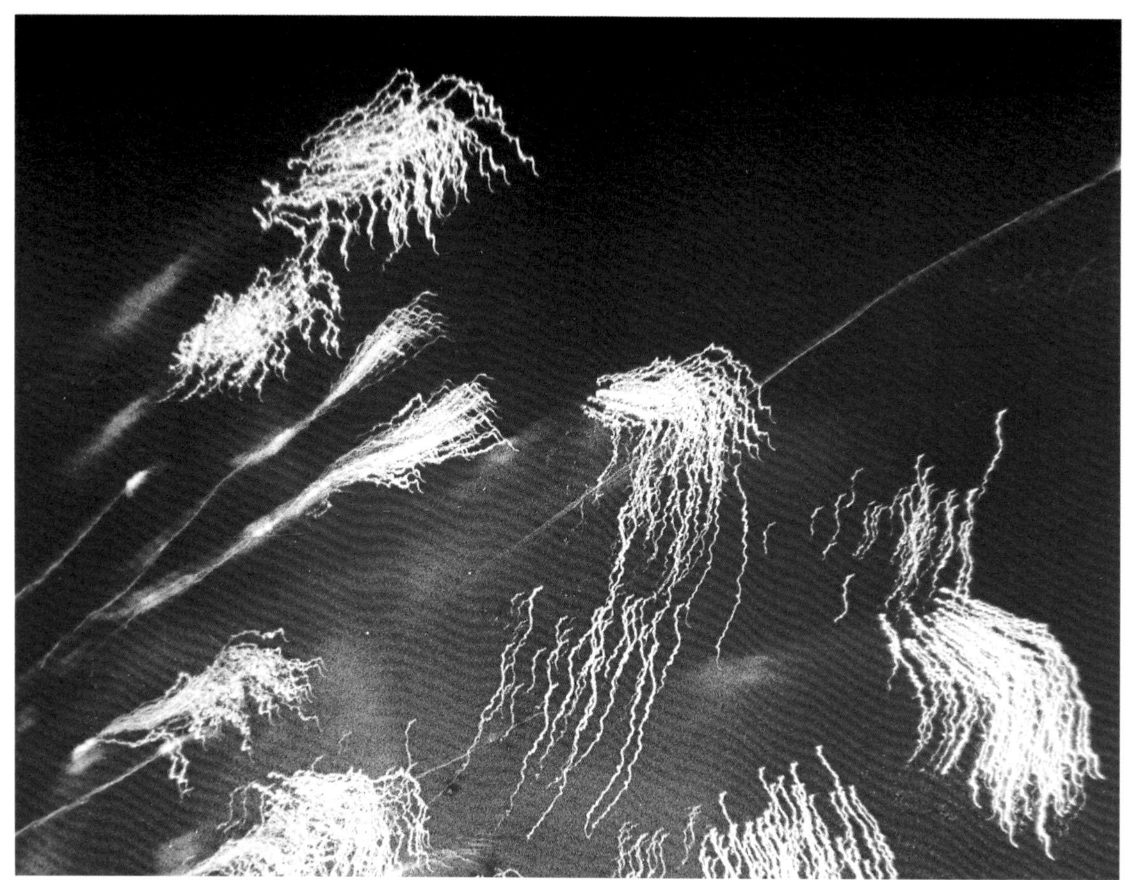

82

83

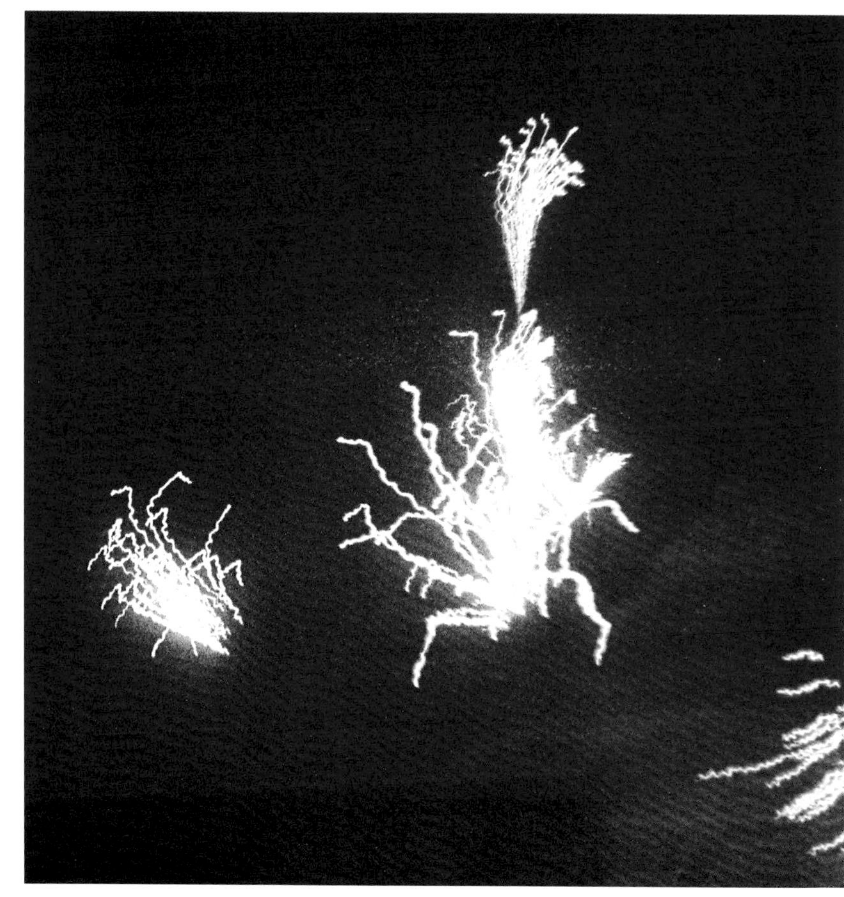

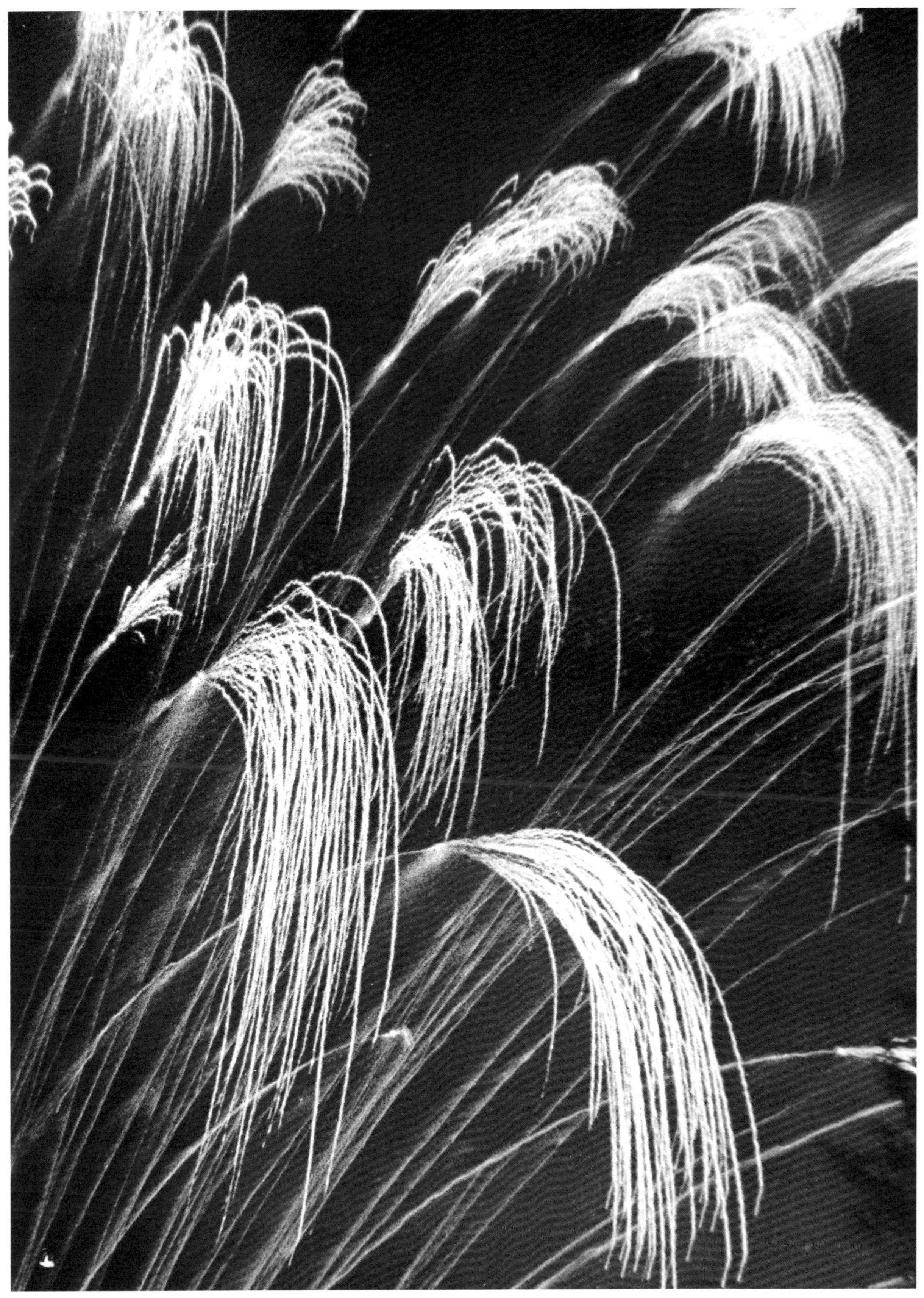

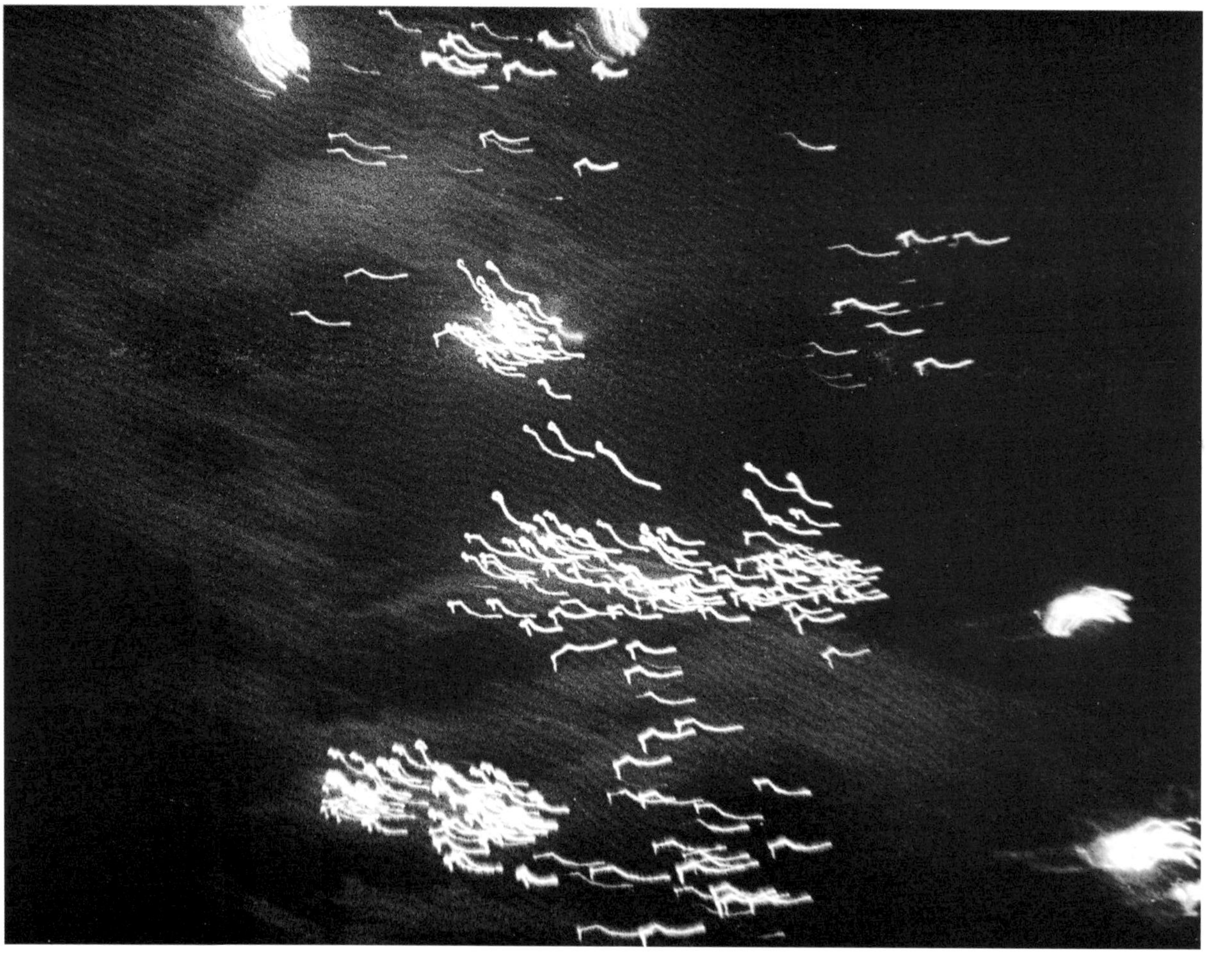

85

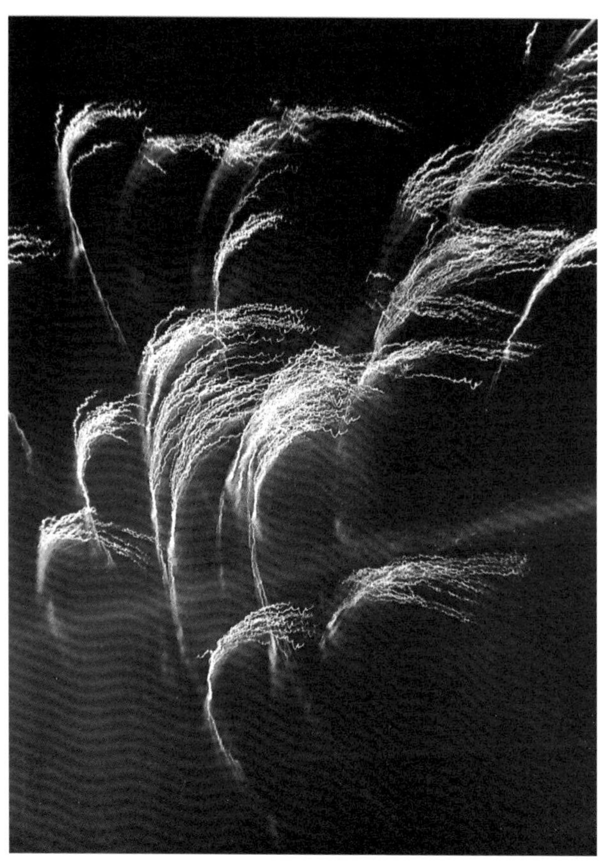
86

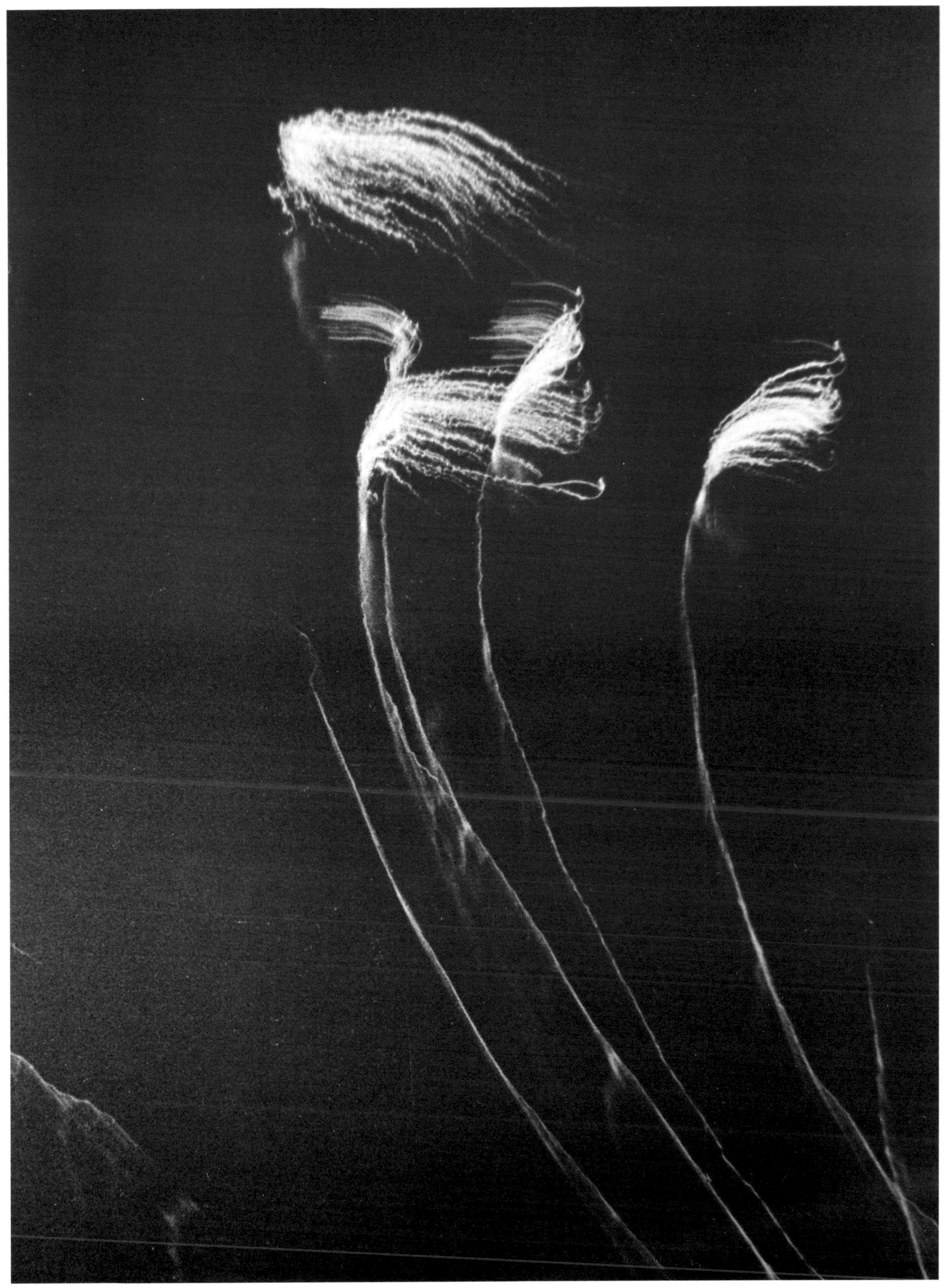

87

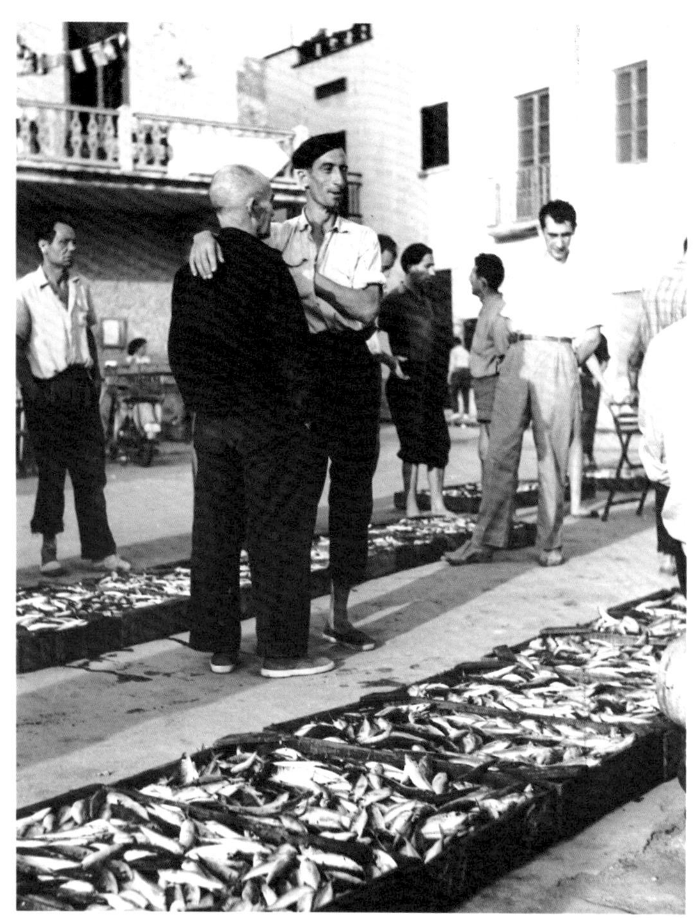

88

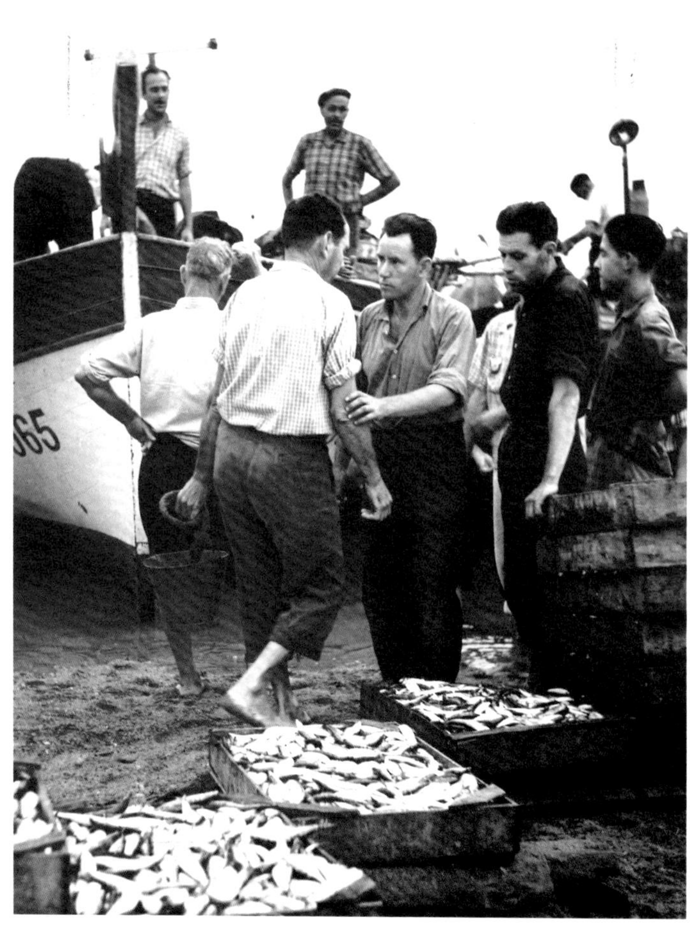

89

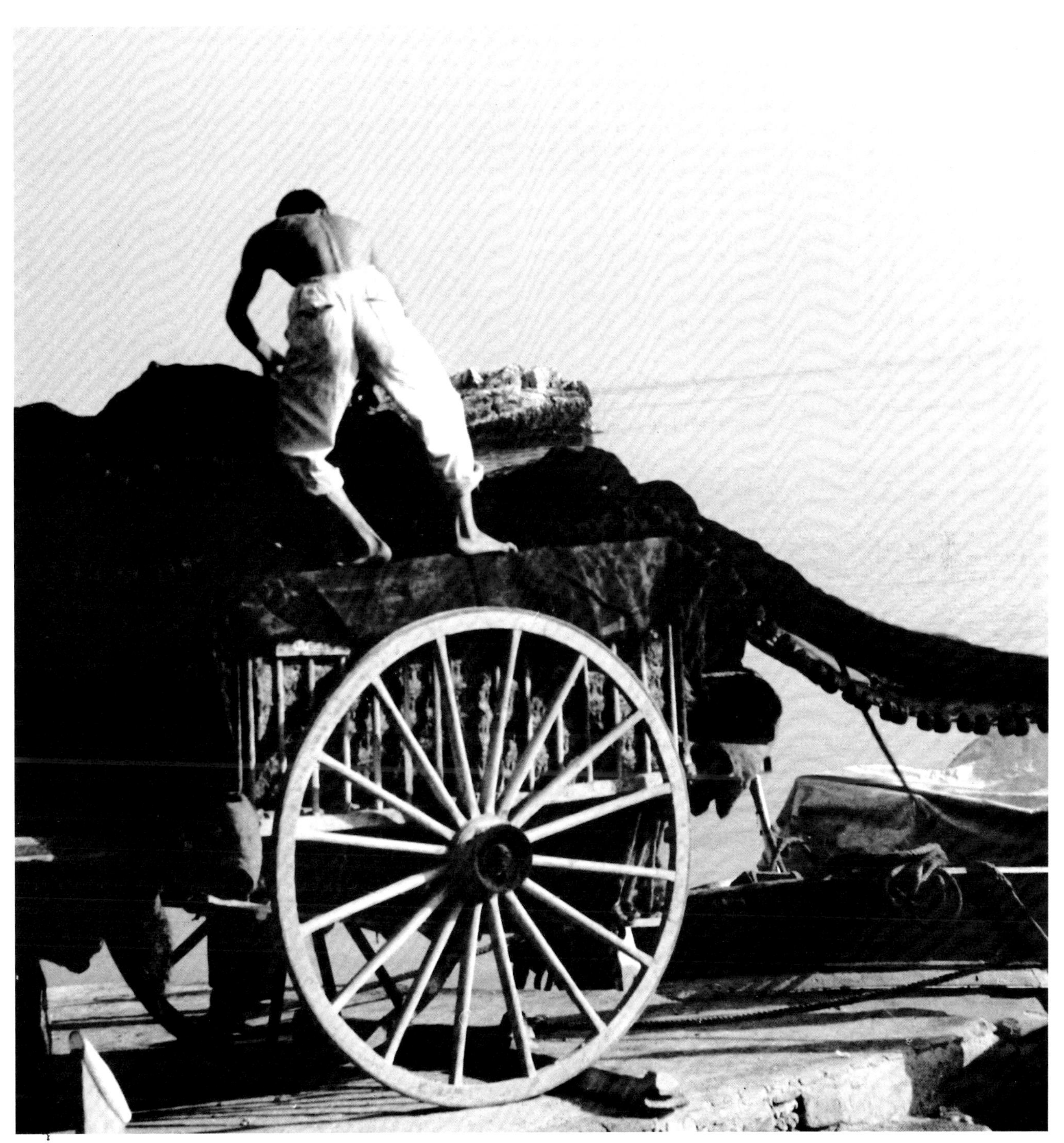

90

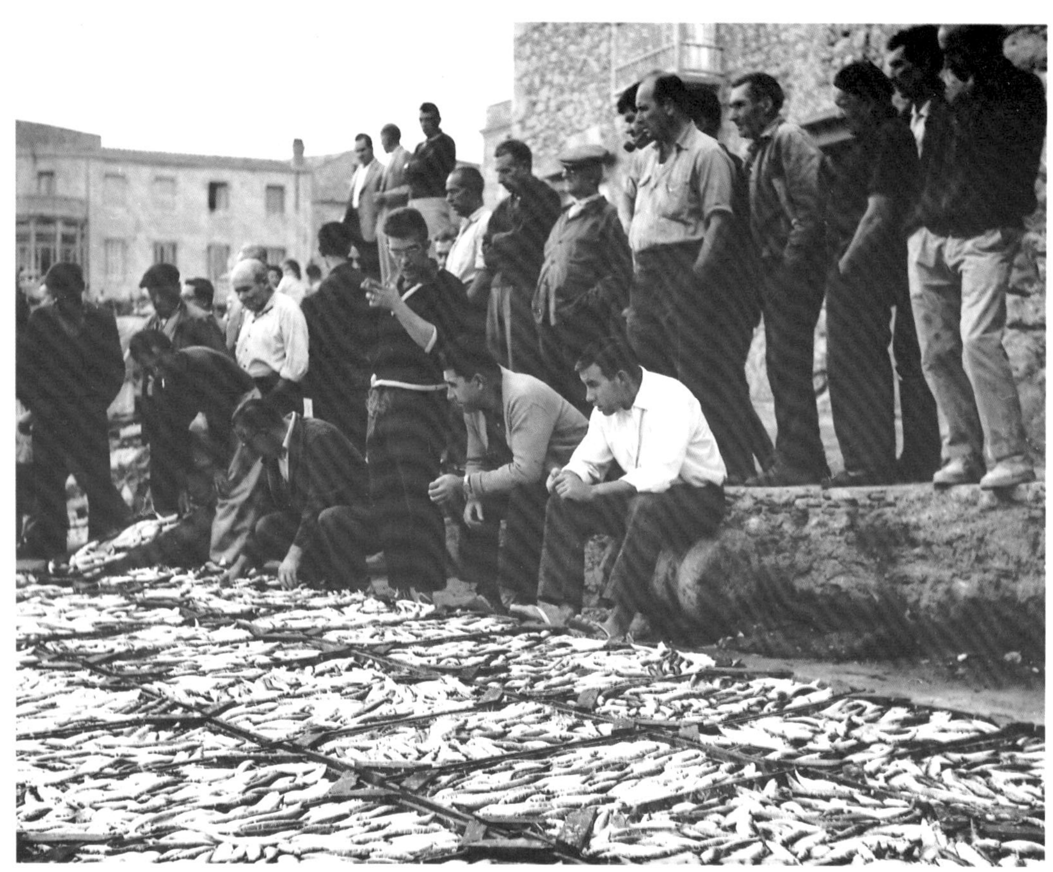

91

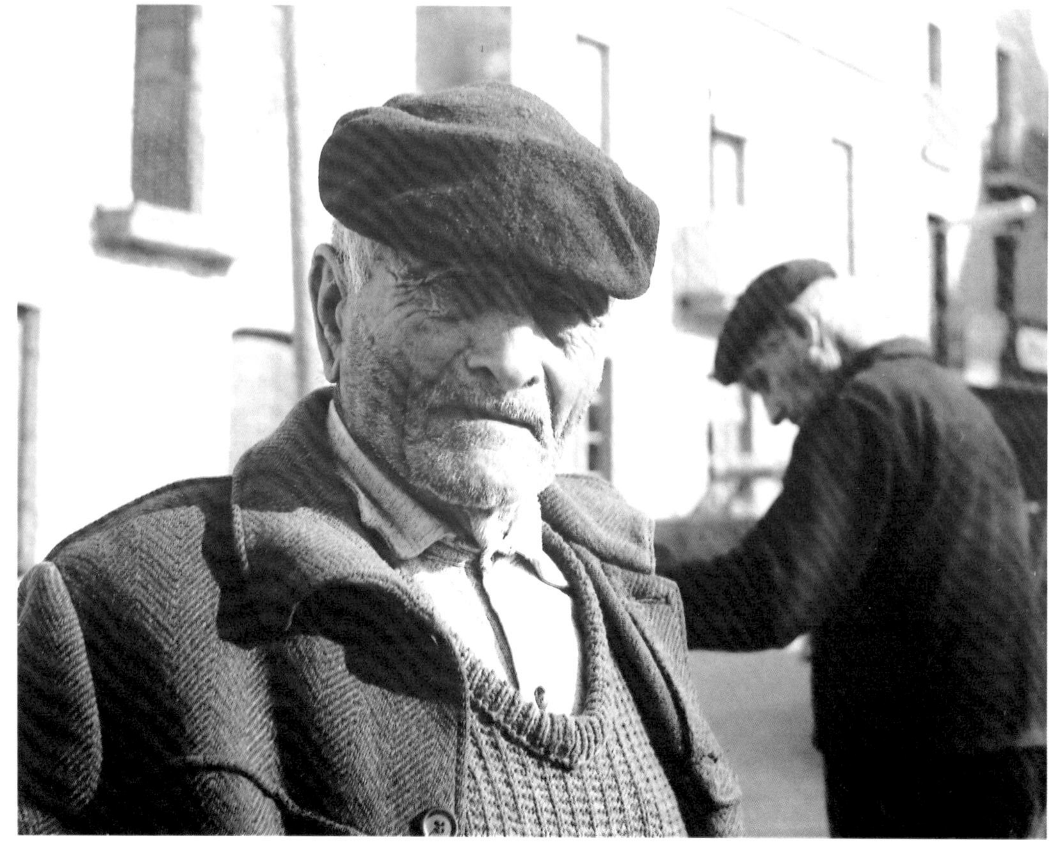

92

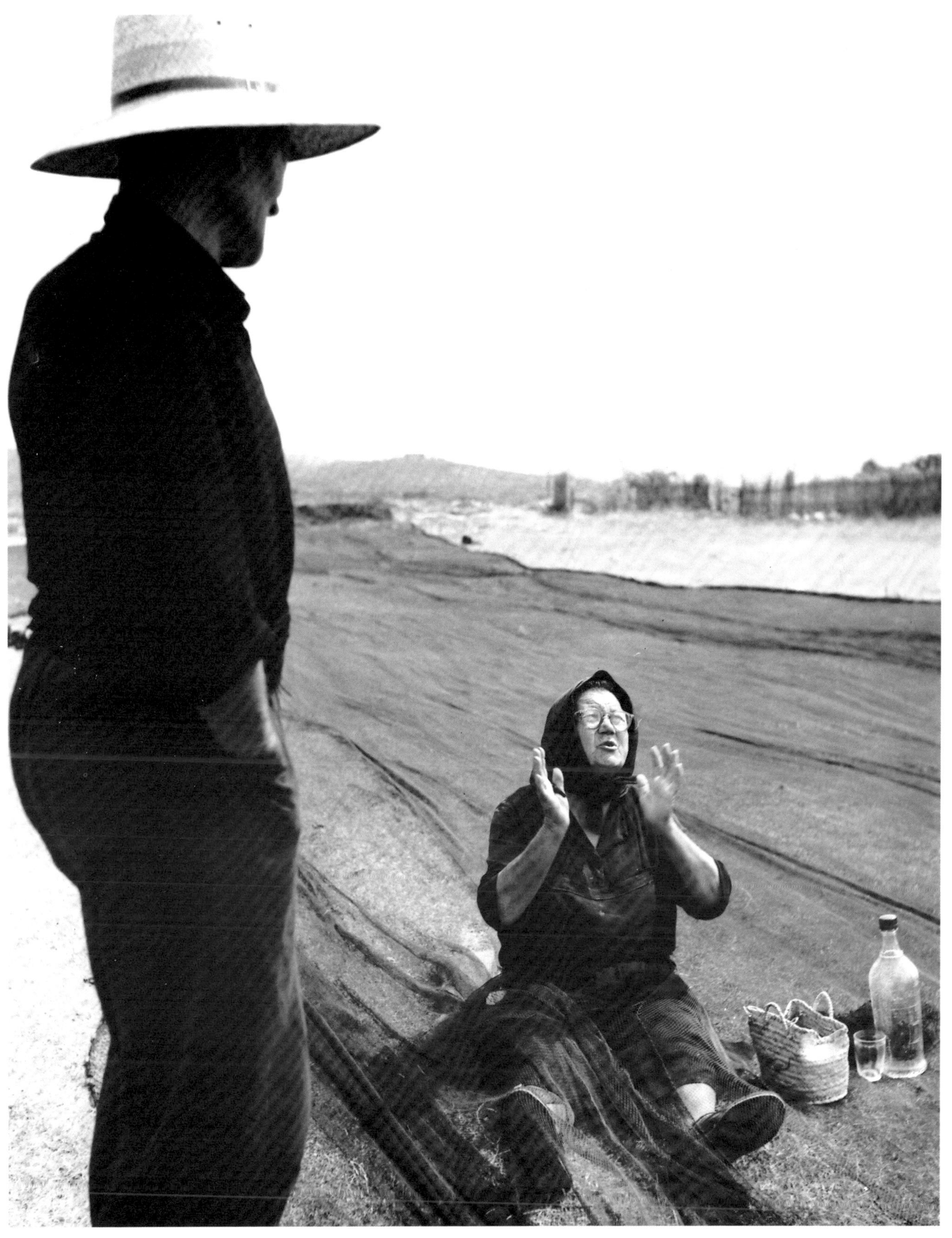

93

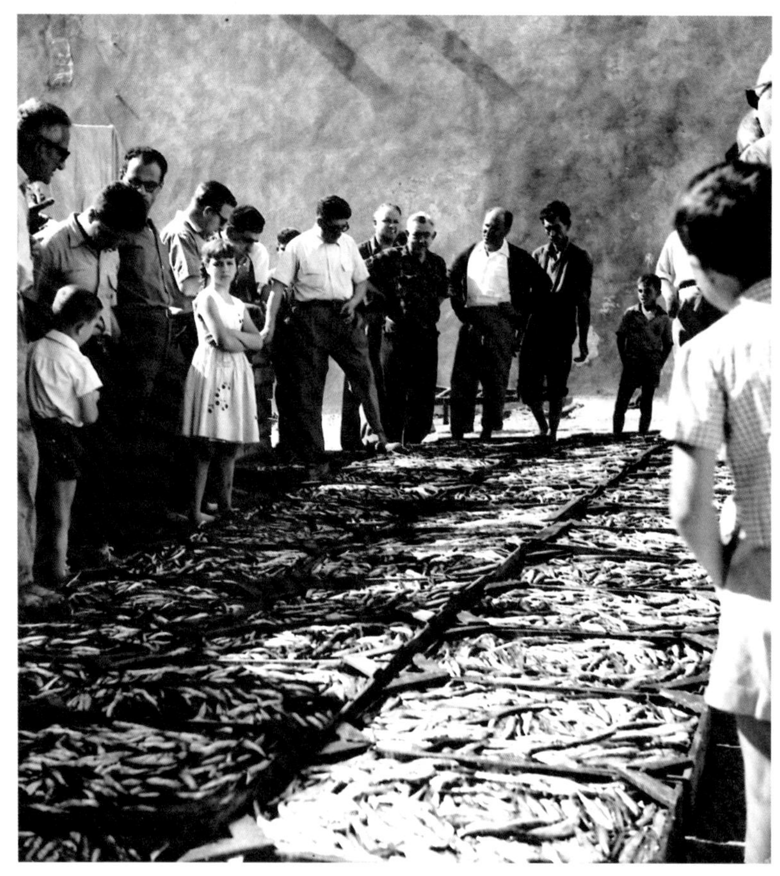

94

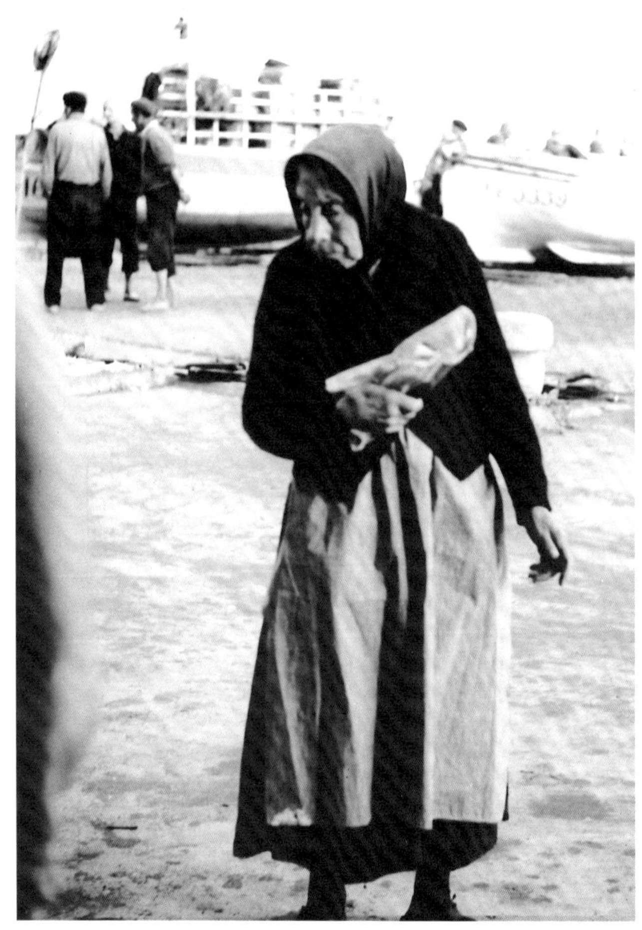

95

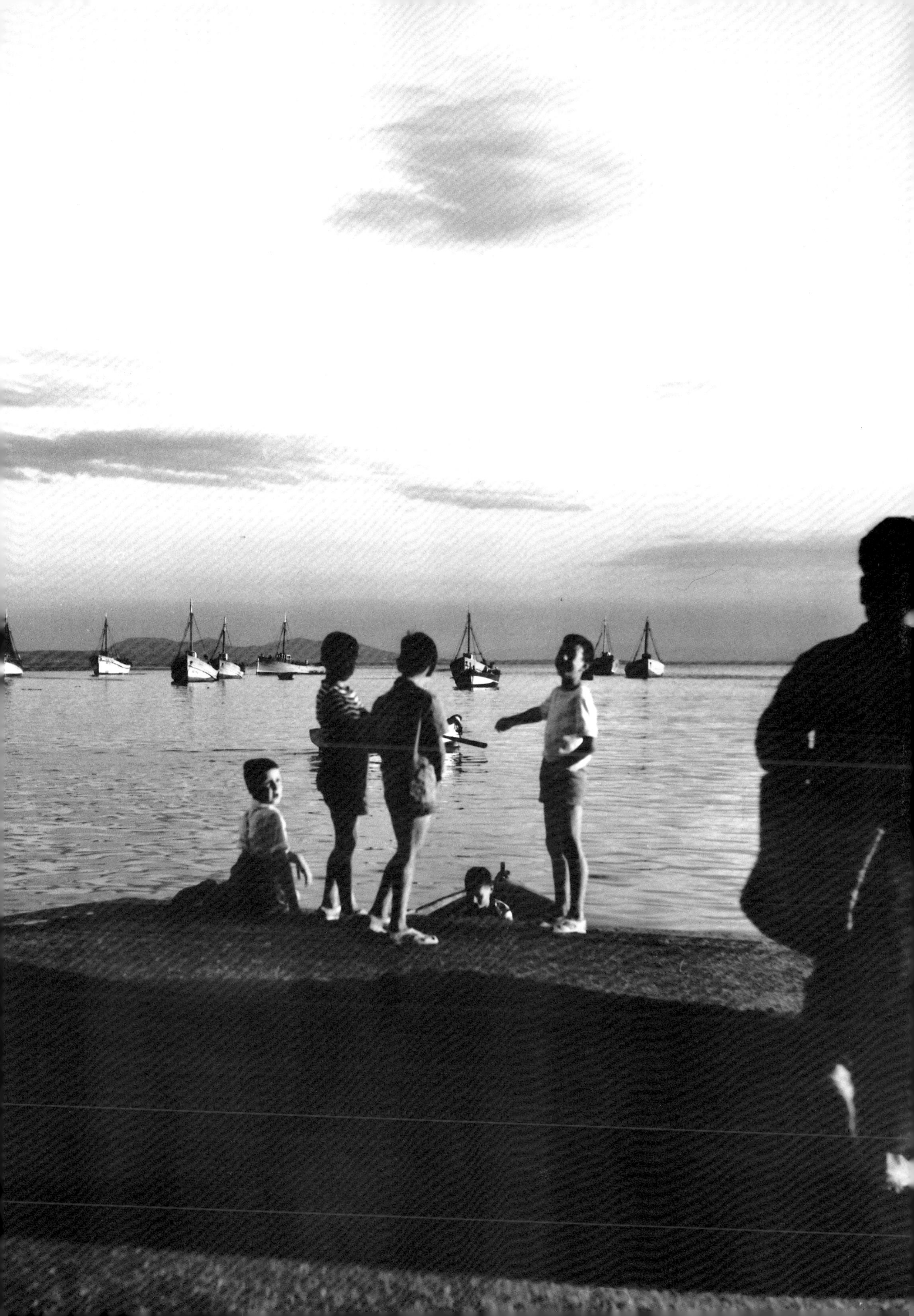

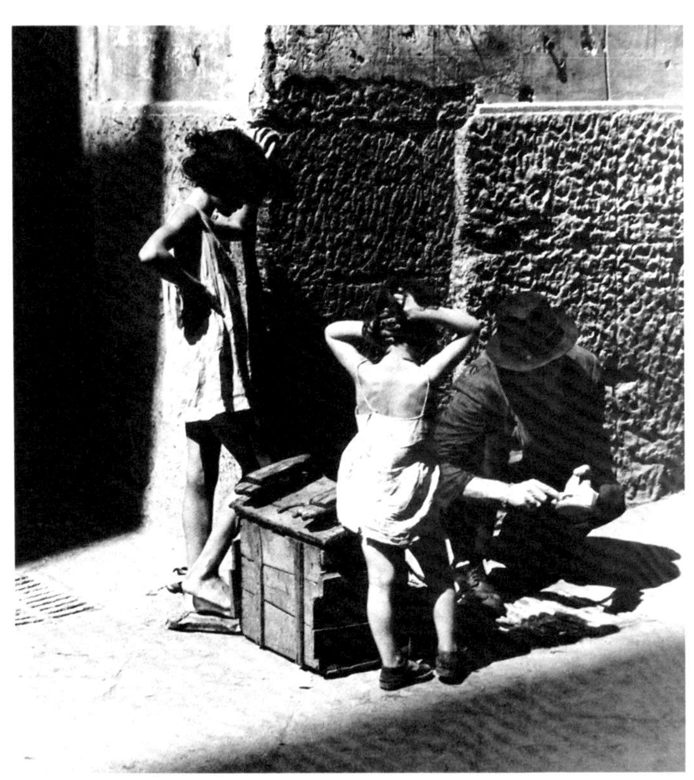

97

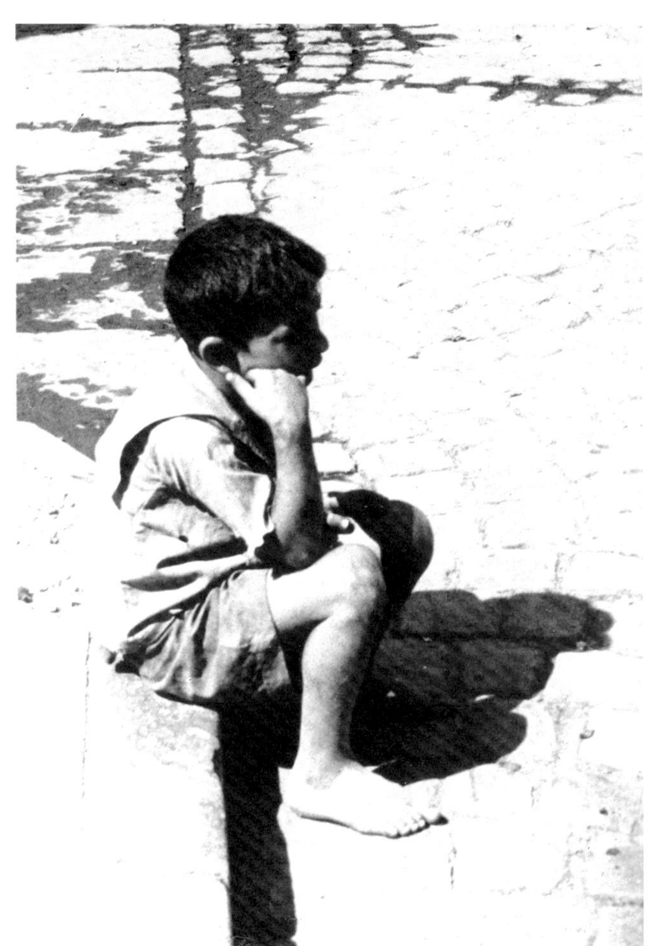

98

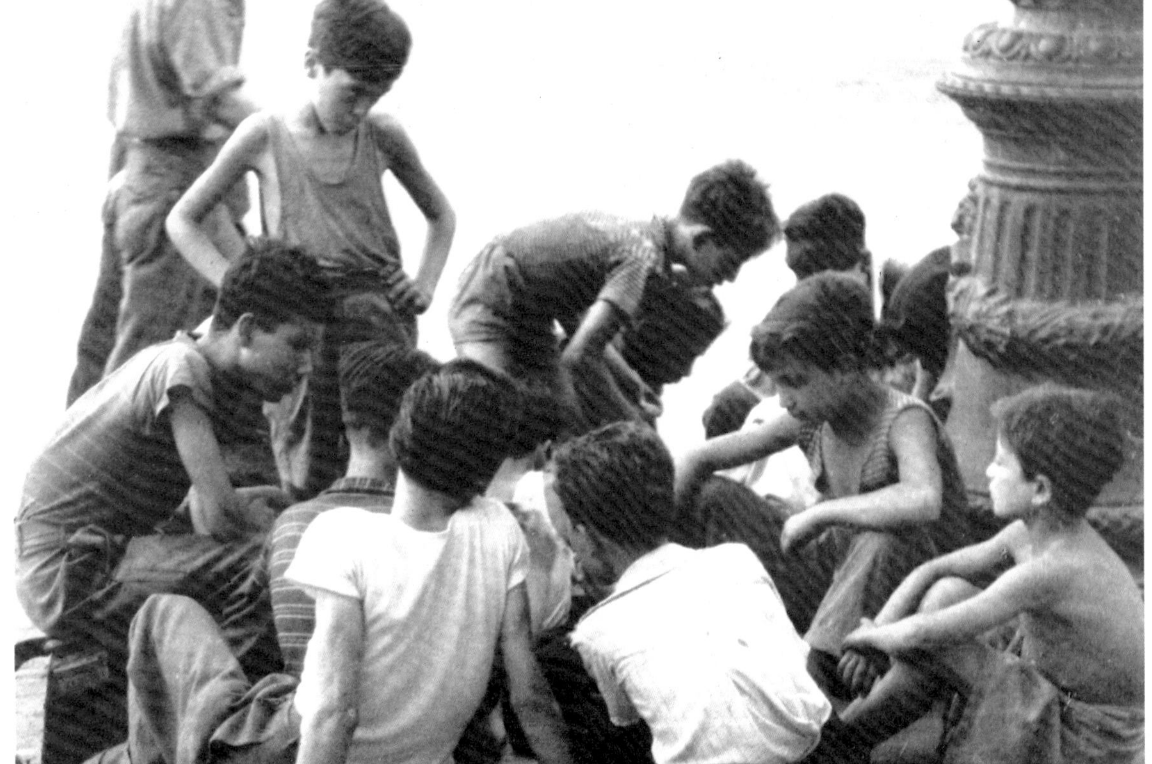

99

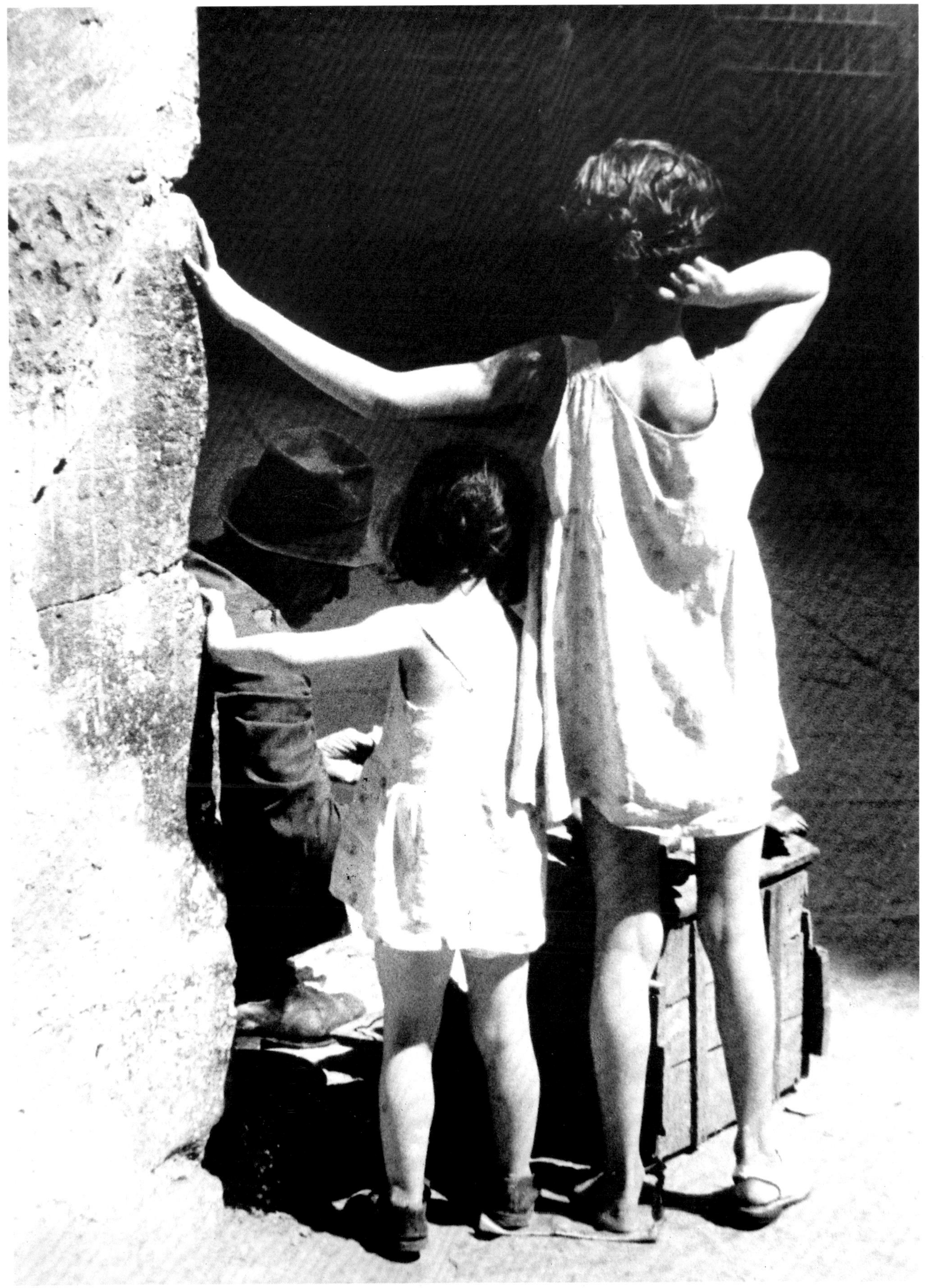

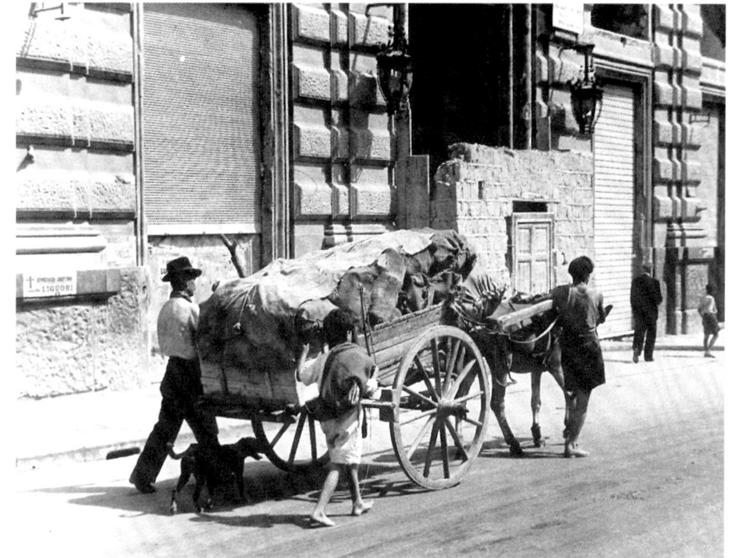

101

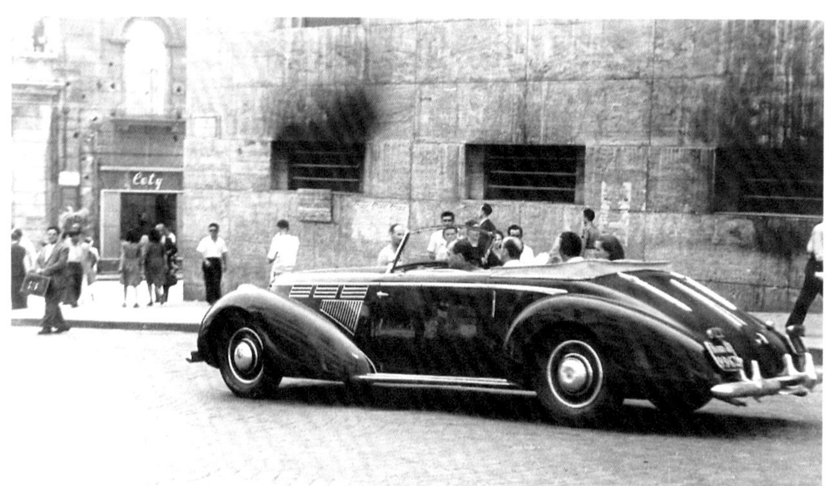

102

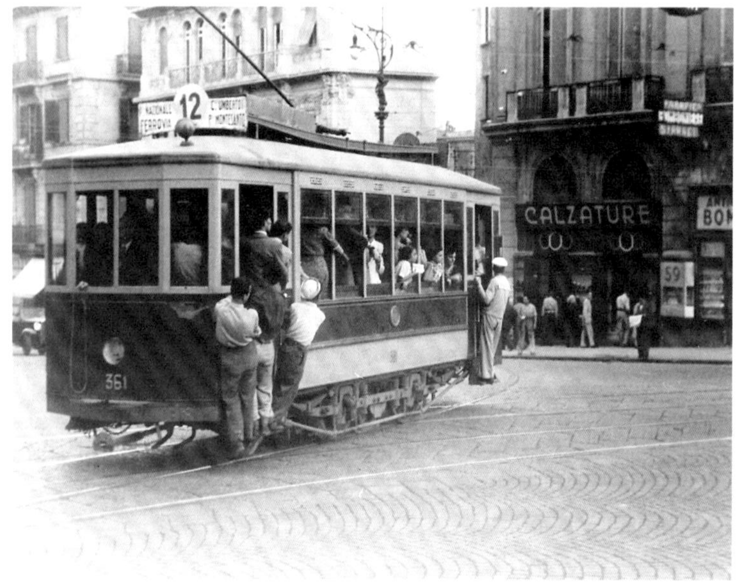

103

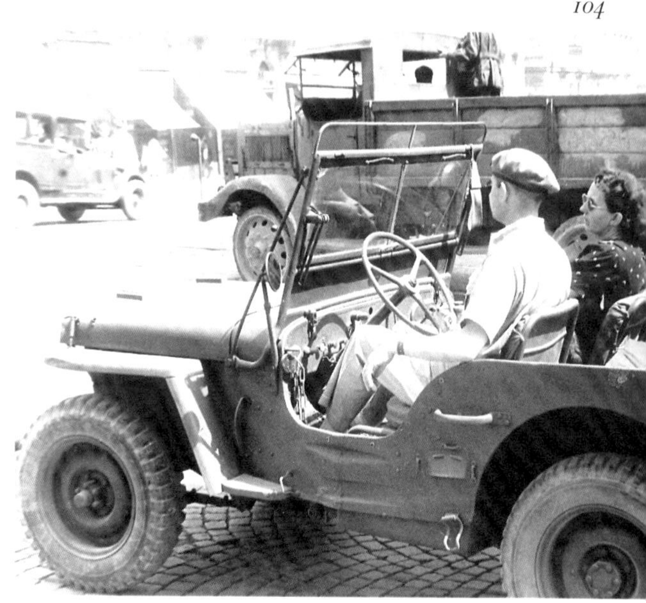

104

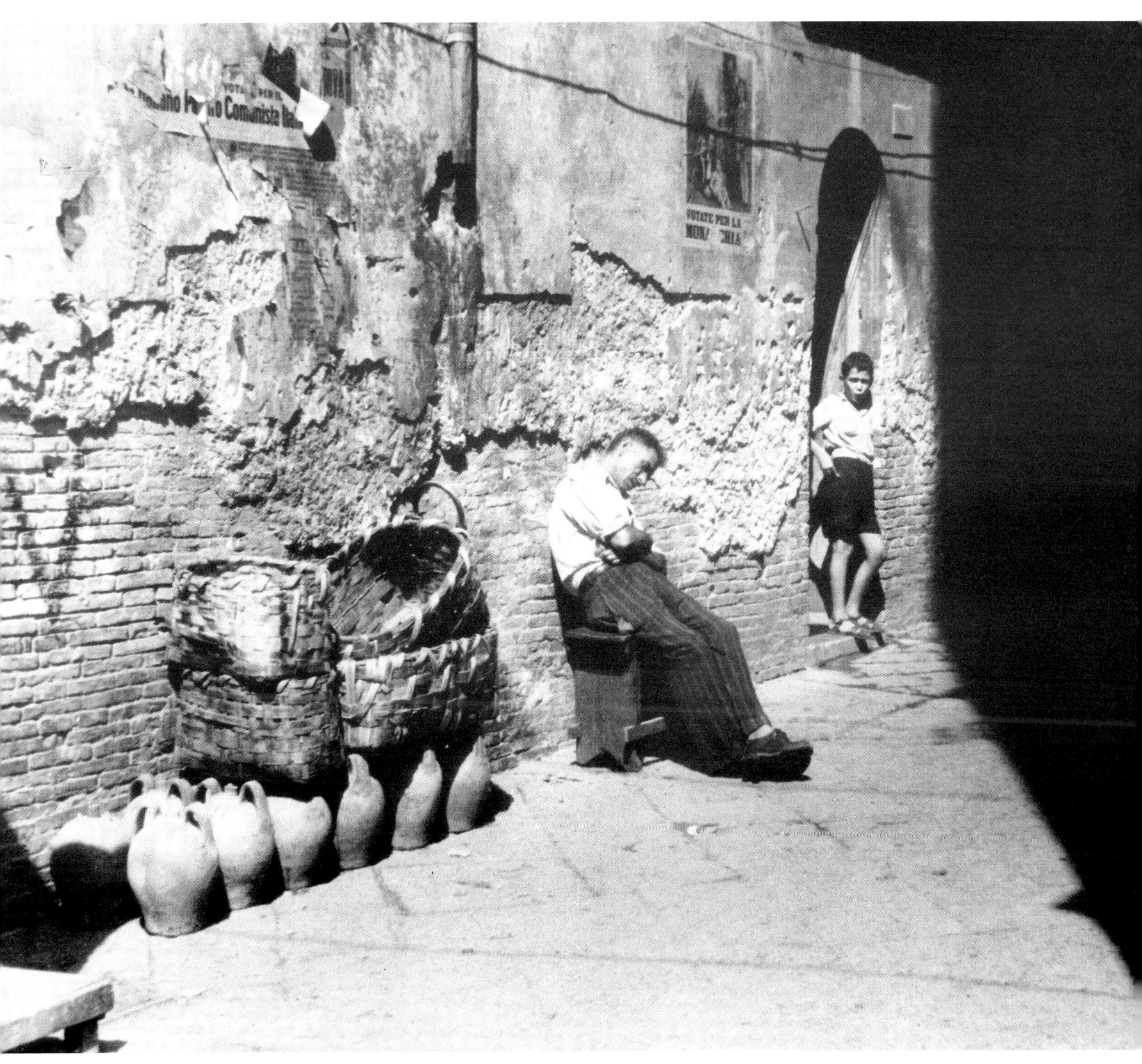
VOTATE PER IL
Partito Comunista Italiano
VOTATE PER LA
MONARCHIA

105

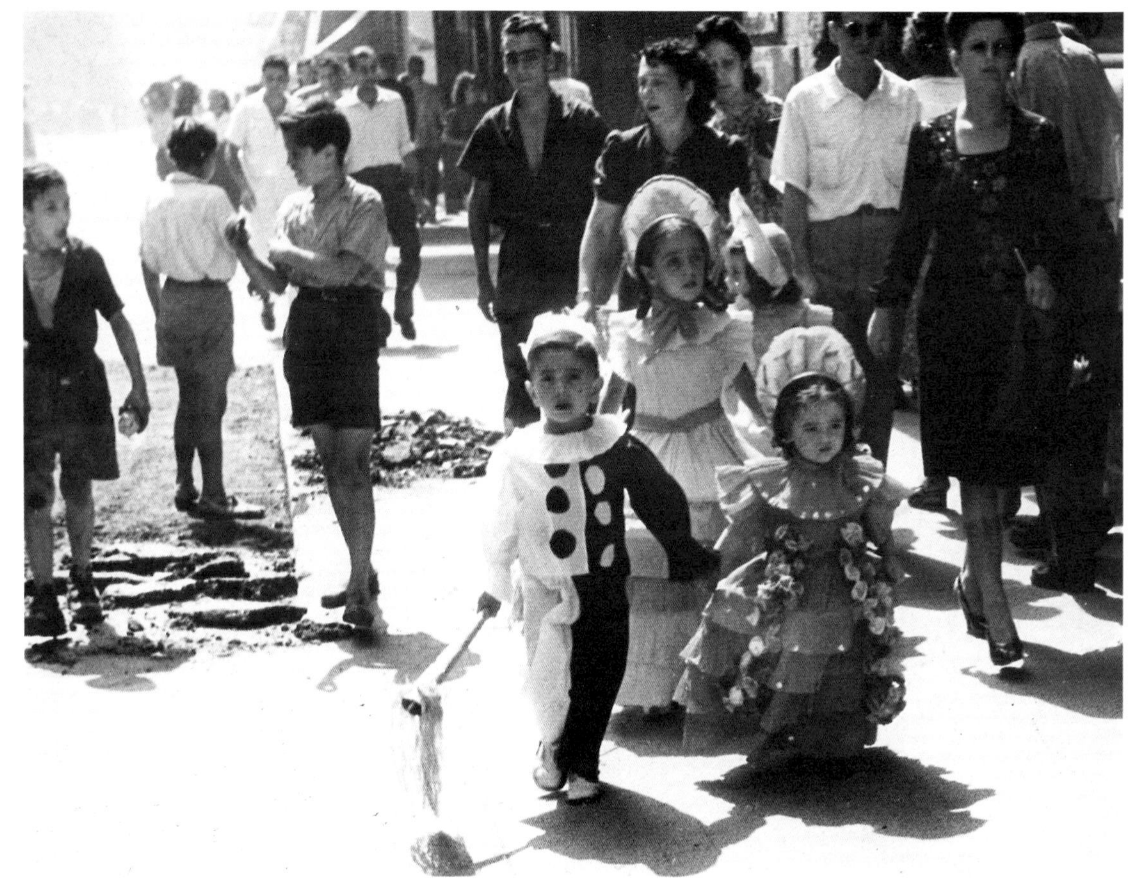

106

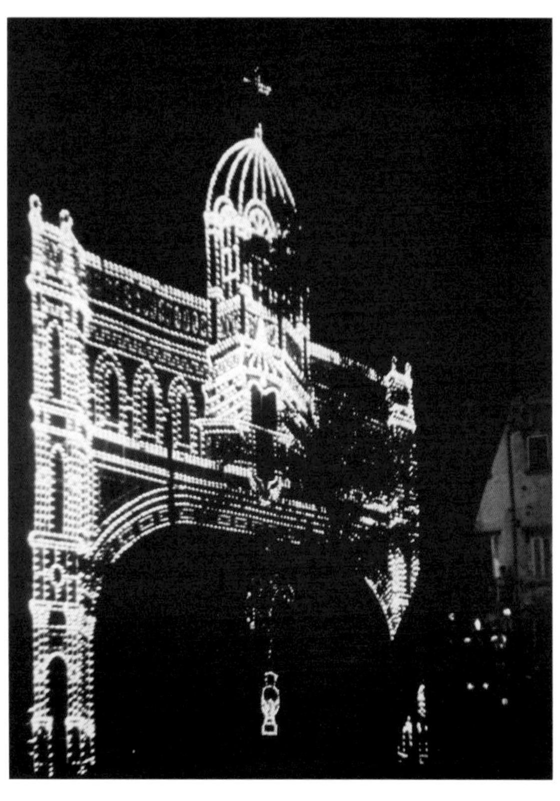

107

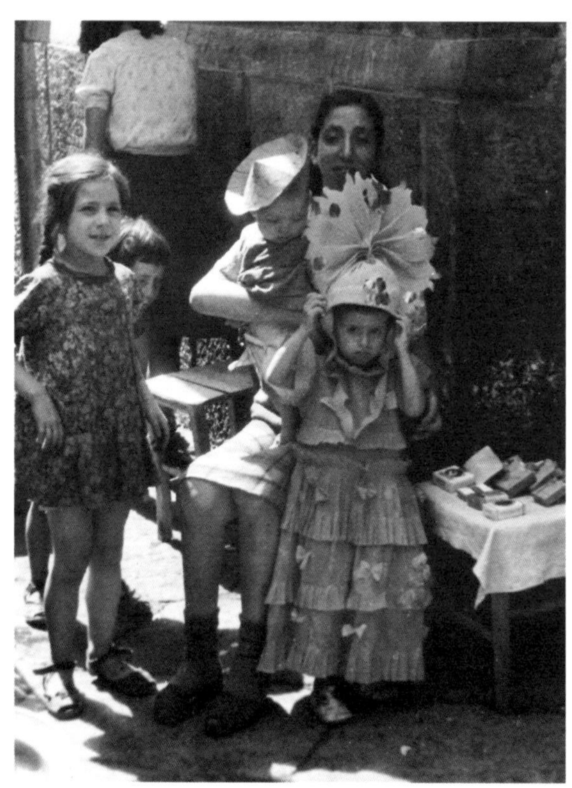

108

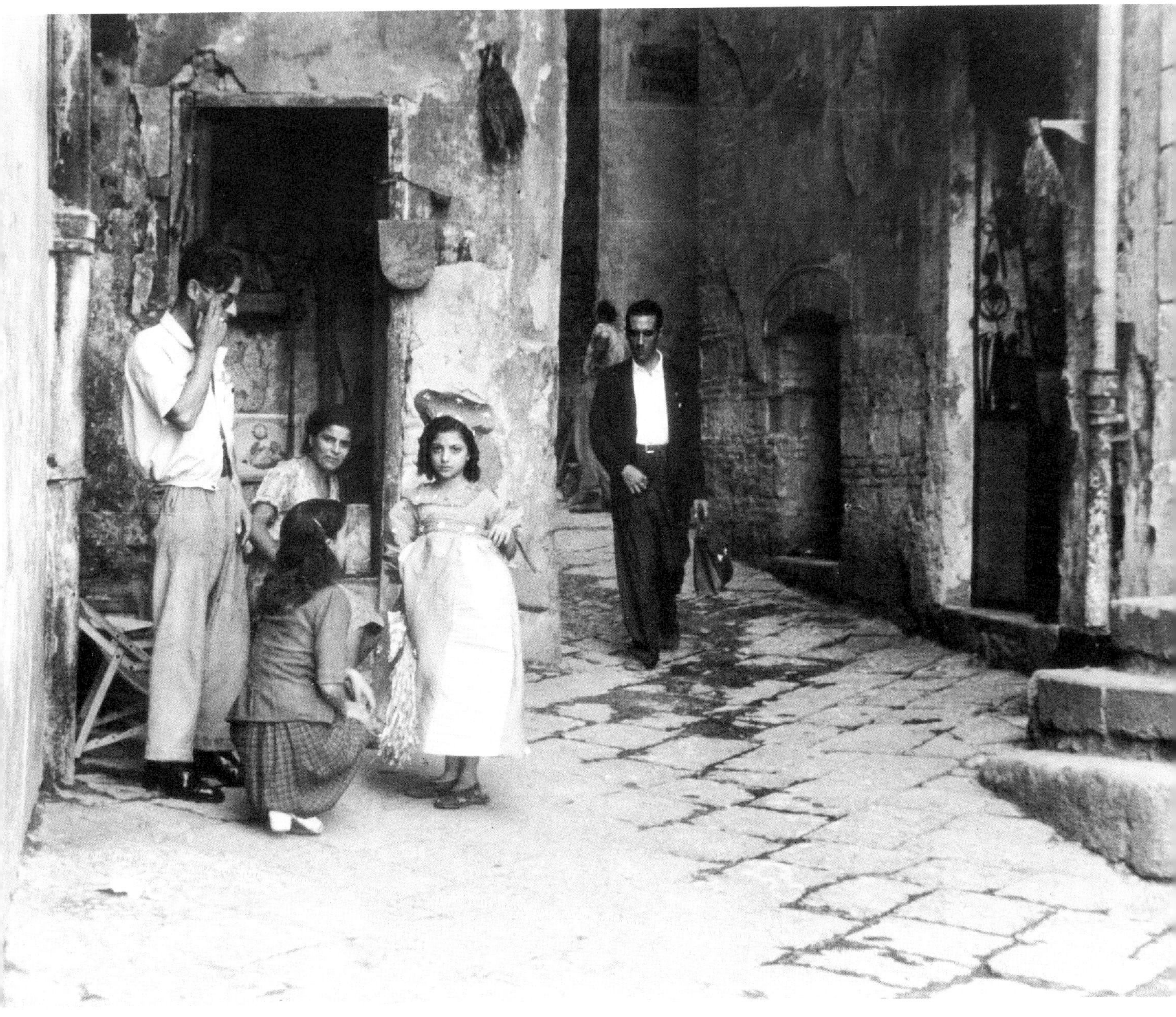

109

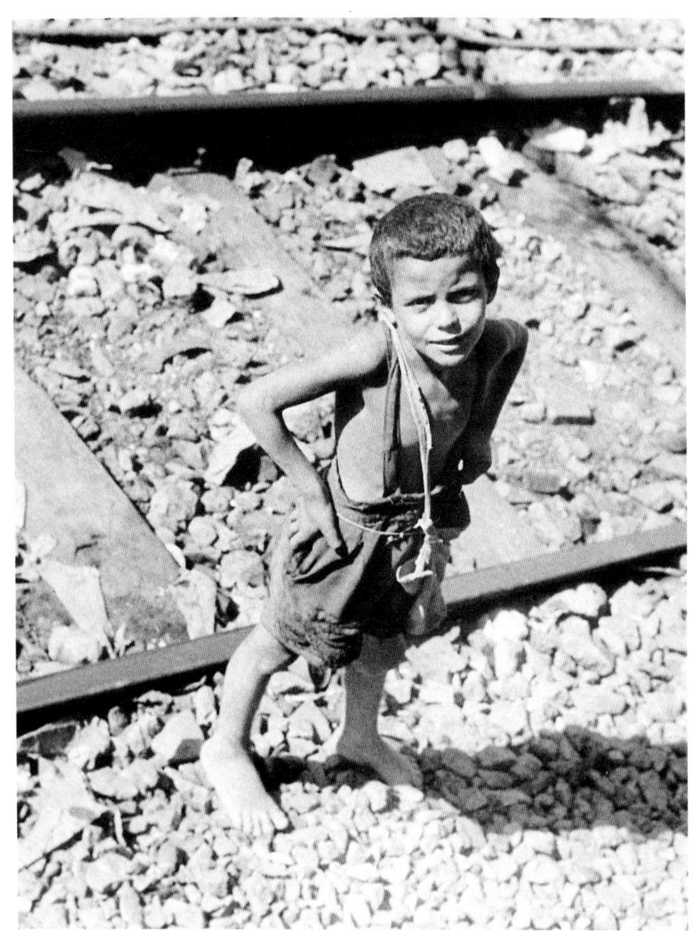

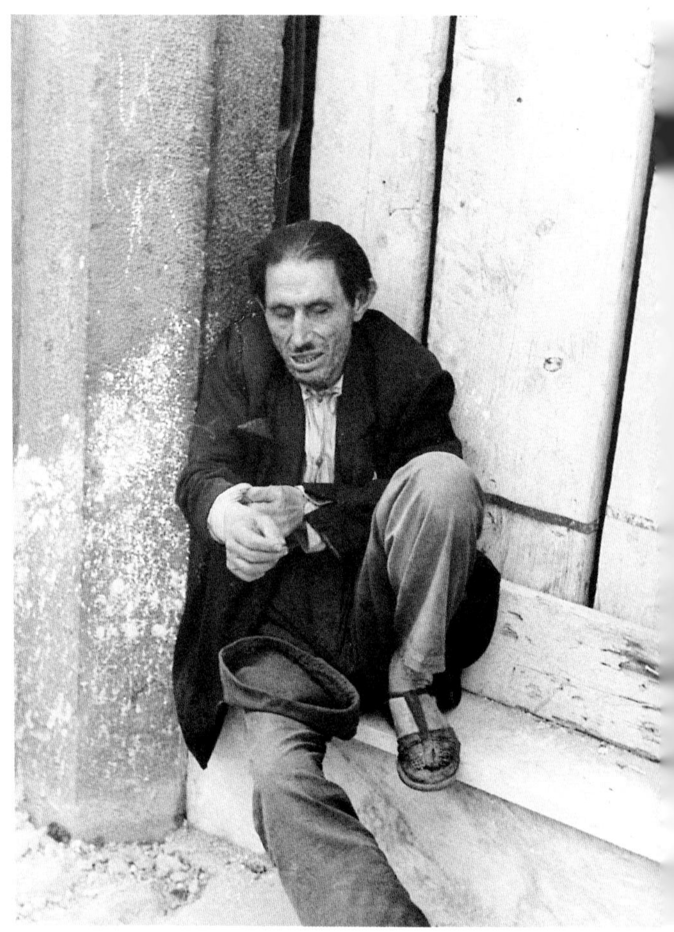

110

11

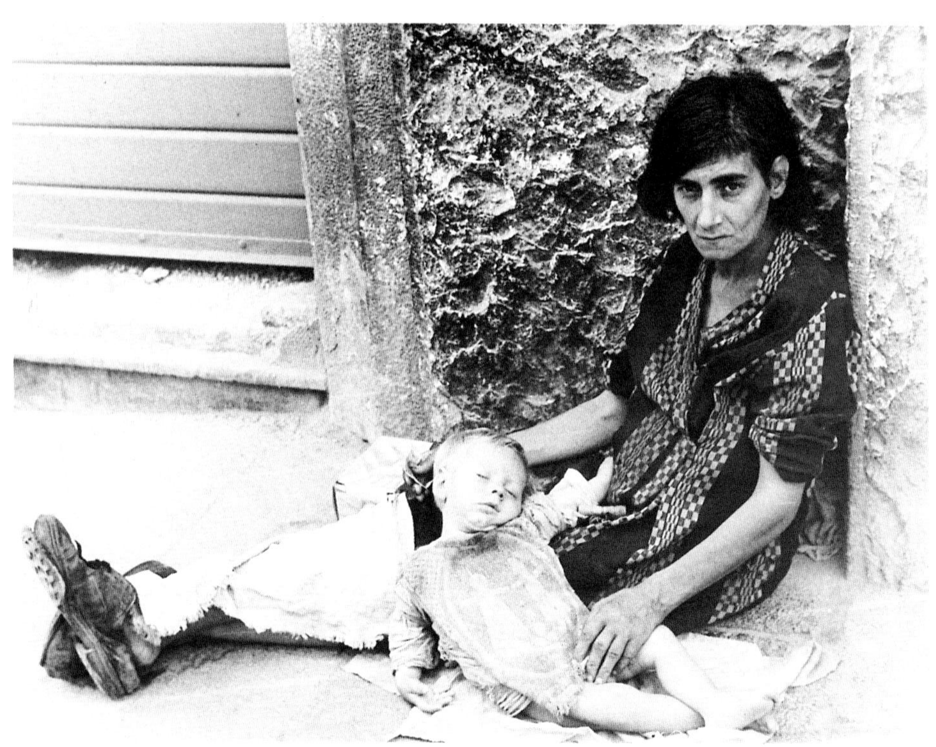

112

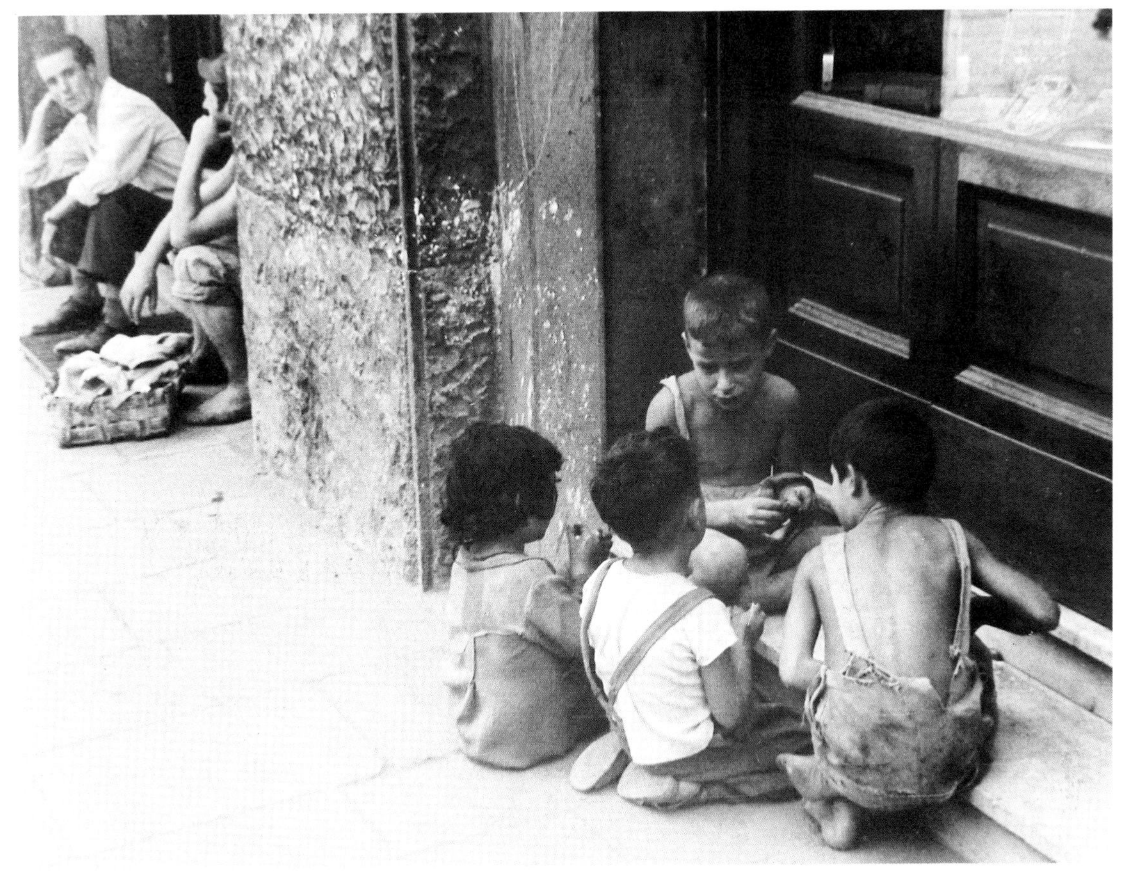

113

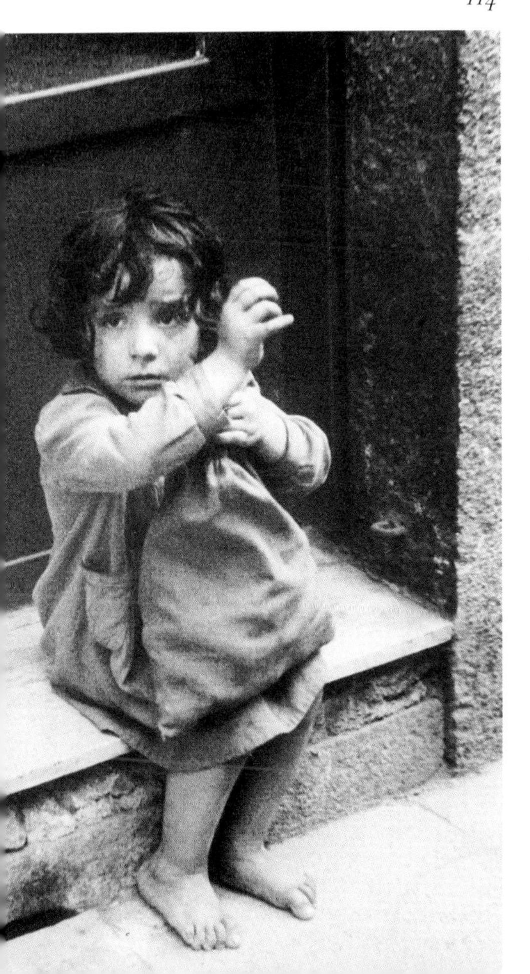

114

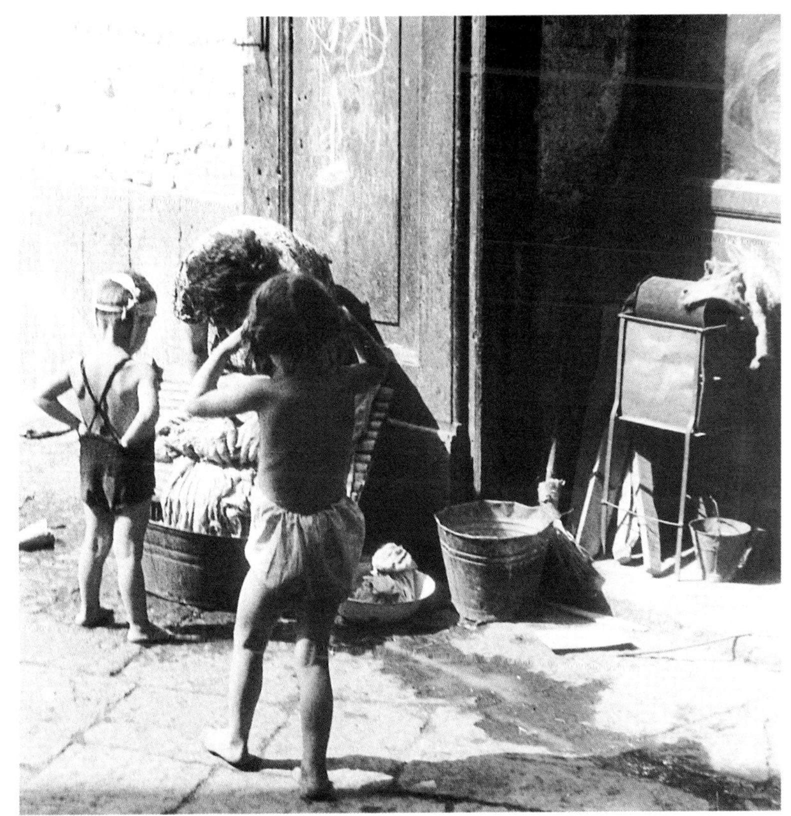

115

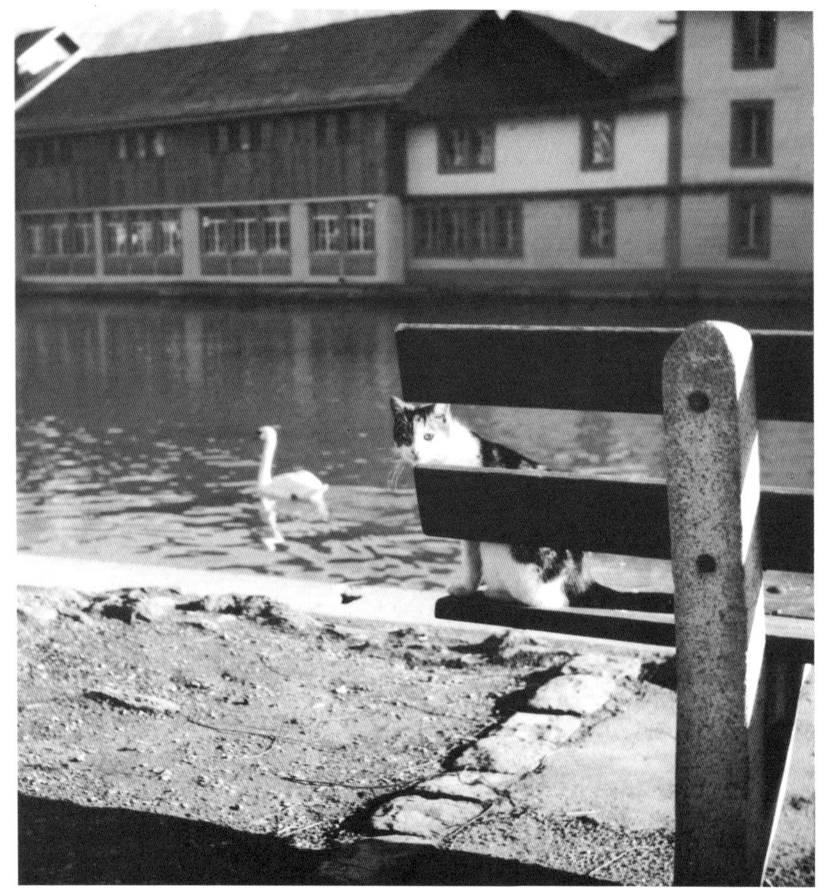

116

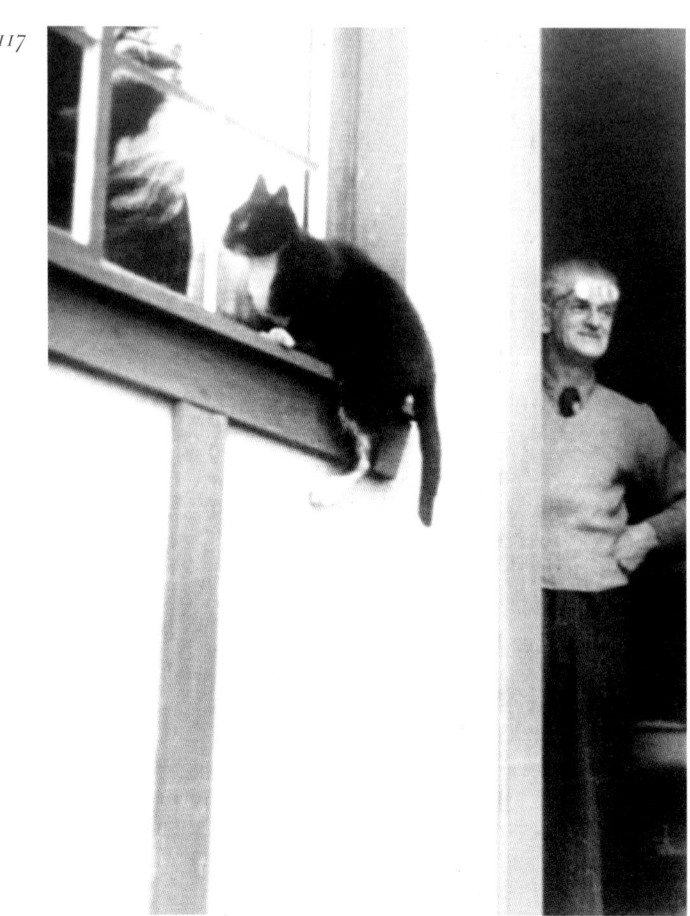

117

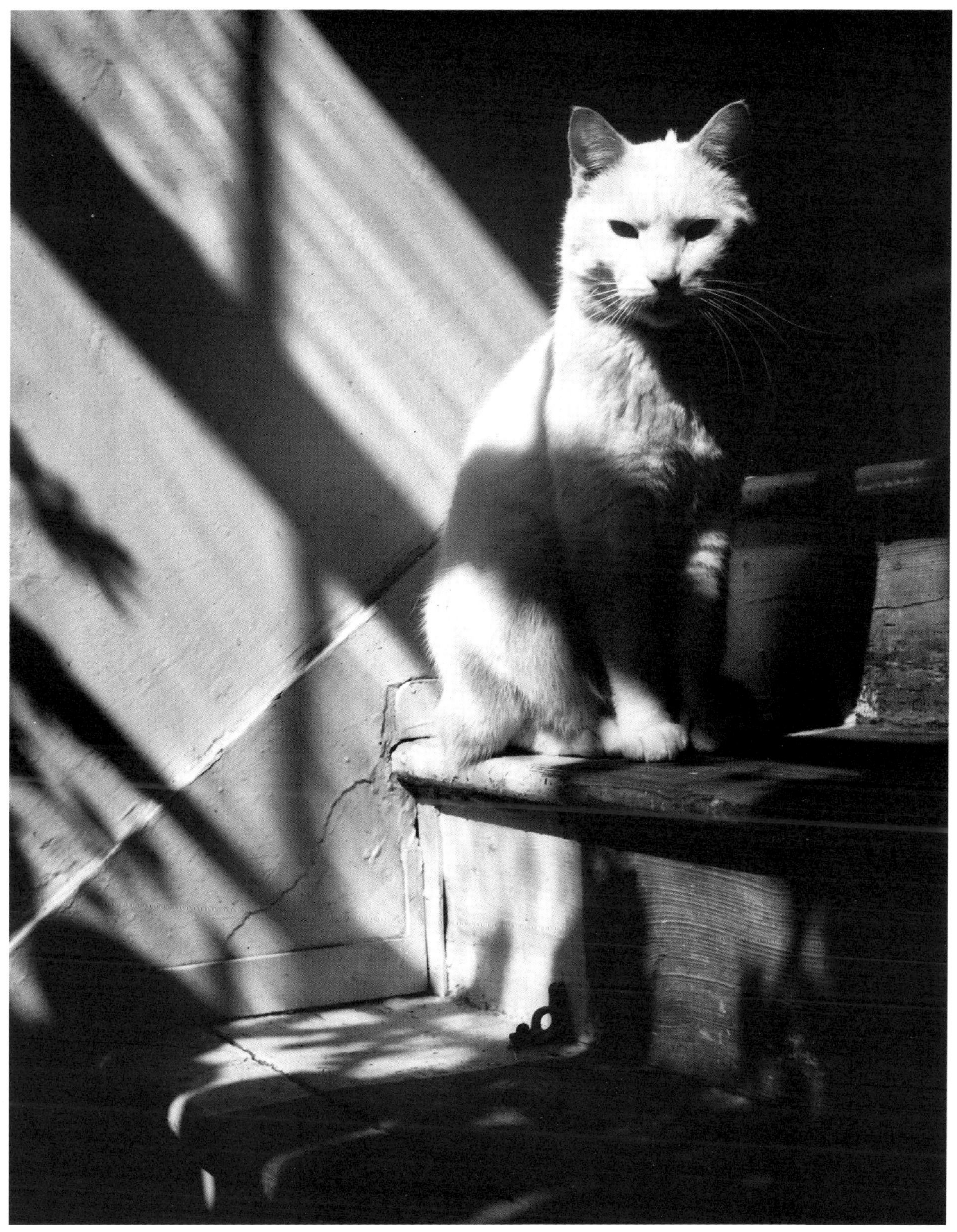

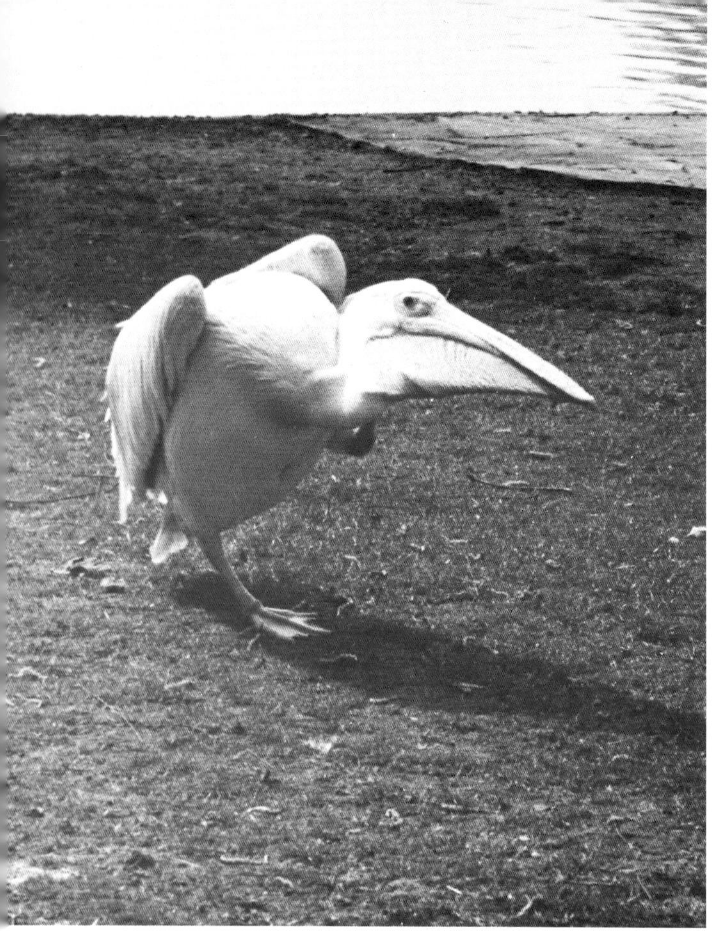

119

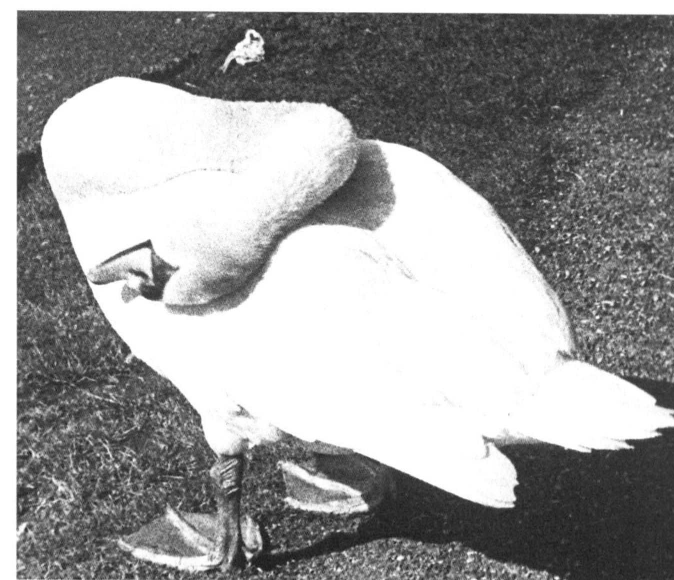

120

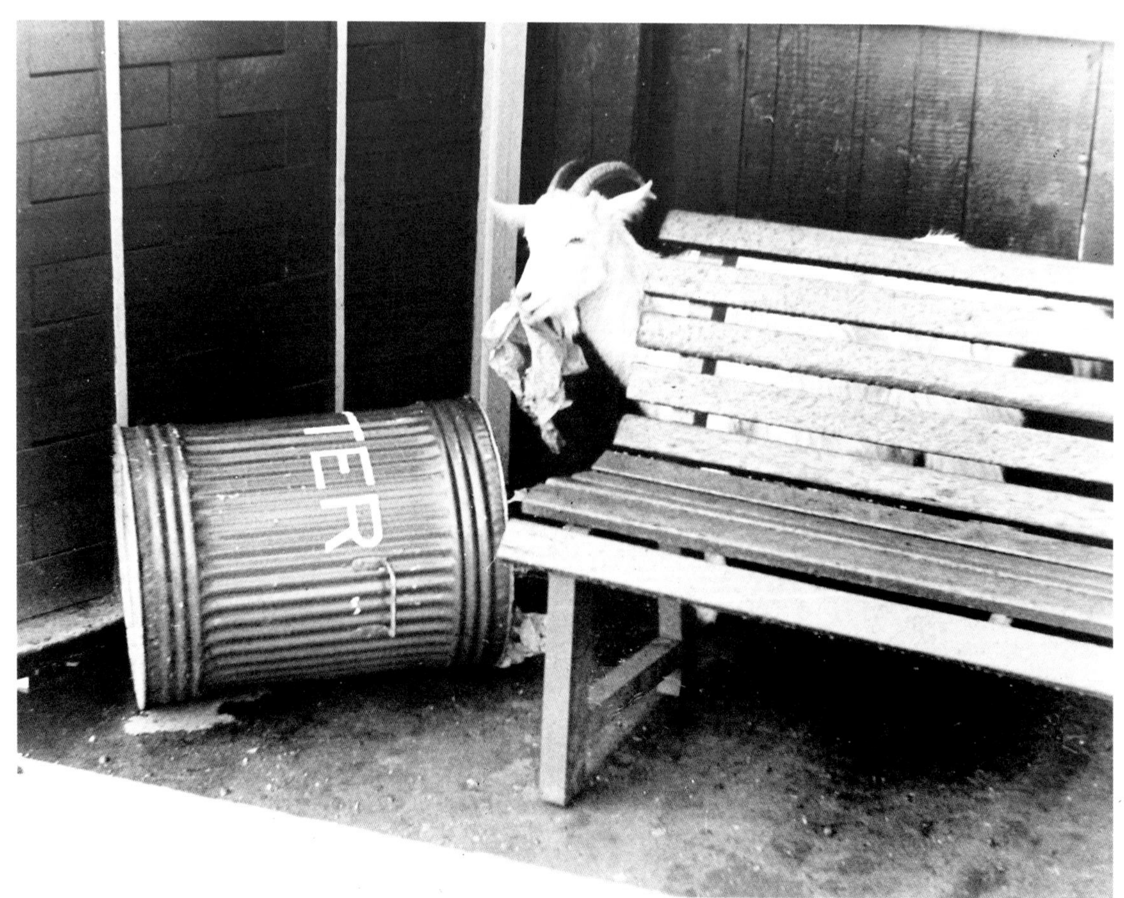

121

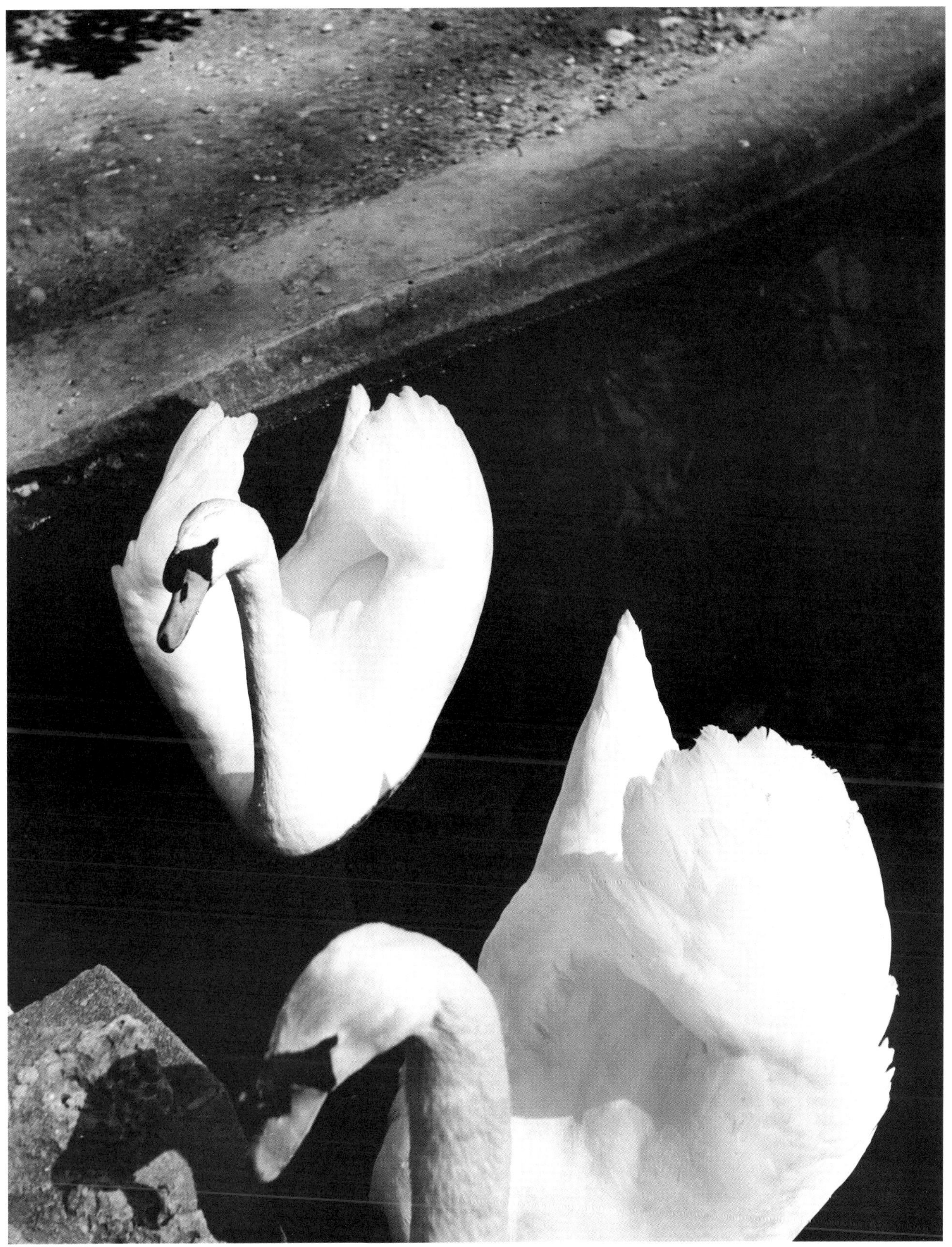

122

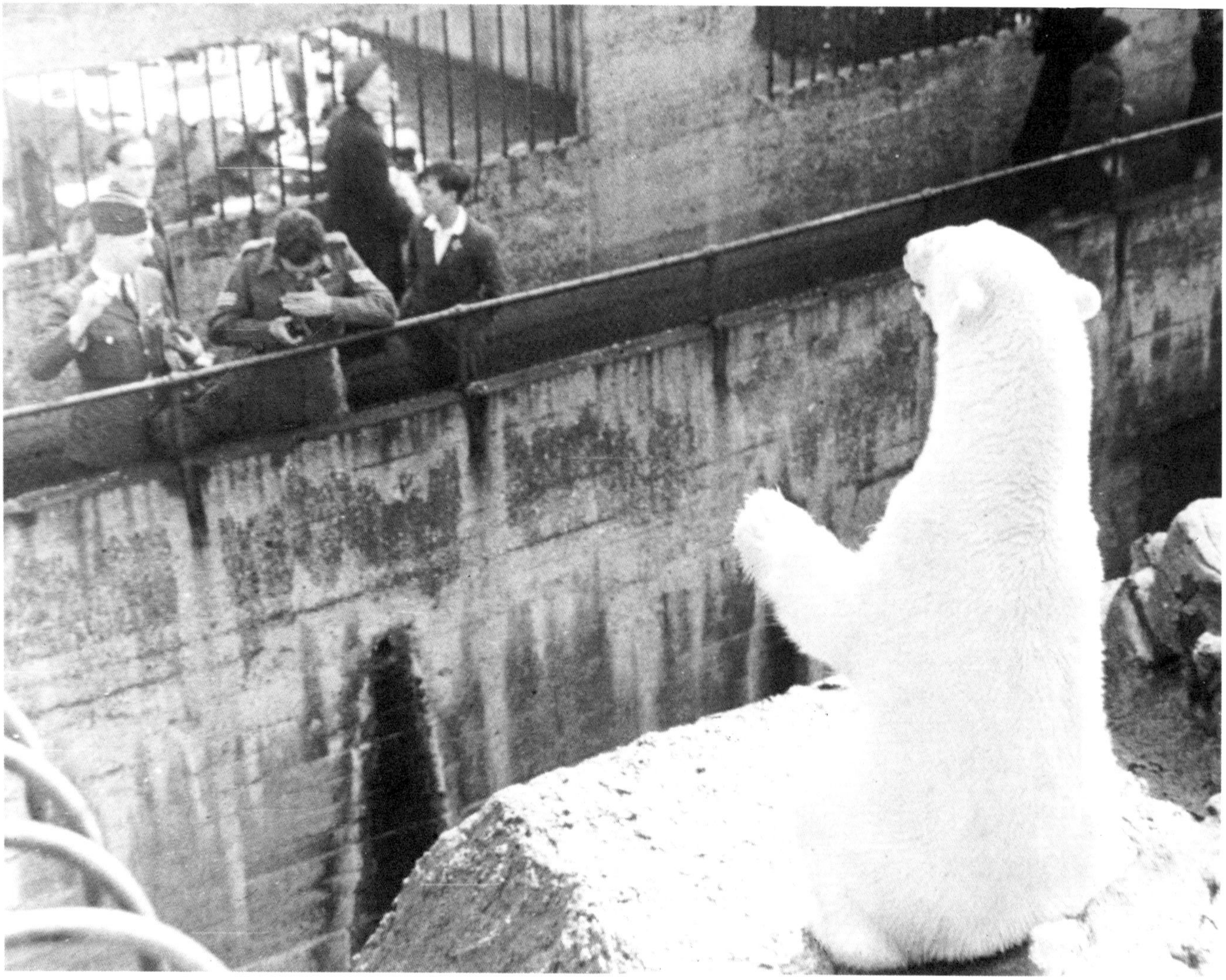

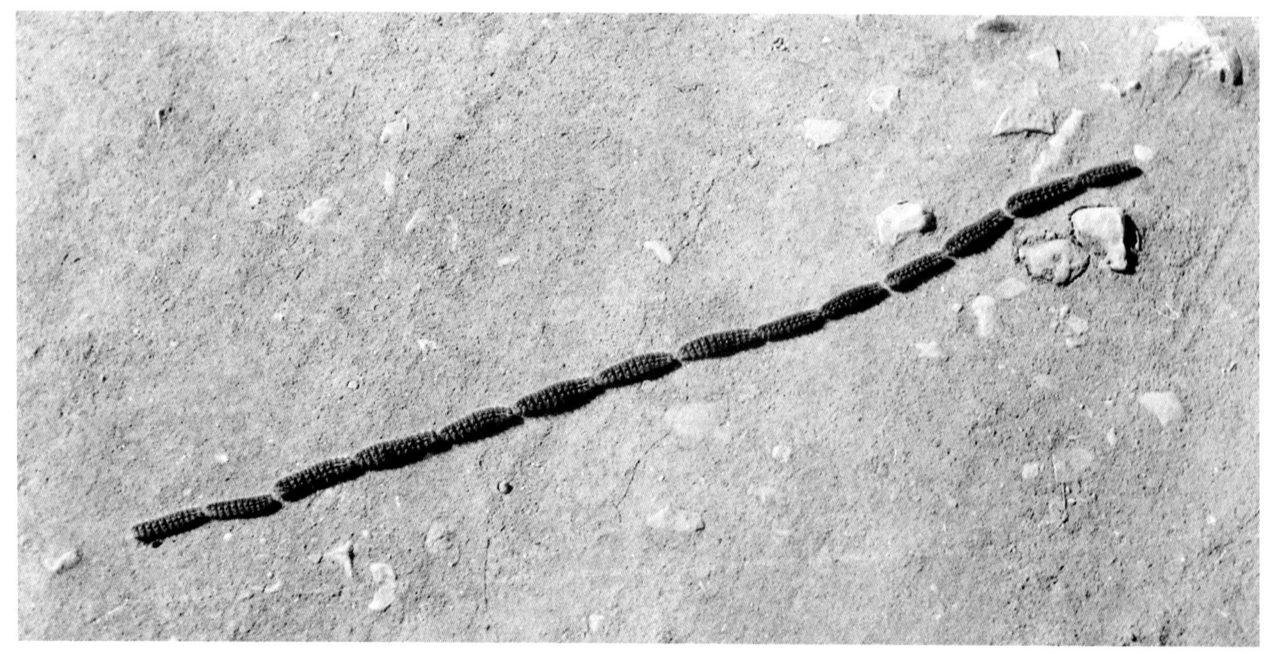

123

124

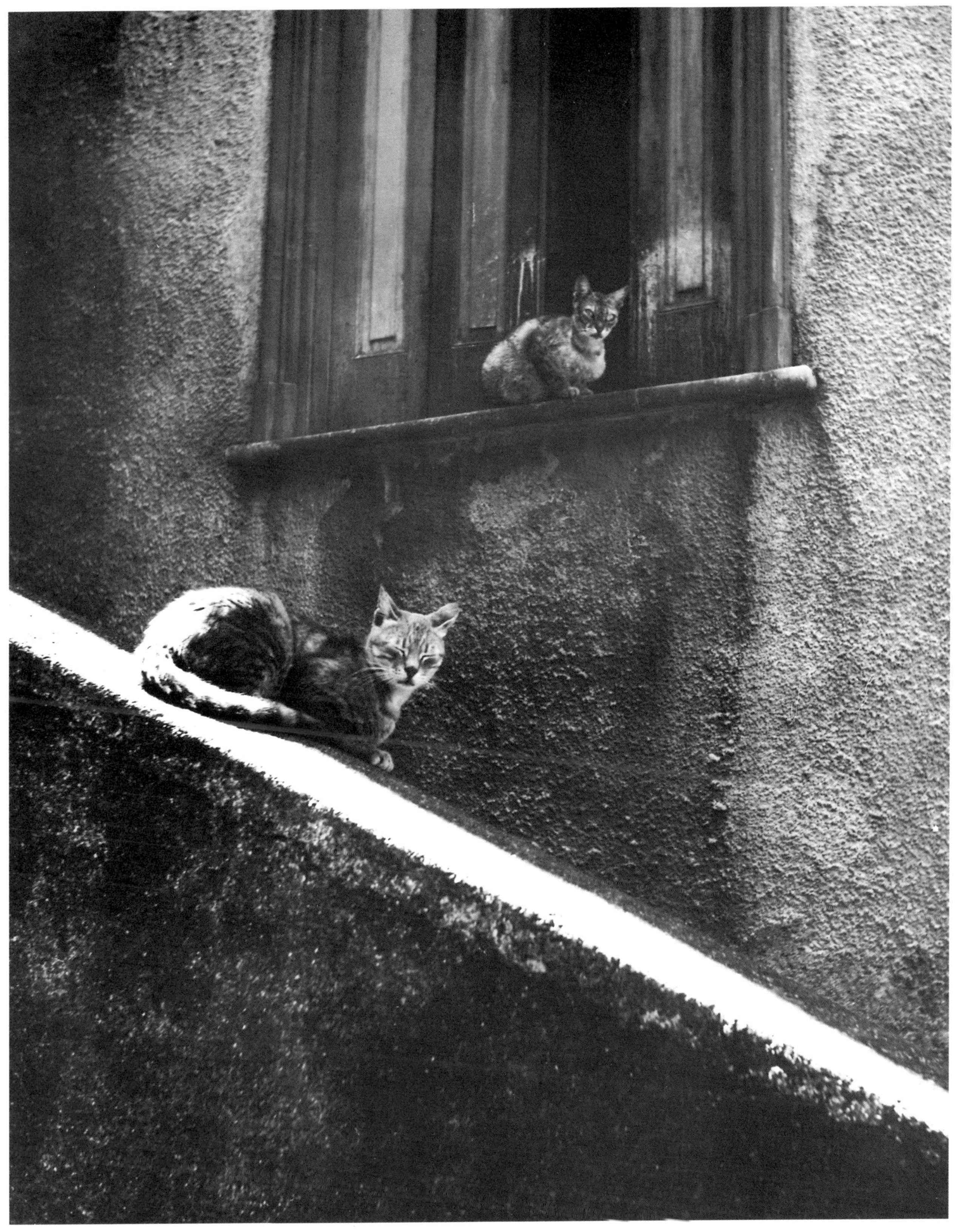

127

126

127

1894
"BRAN"
1898-97.
R.M.J.
IN
MORY OF
"SAAC"
UST 7TH 1896.
JULY 6TH 1894.
"GIOIA"
ADDIJ! ADDIJ! E'N'
ALDRA VOLD'ADDIJE
LA LUNDANANZA TUE
LA PENA MIJE.
14. APRILE 1900.
IN
FAITHFUL
REMEMBRANC
AT ALL TIMES

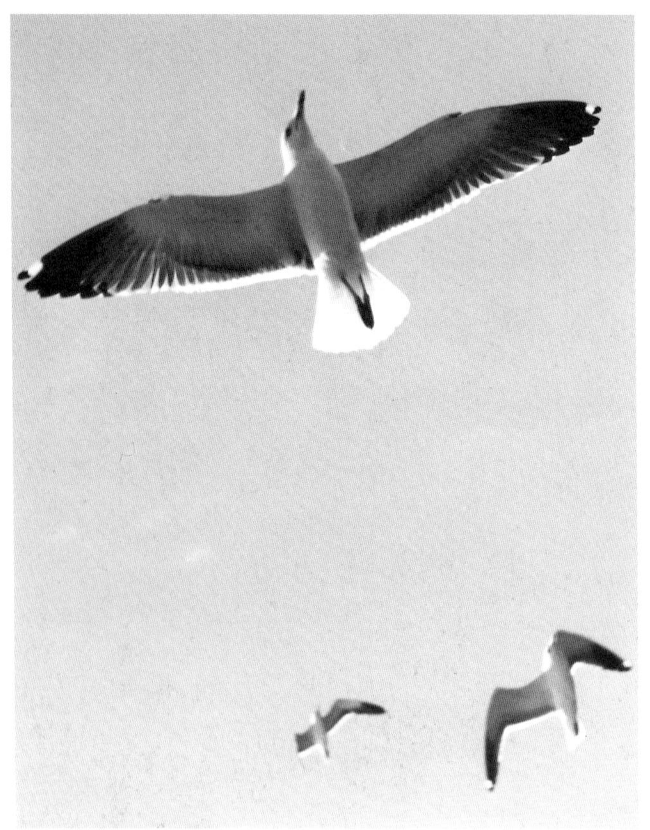

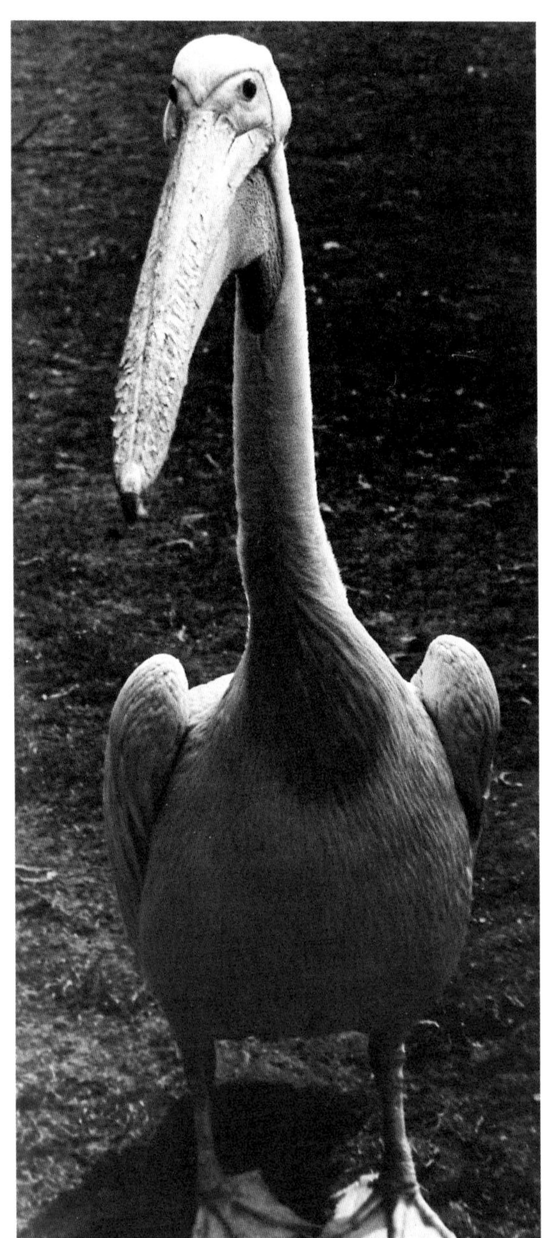

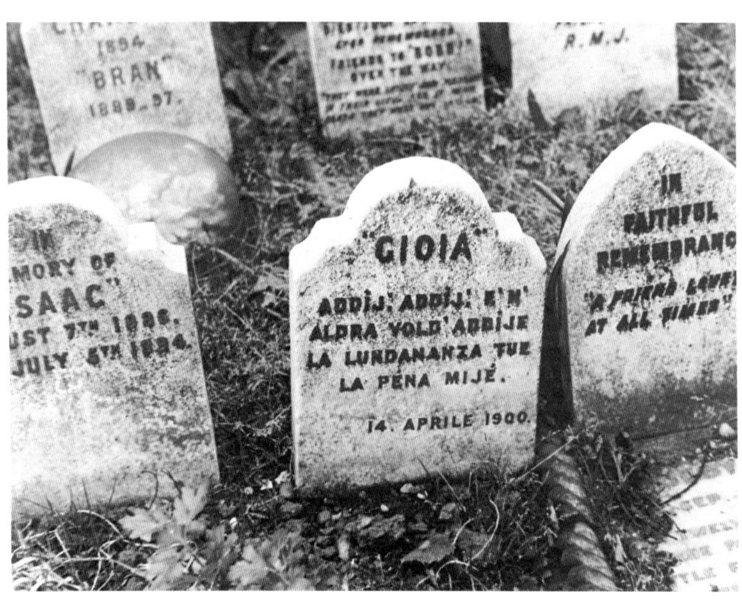

128

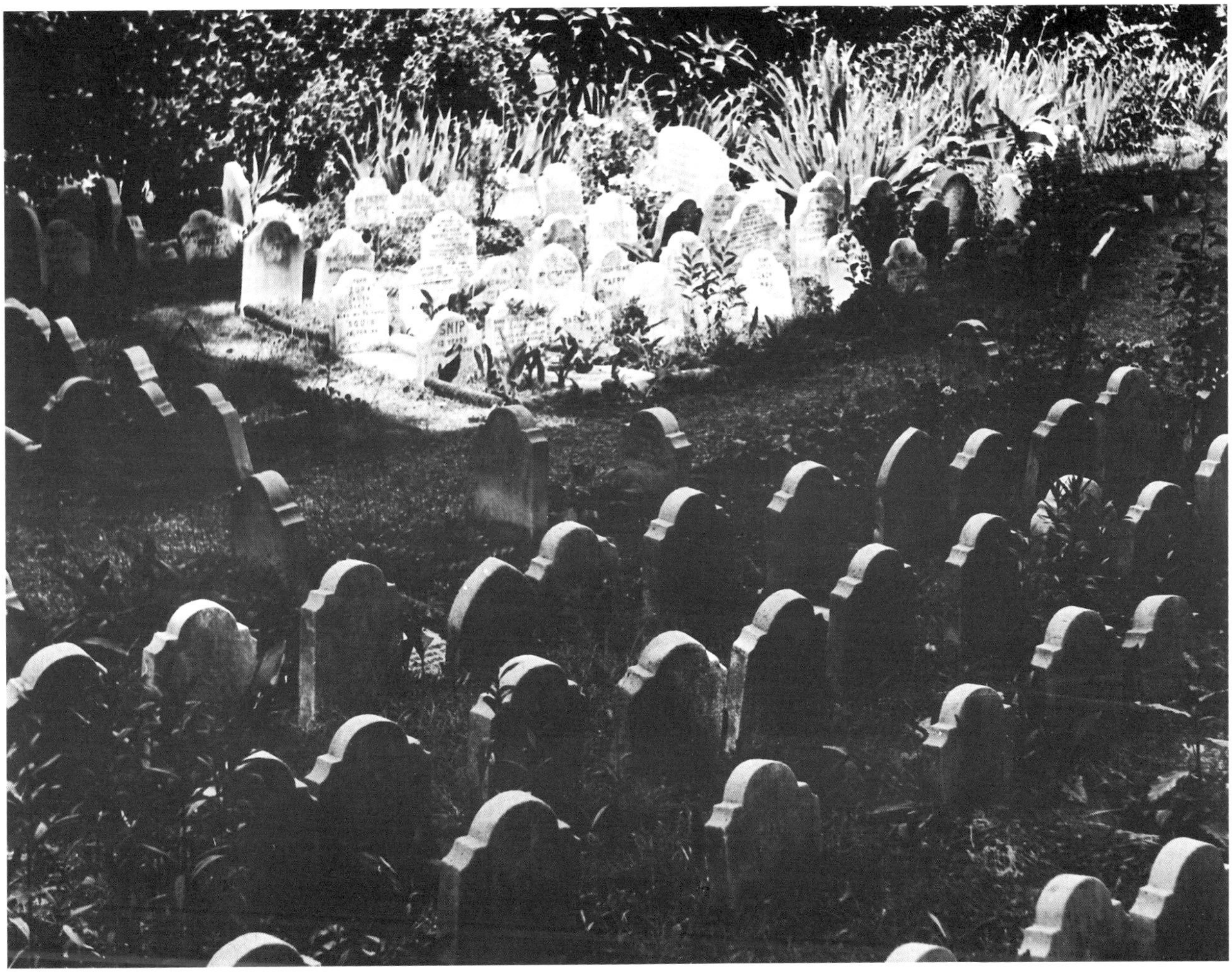

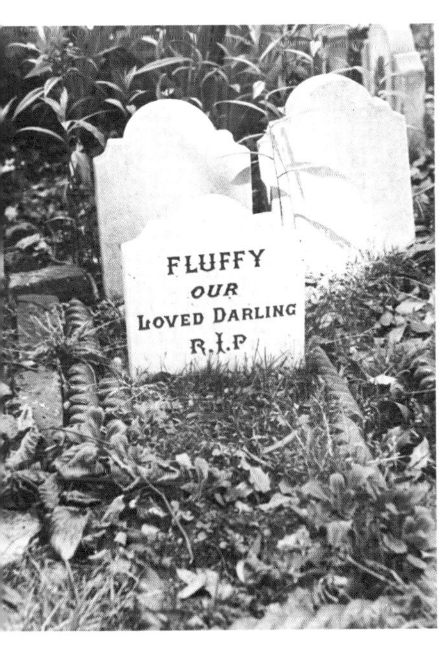

129

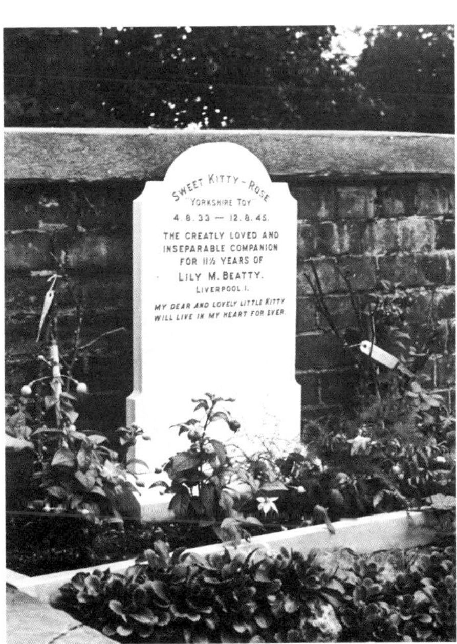

130

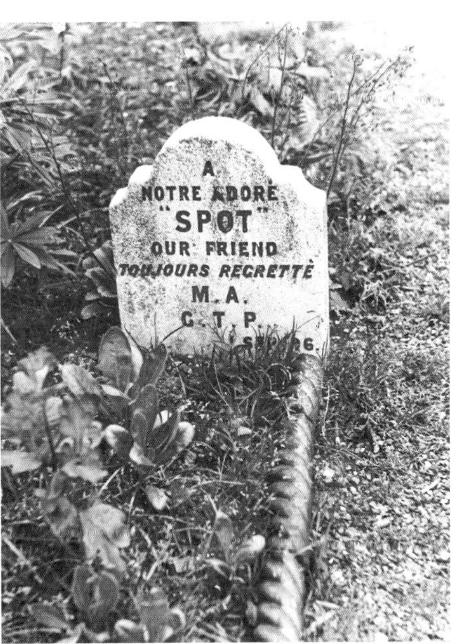

131

132

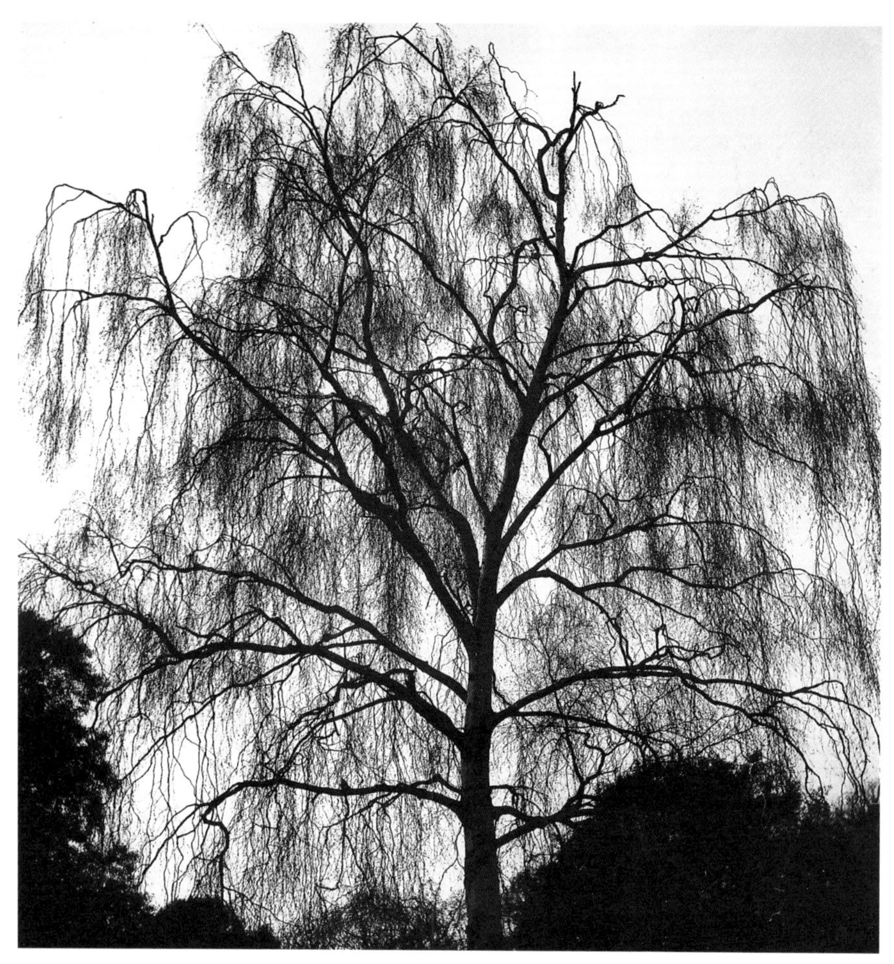

133

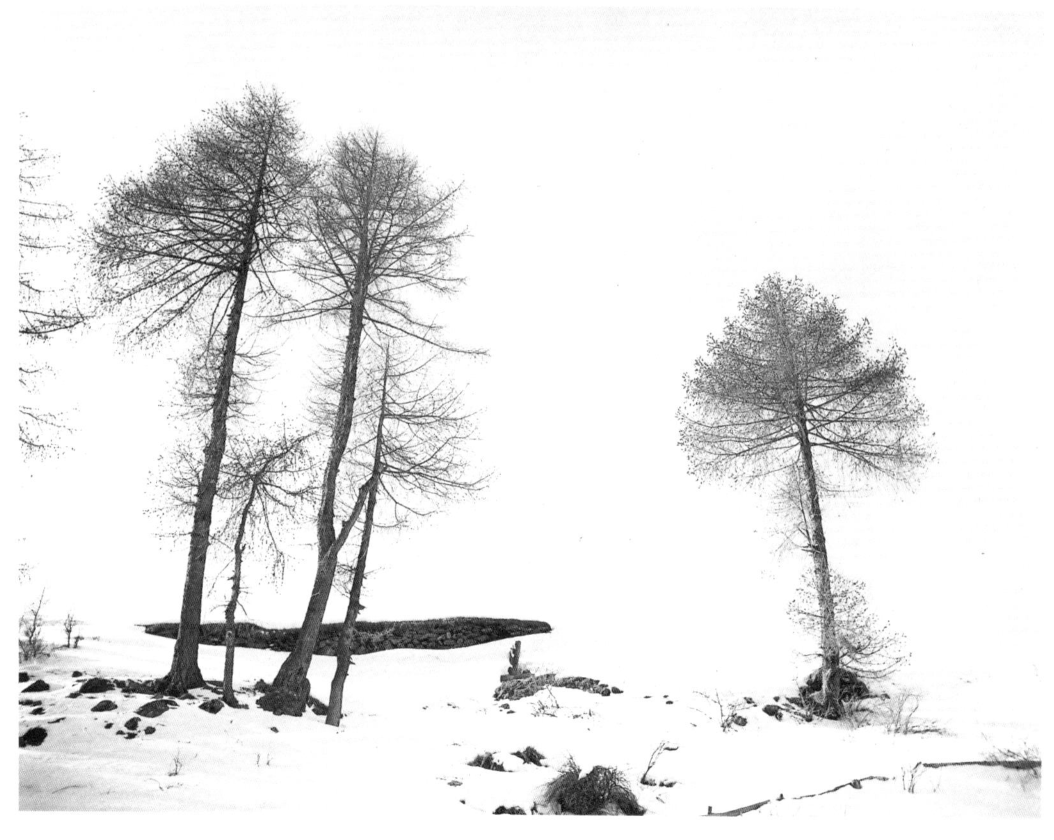

134

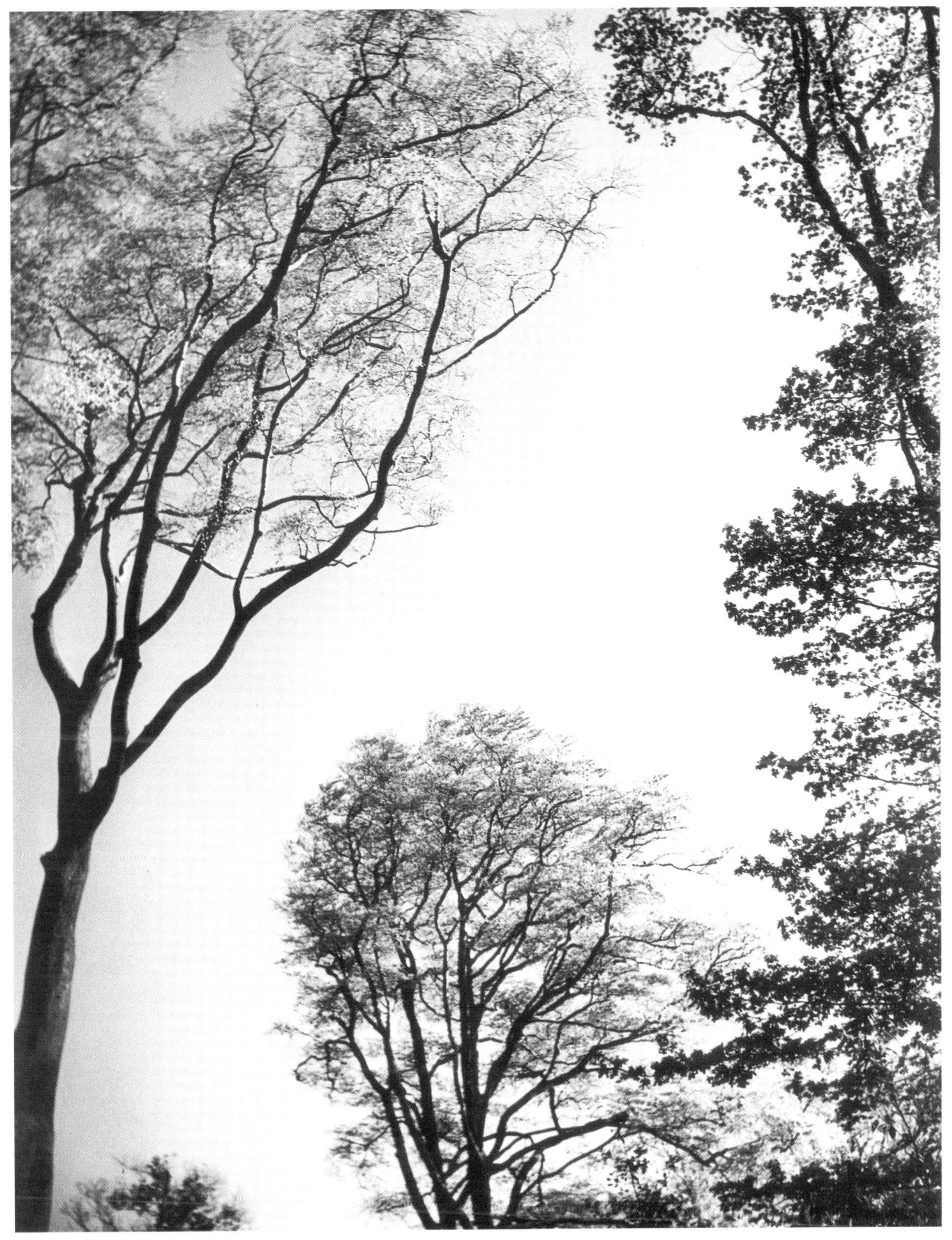

135

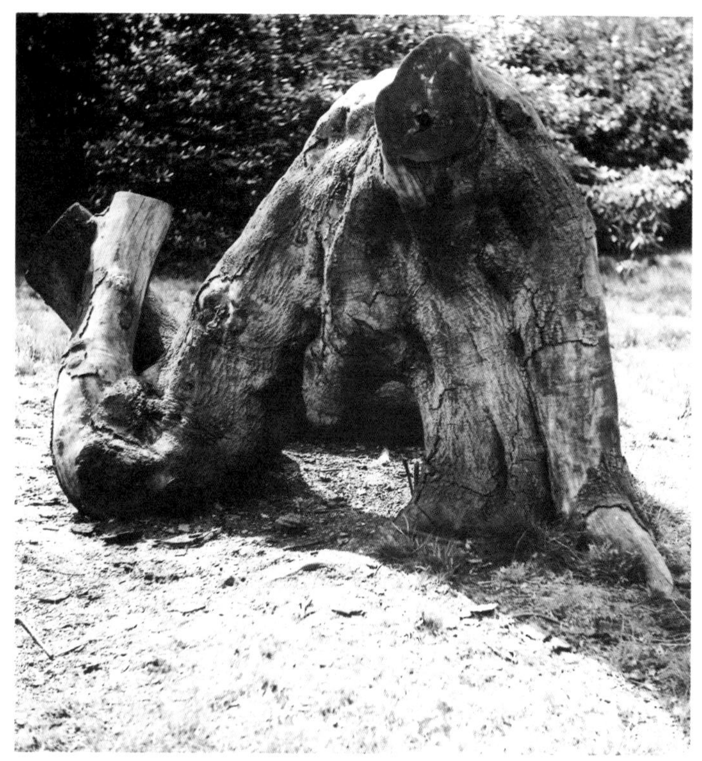

136

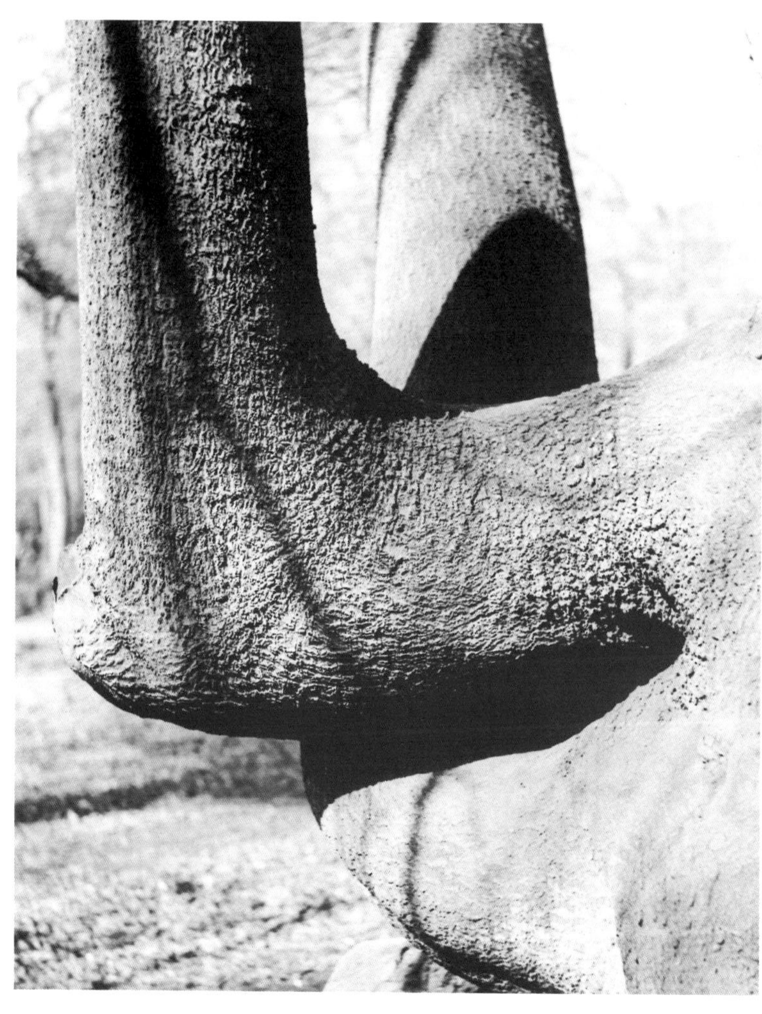

137

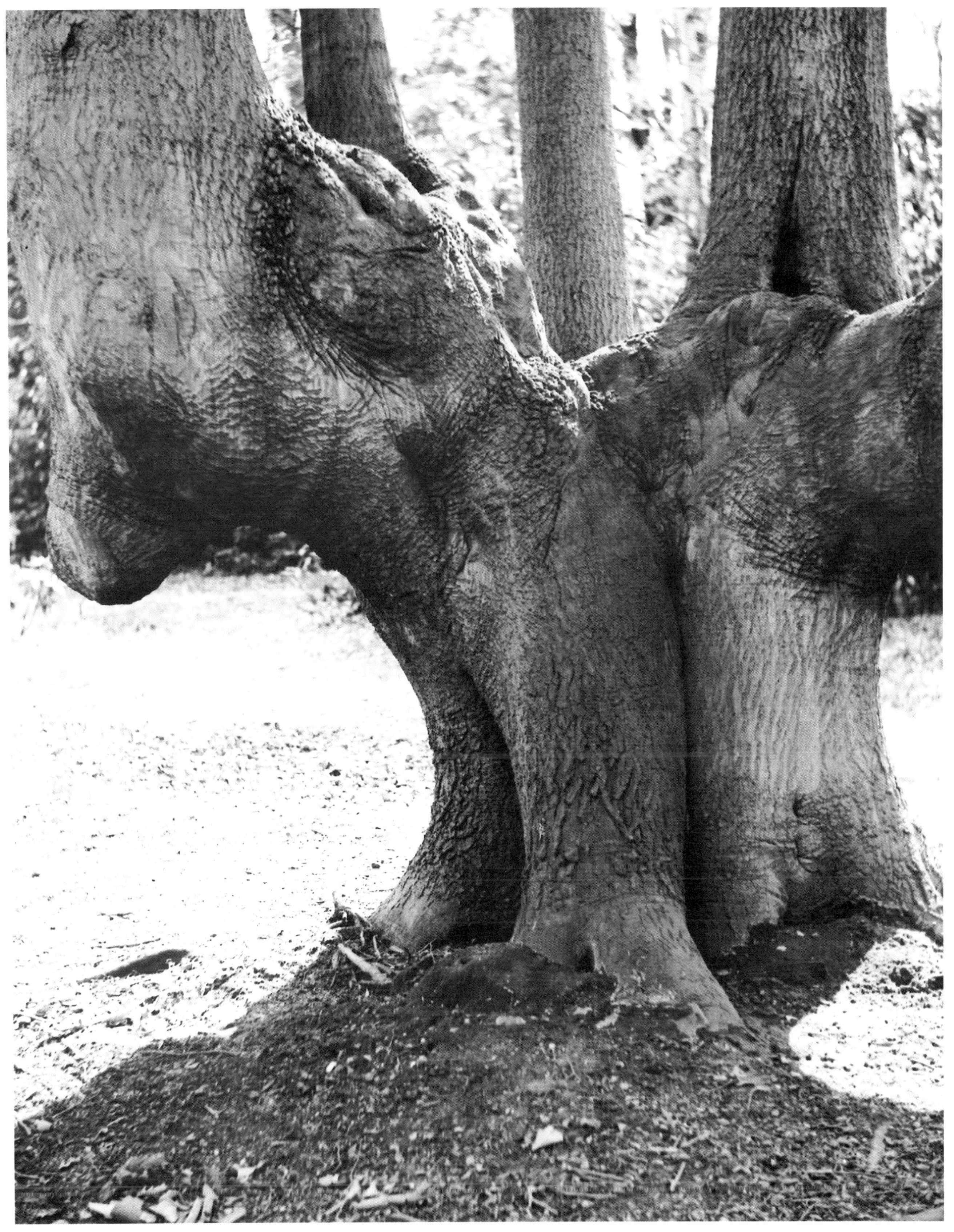

138

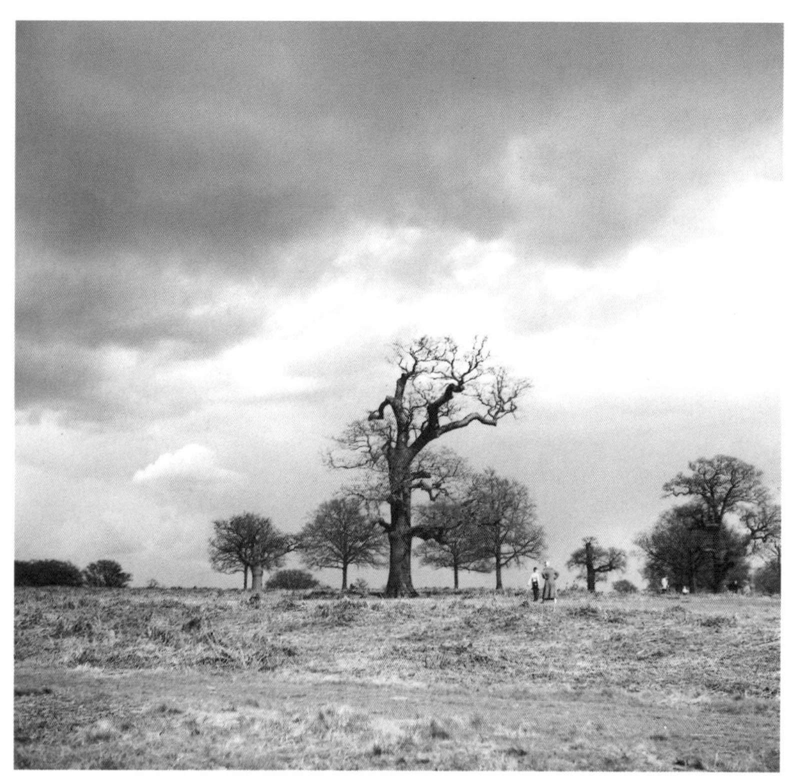

139

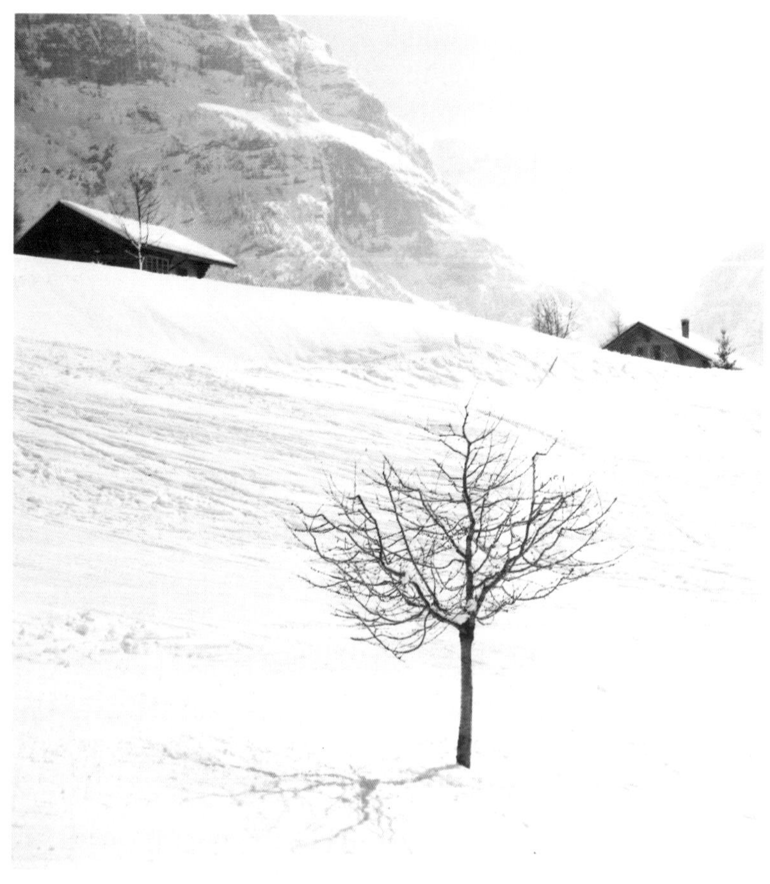

140

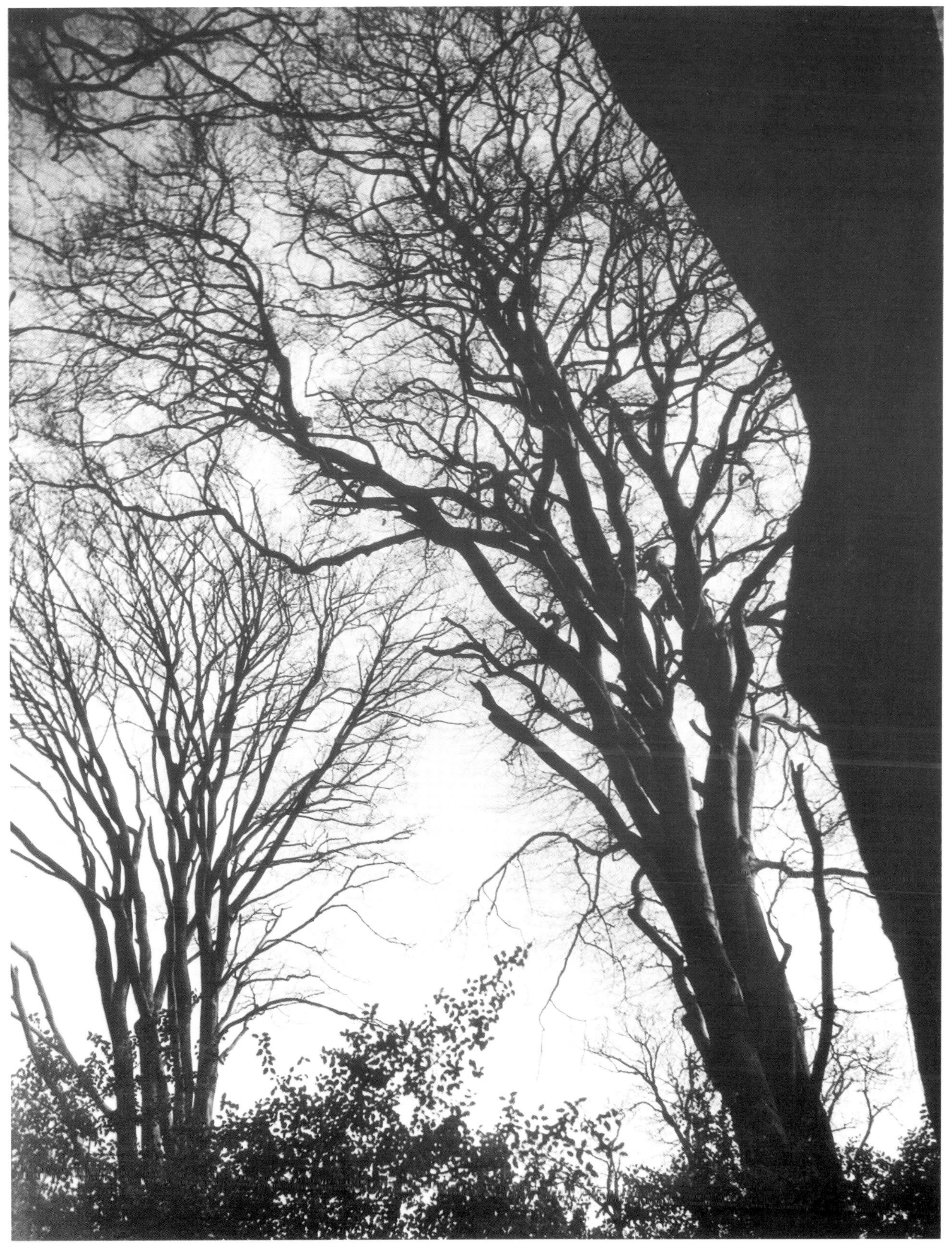

141

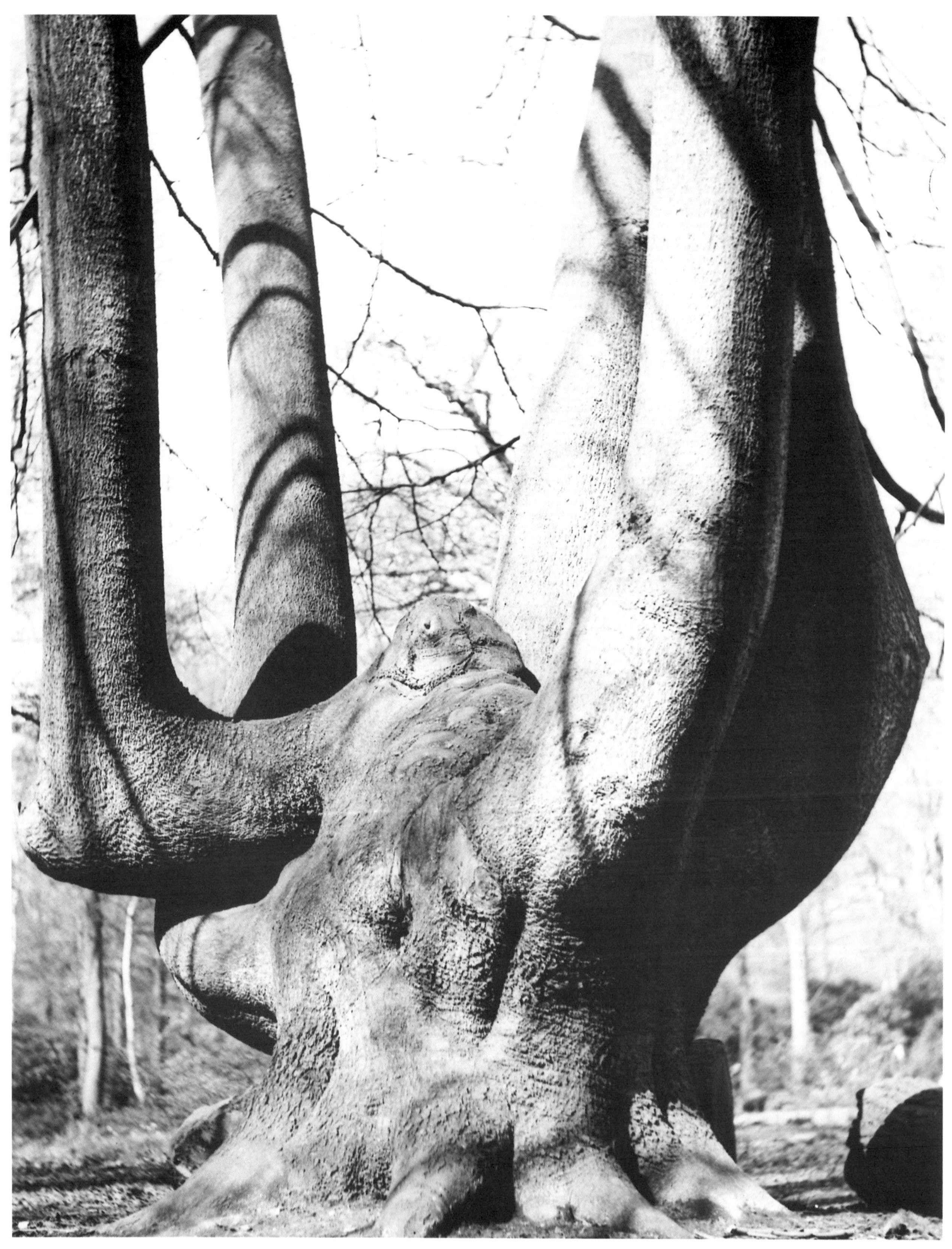

142

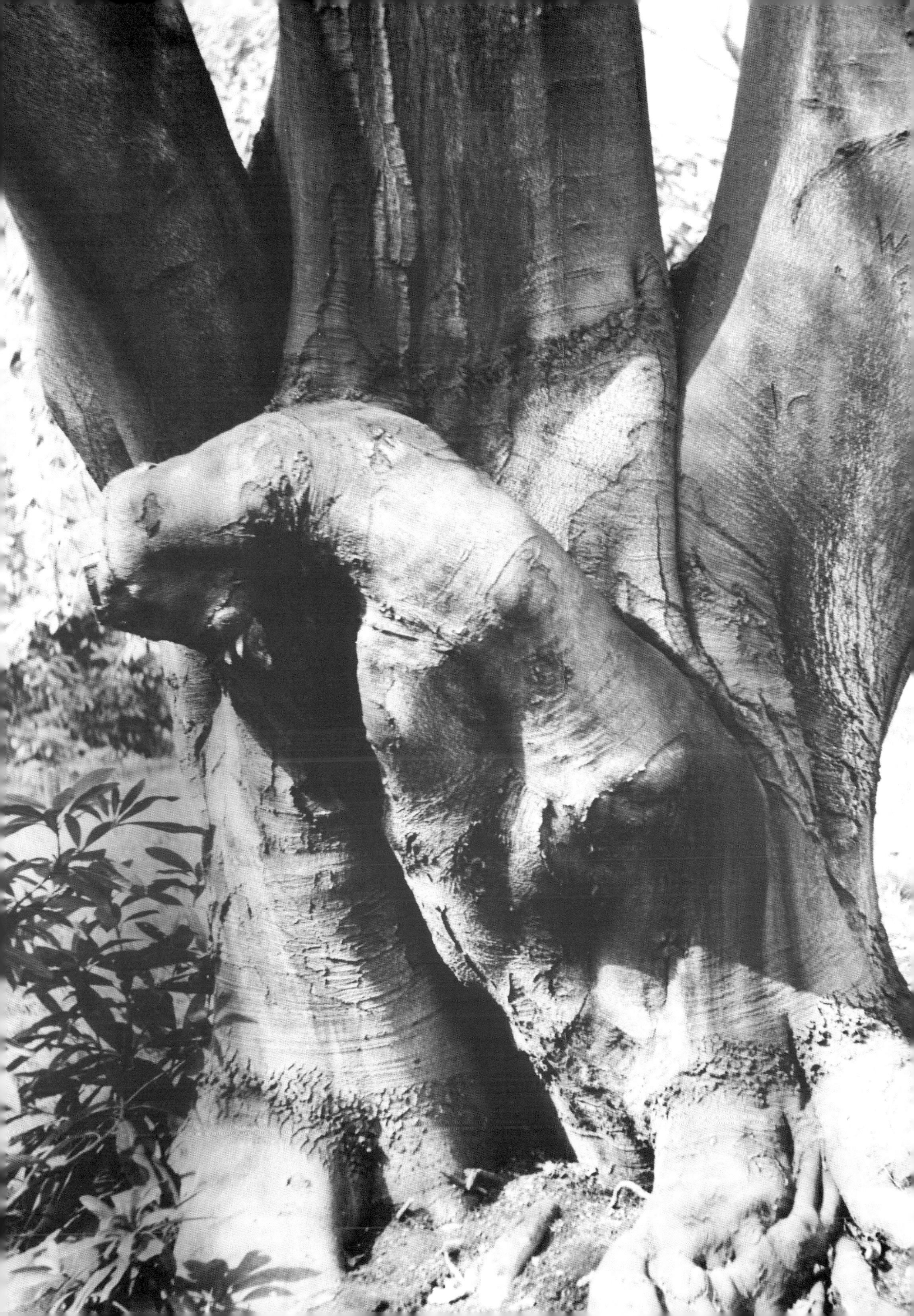

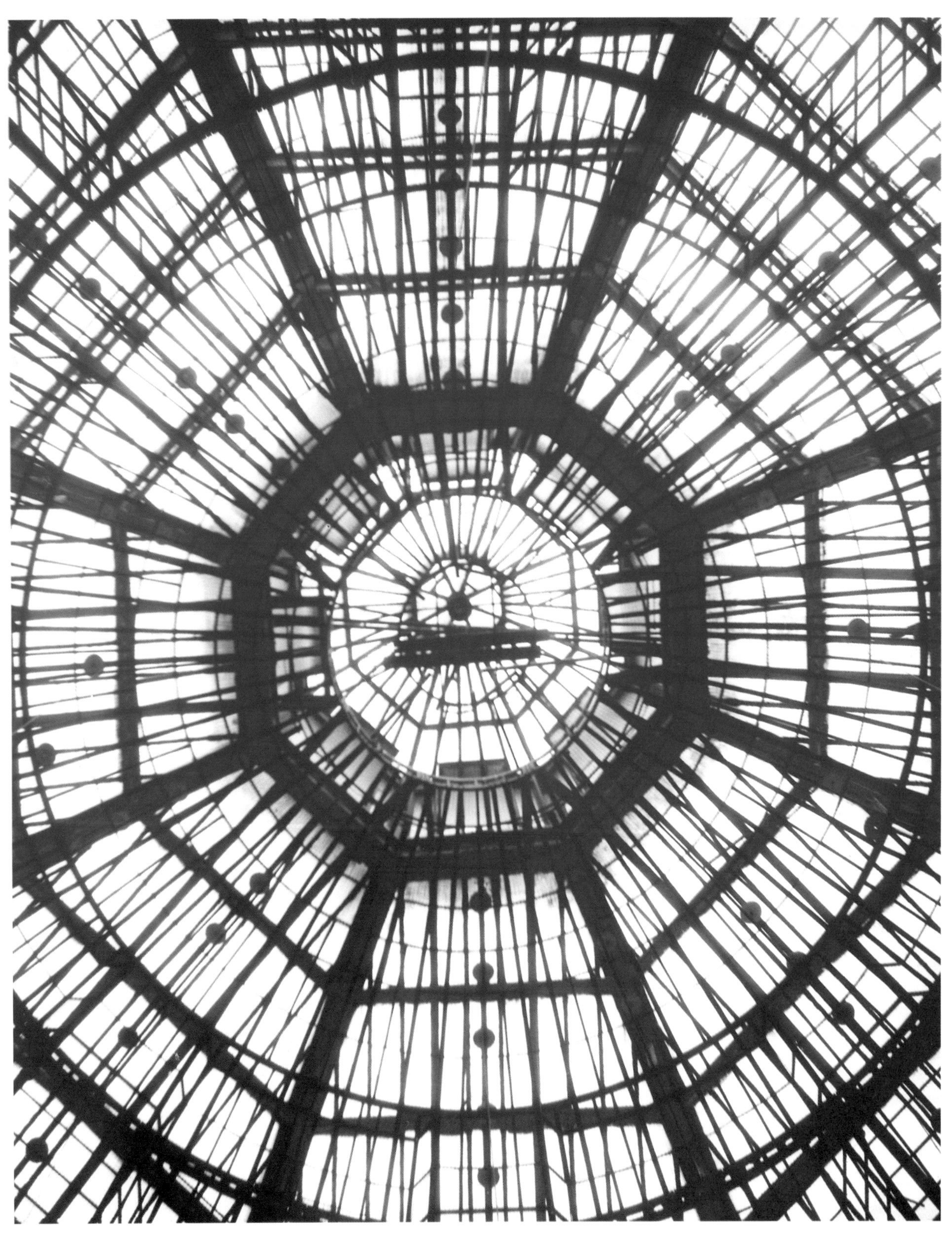

144

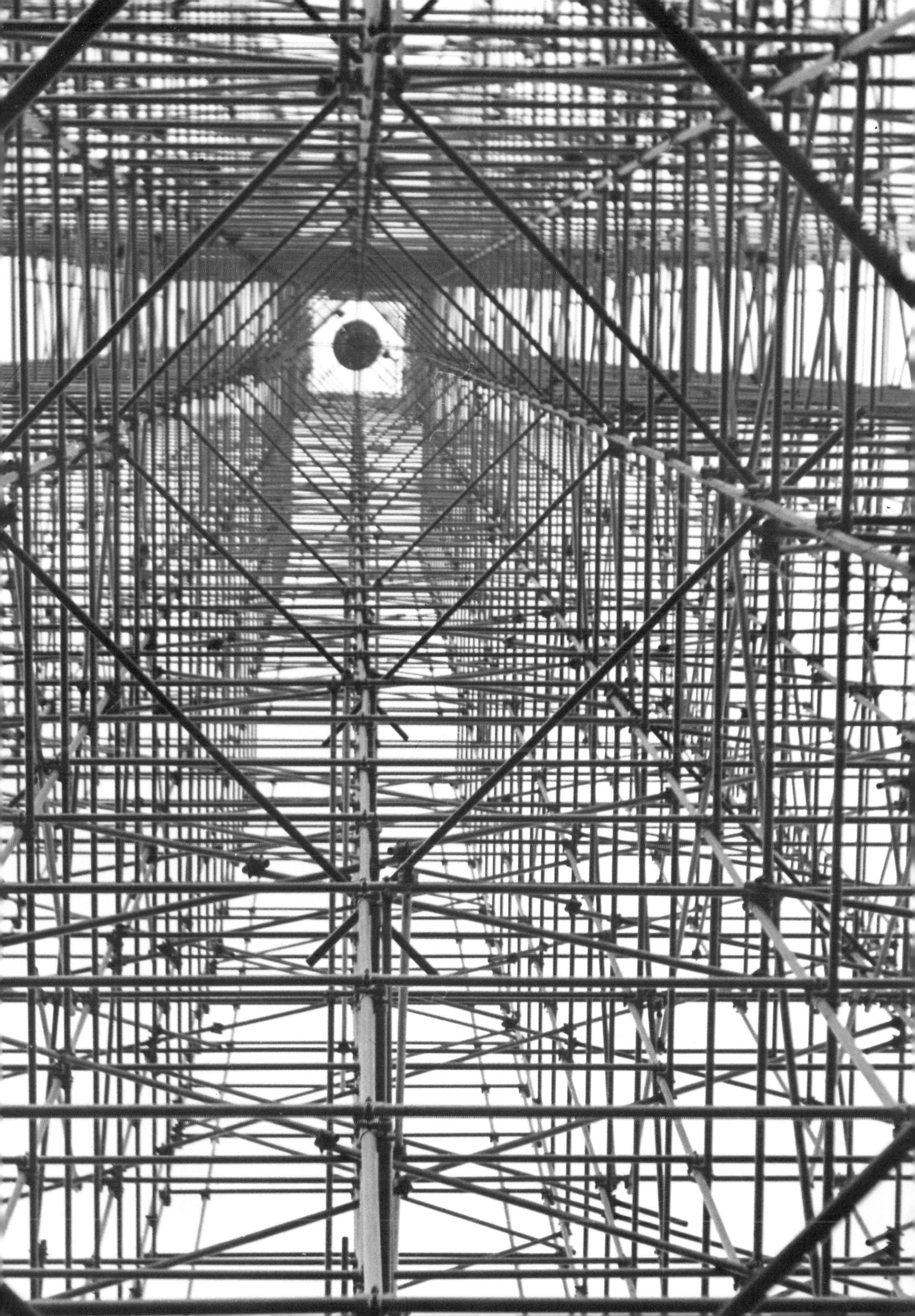

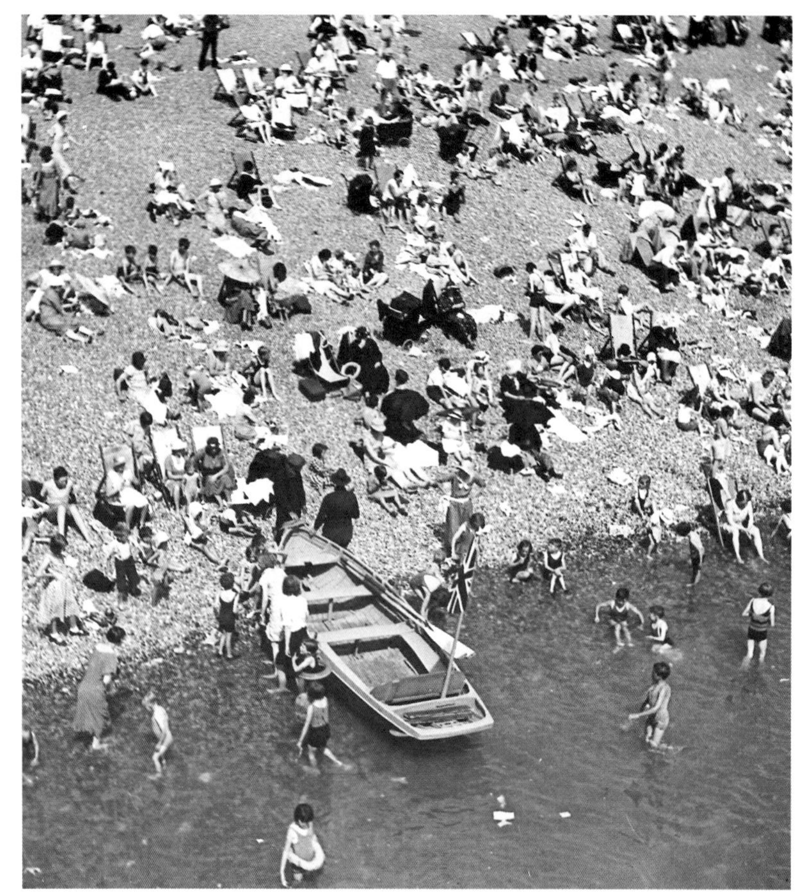

146

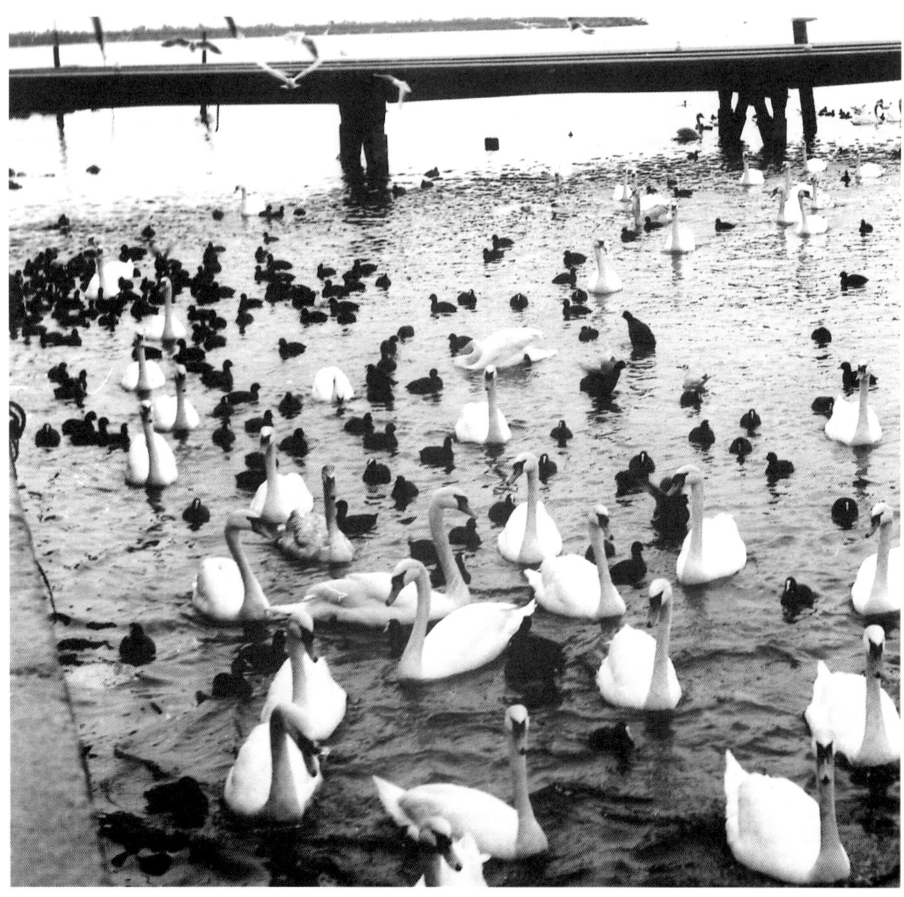

147

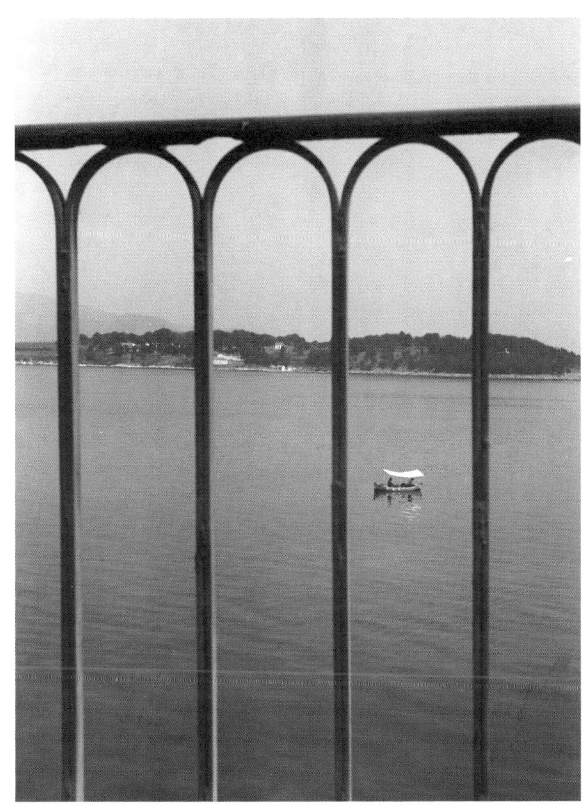

149

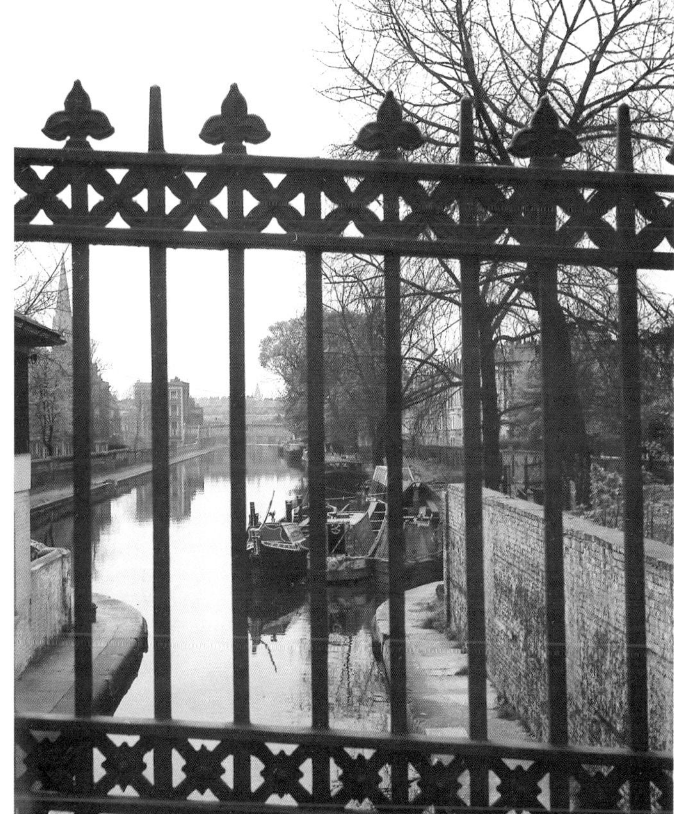

150

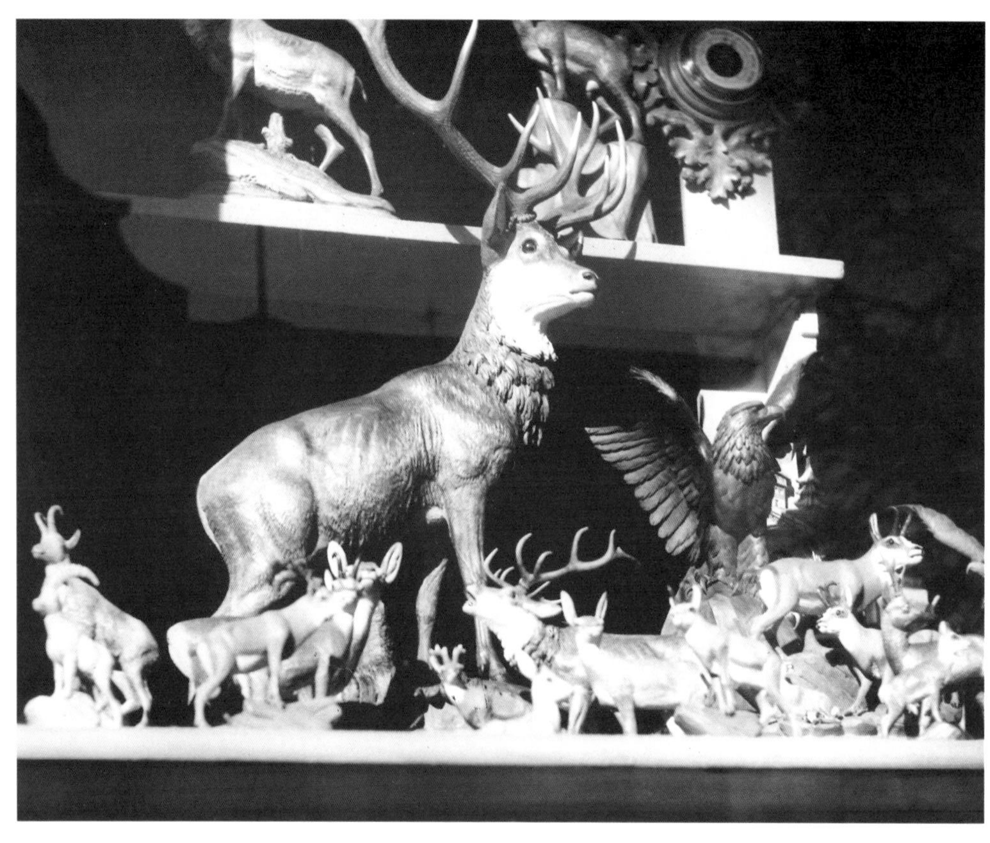

151

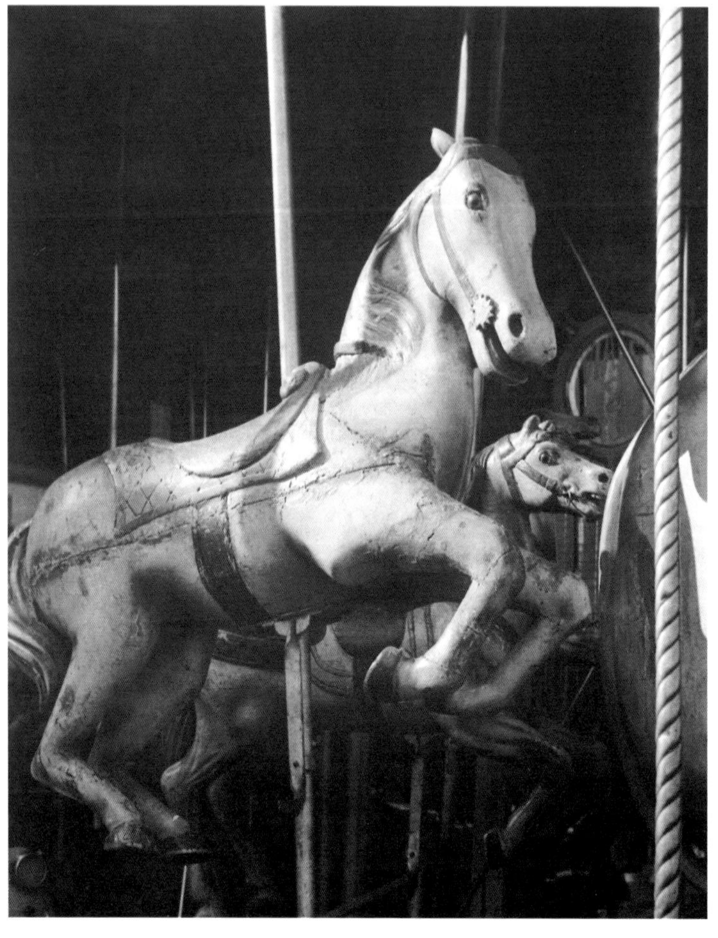

152

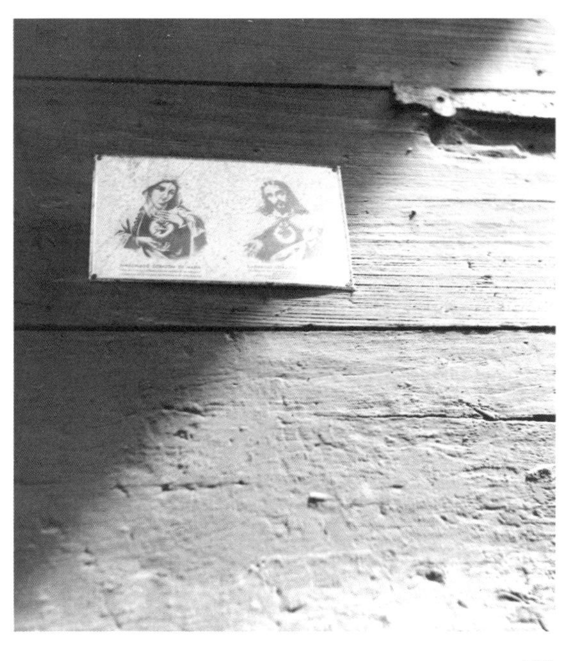

153

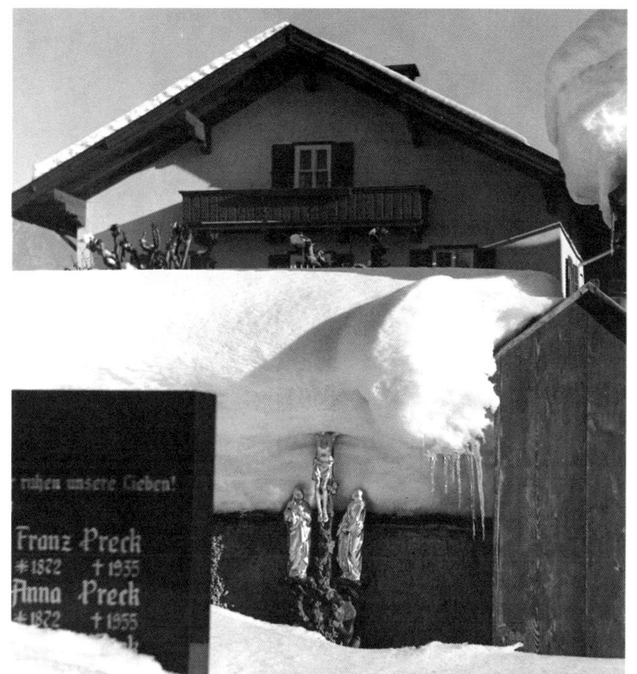

154

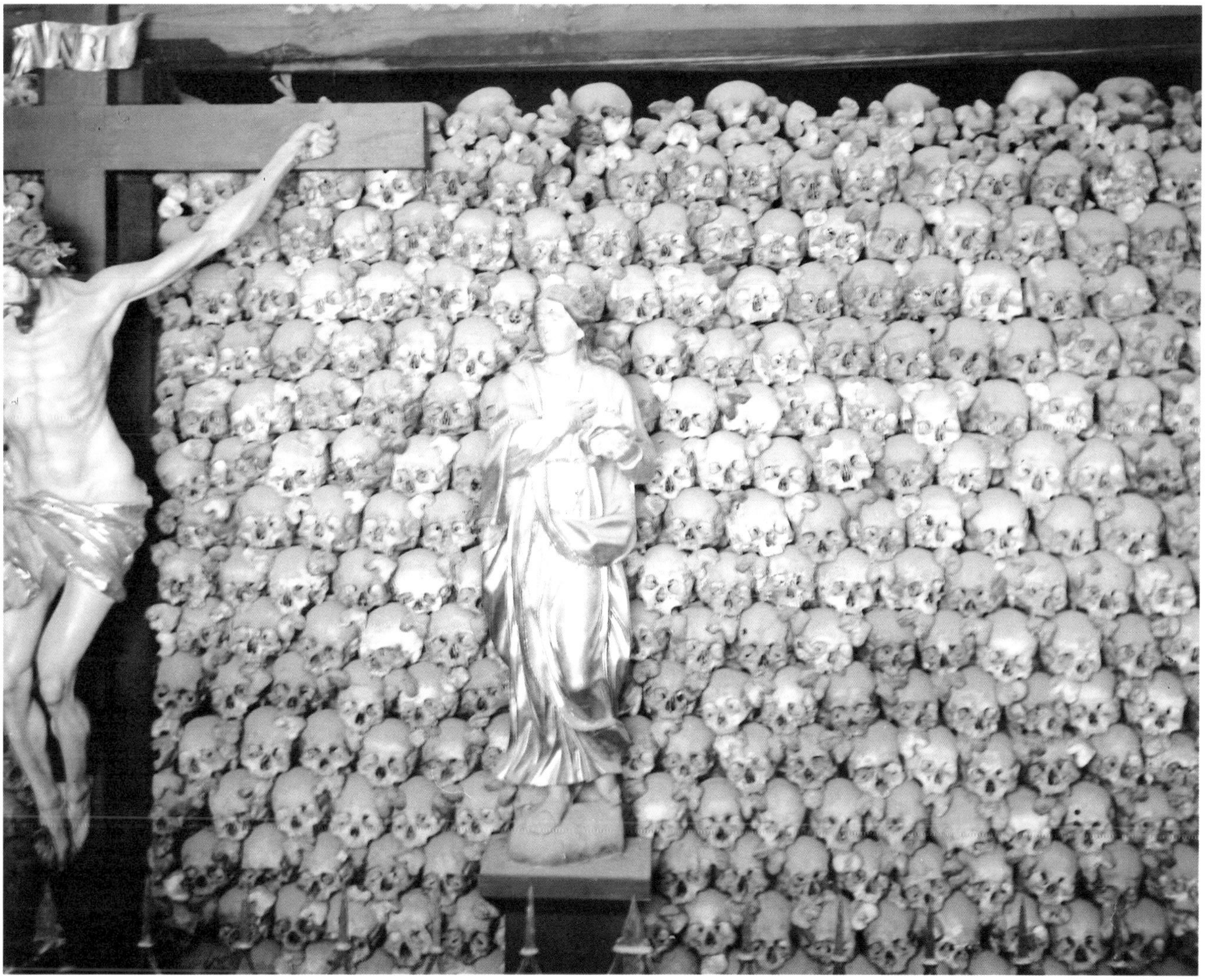

156

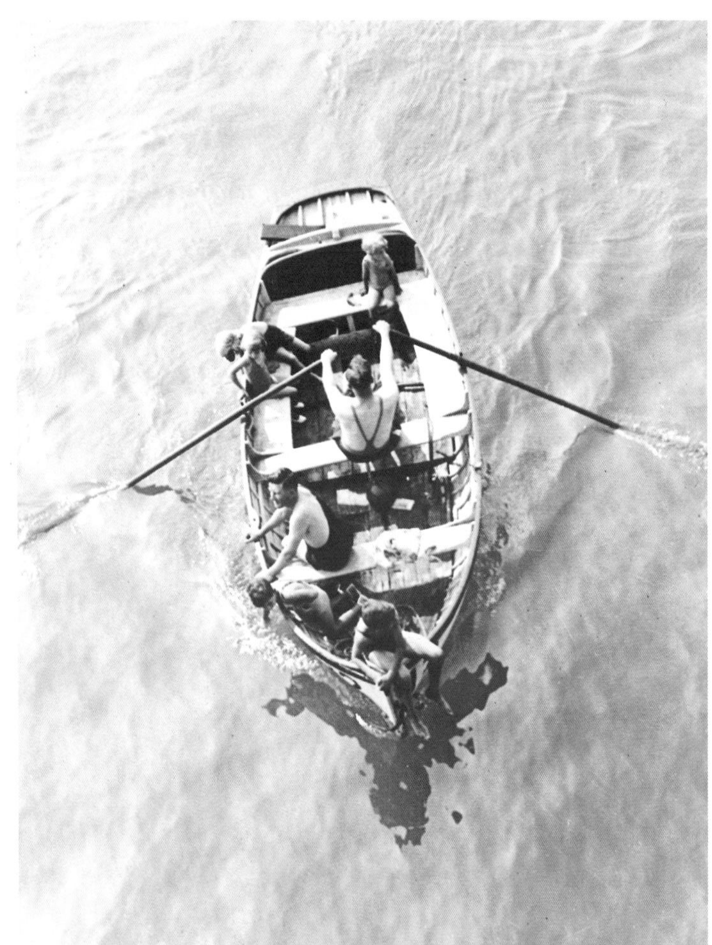

156

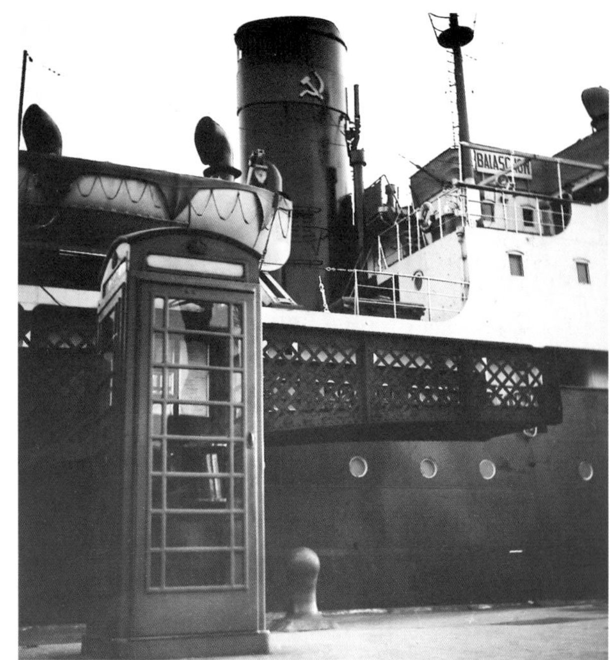

157

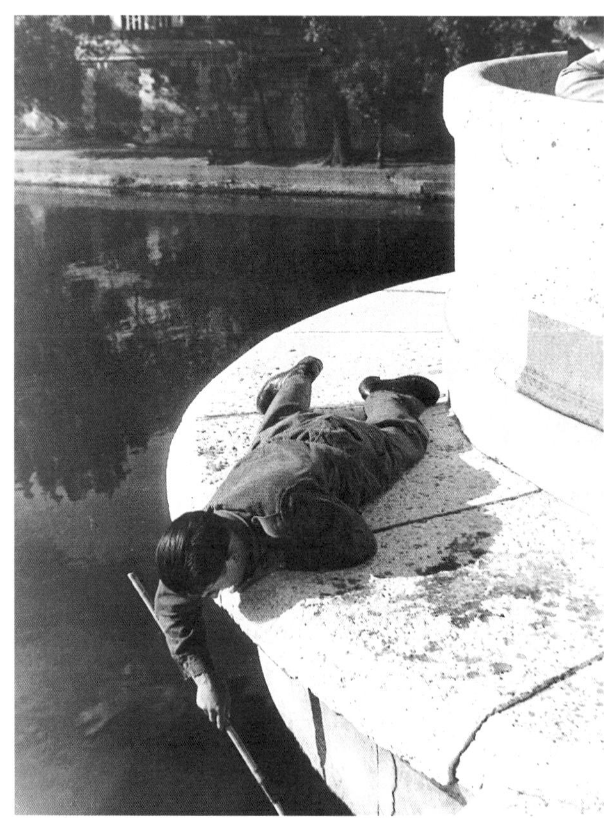

158

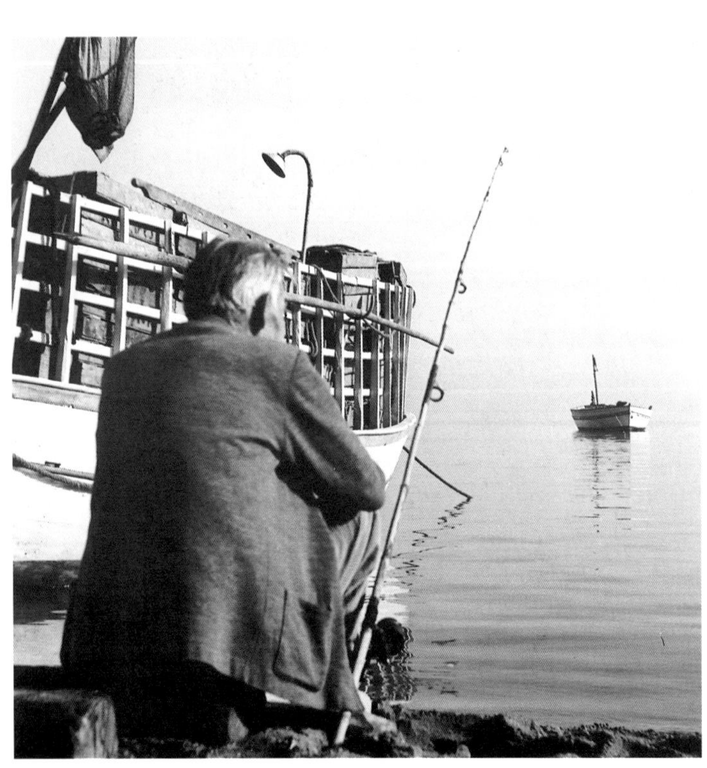

159

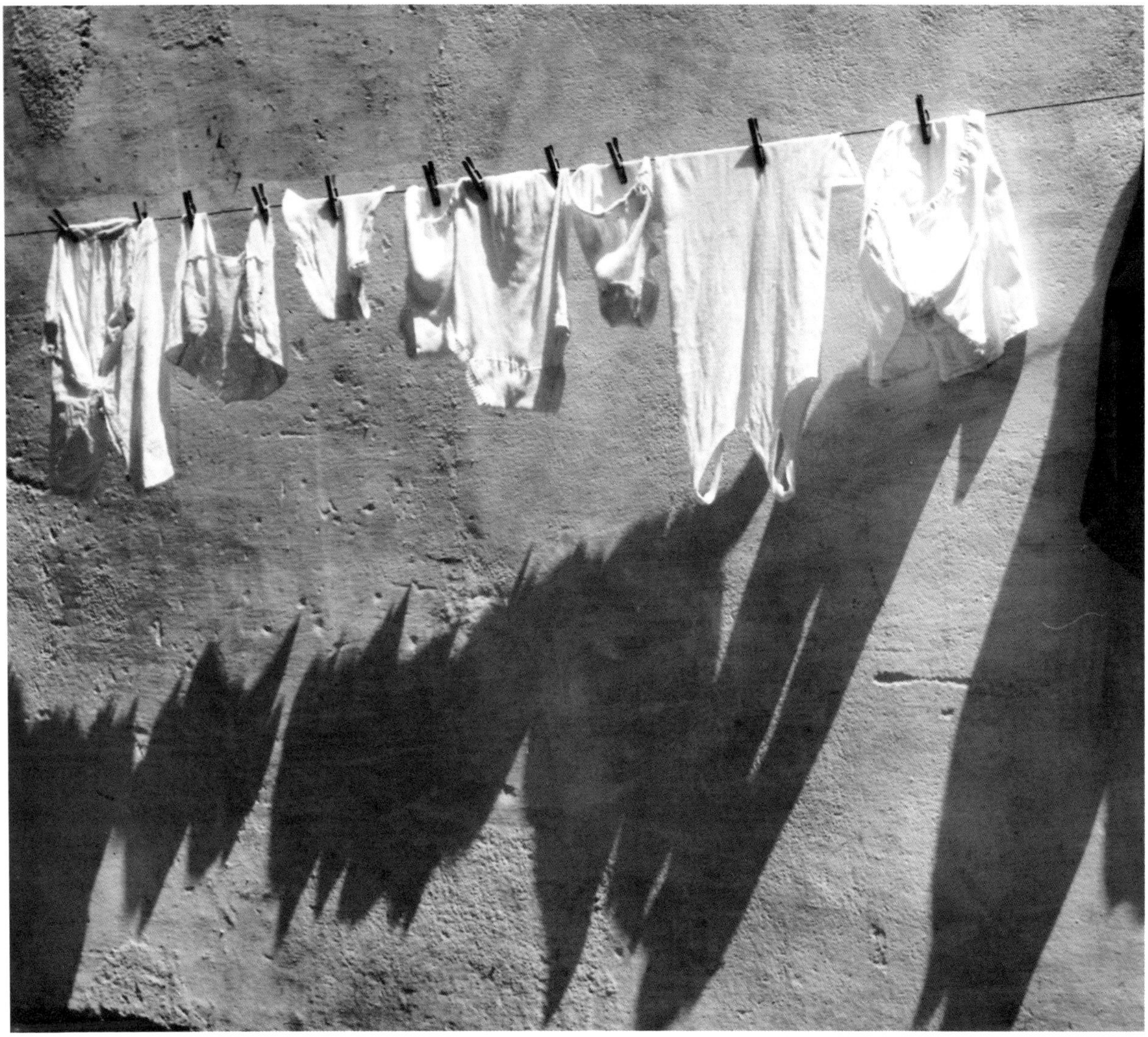

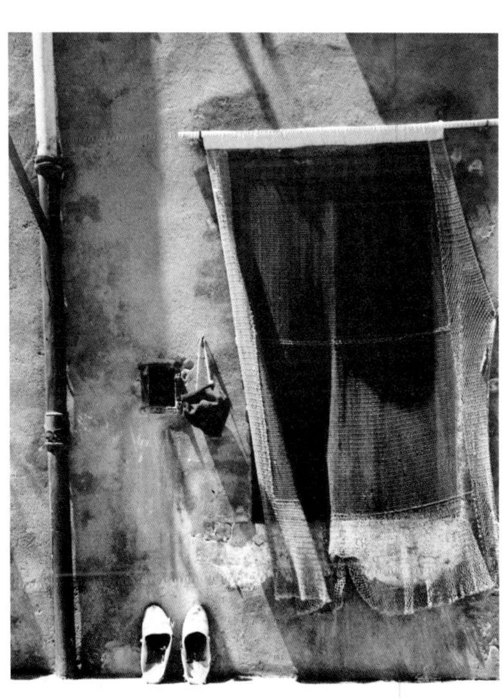

160

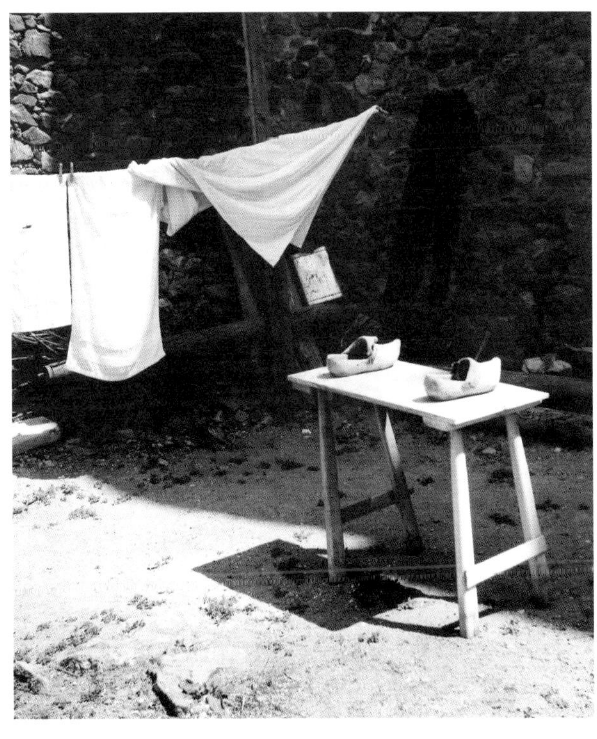

161

162

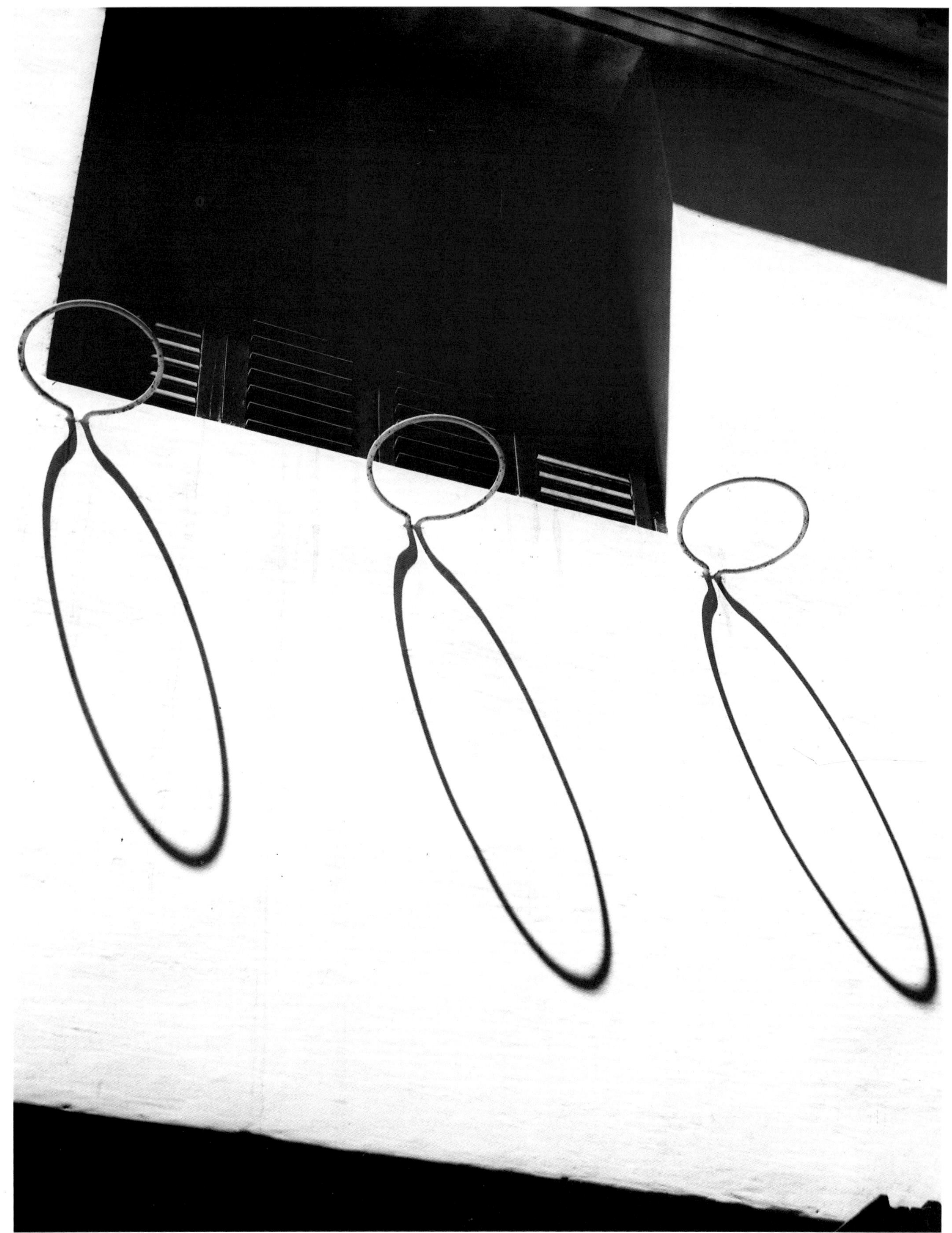

163

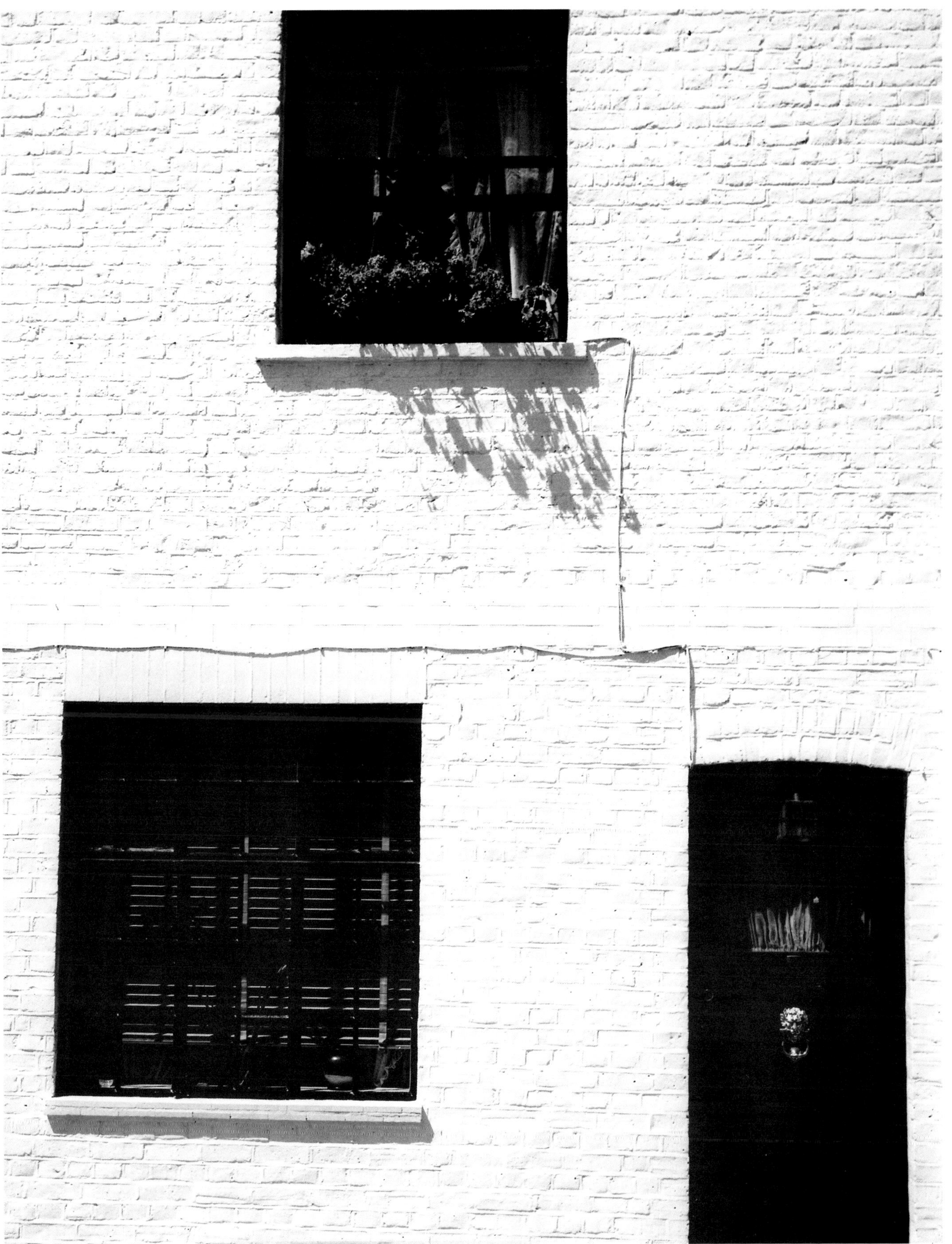

164

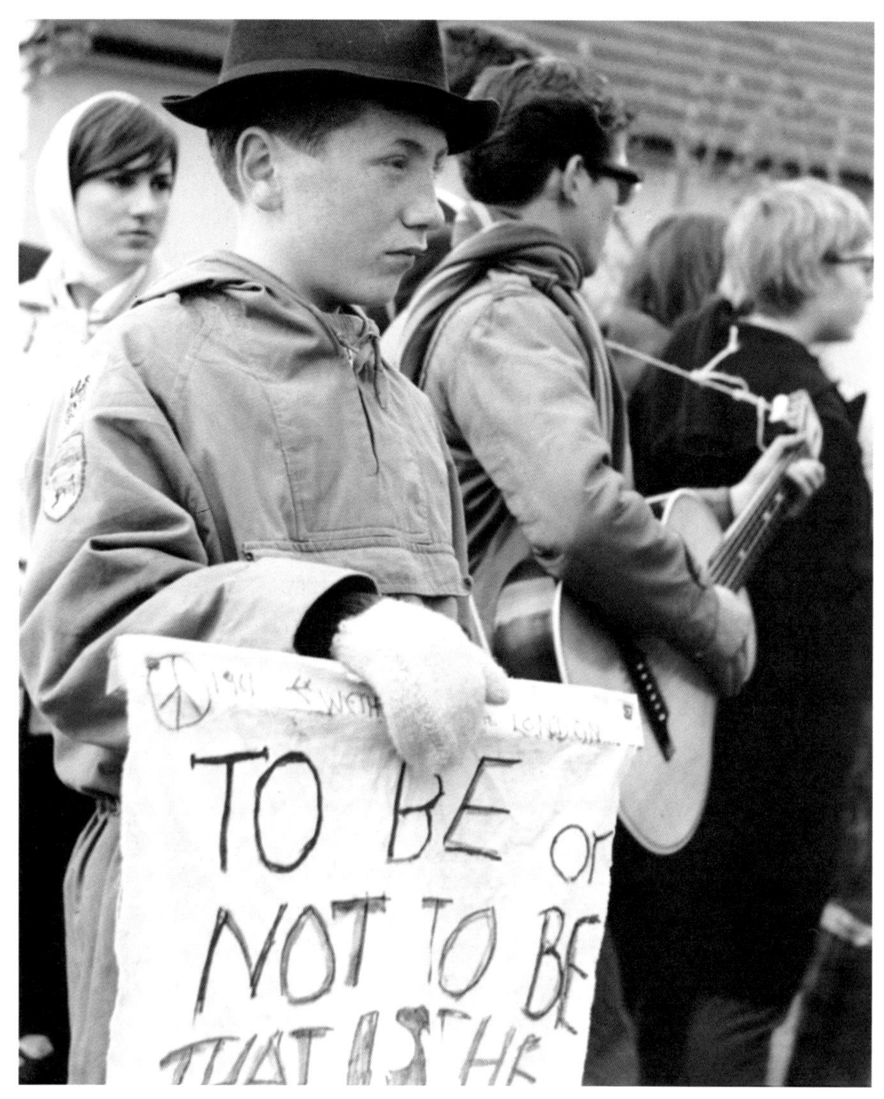

165

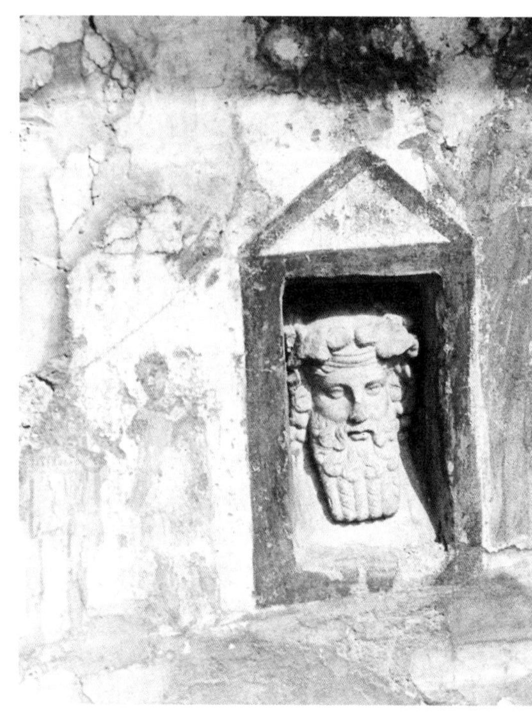

166

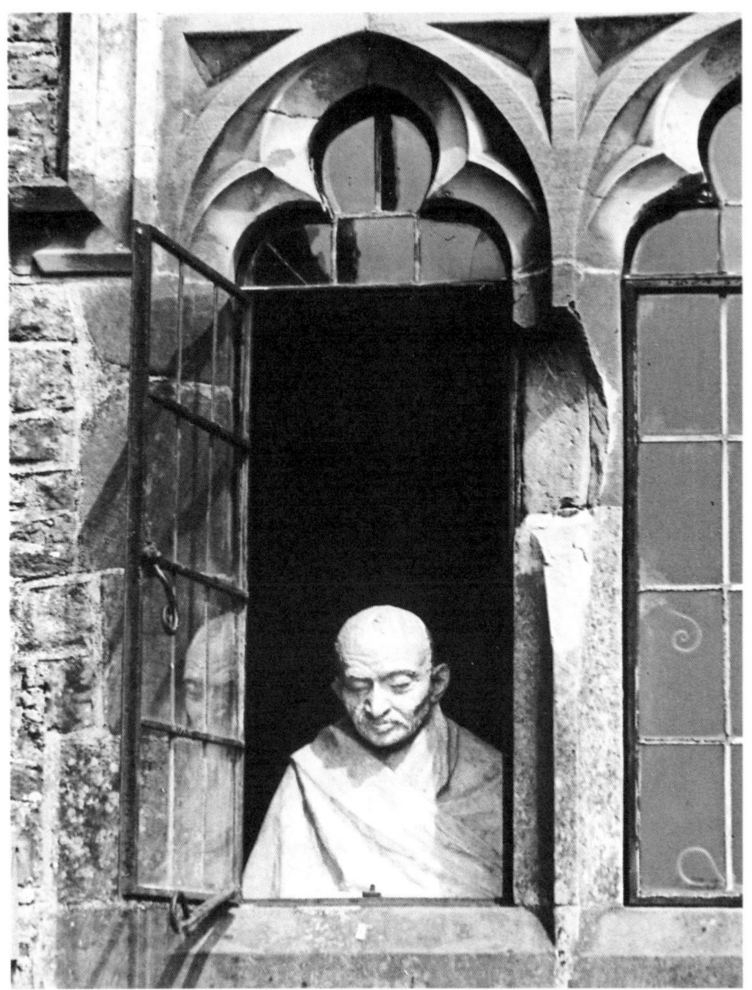

167

168

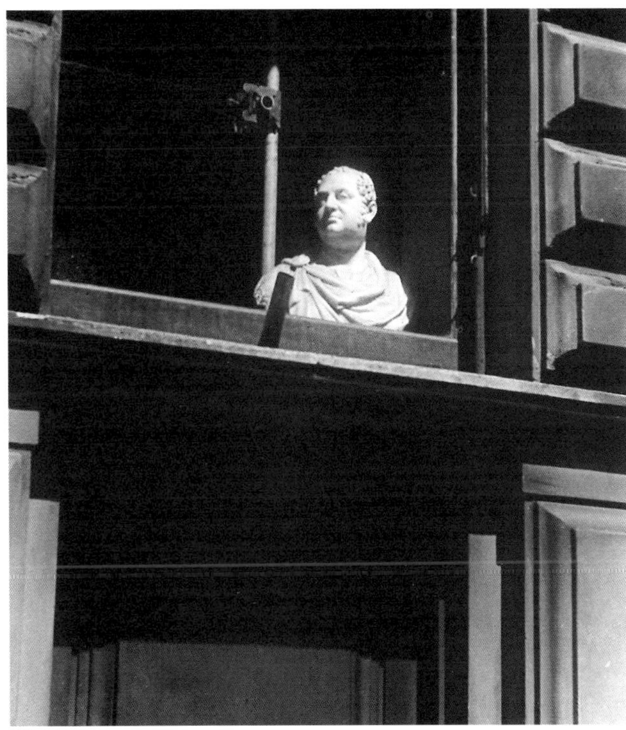

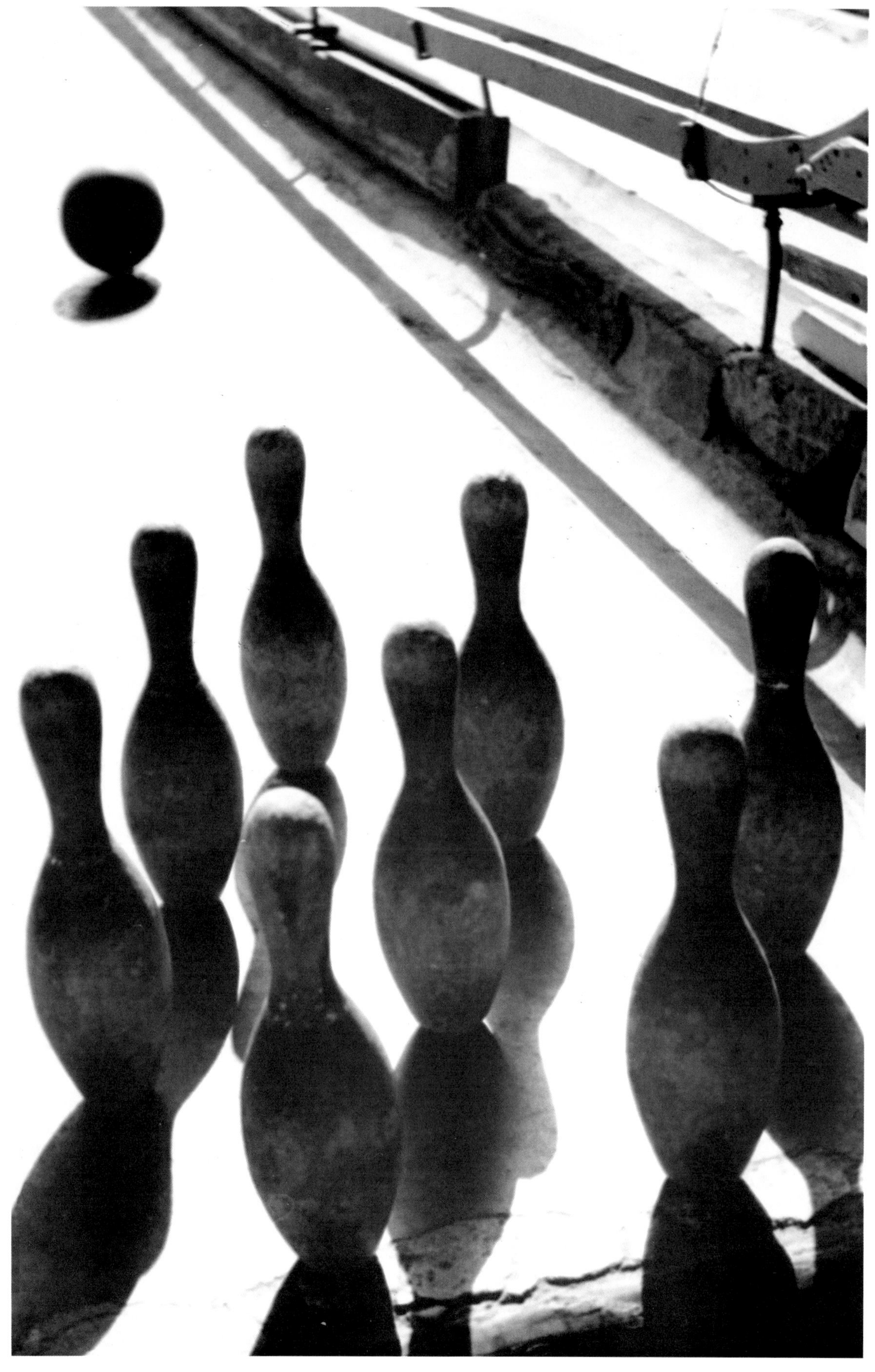

169

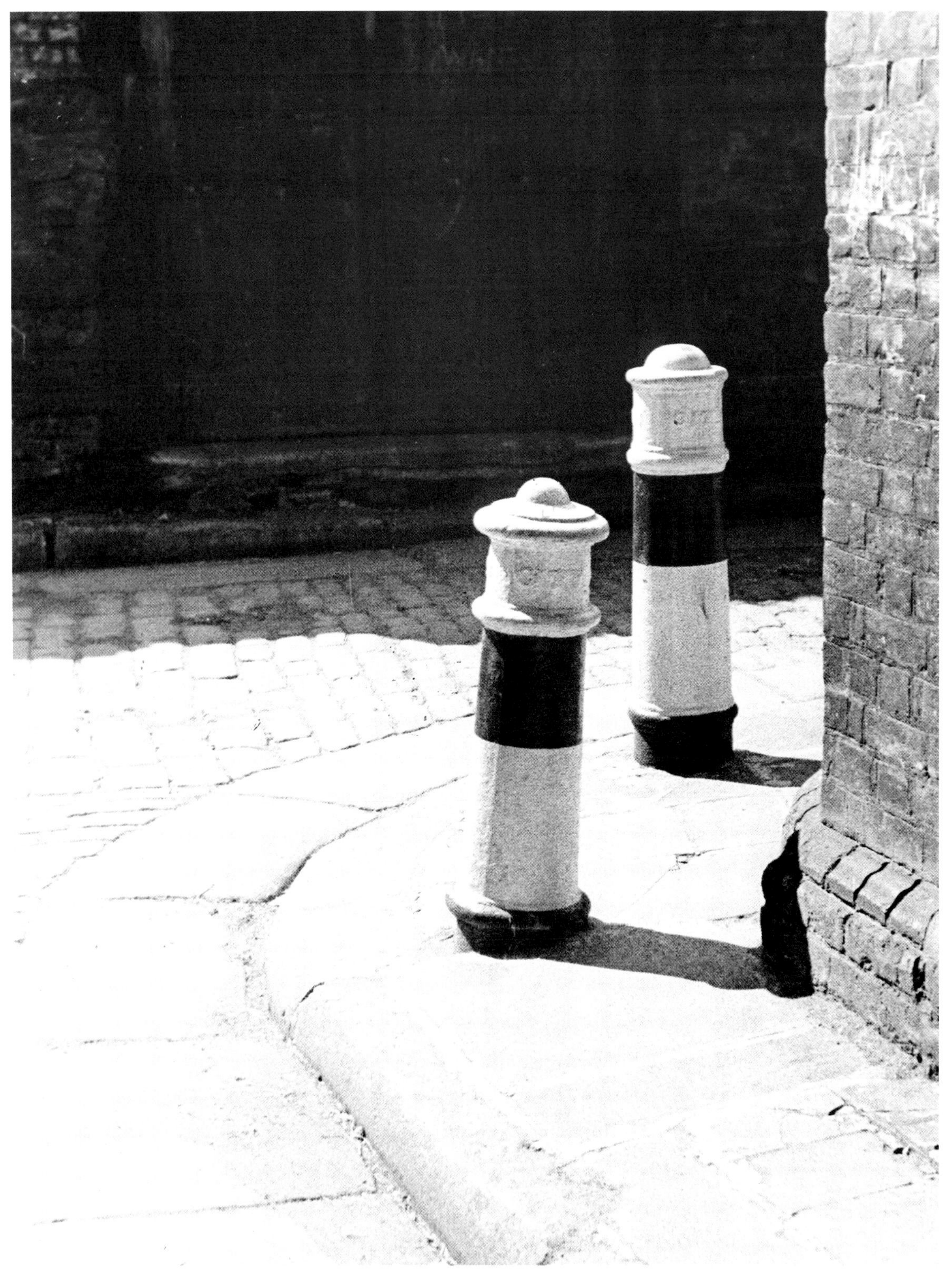

170

NOTES

*The photographer suggests that the Notes should be read if, and
when, you think the photographs are worth looking at a second
time! And then only out of curiosity — wanting to know where and
when they were taken and any other information he can provide!*

I Singles

1. Kew Gardens.
2. Timber in the Russia Dock, London Docks, 1950s.
3. Bruges, Belgium.
4. Beach Scene, Dieppe.
5. Narbonne, France.
6. Gypsy Children at Cerbere Frontier Station.
7. Outside the Tate Gallery.
8. An East End road cleaned up for the Festival of Britain, 1951.
9. Alley off Bond Street, London, 1936.

II Paris, Parc de Sceaux

10-12 A delightful park near Paris, not well known, yet it can be reached by the metro.

III Paris, Jardin des Plantes

13-18 The daily gathering in the Jardin des Plantes of retired Parisians enjoying games of chess, draughts and cards in the spring sunshine.
19. Conversation piece with Sacre Coeur in the background.
20. Montmartre – Place du Tertre.
21. Jardin des Plantes, the grandmother hen with her Chicks!

IV Paris

22. Jardin du Luxembourg during a filming session.
23. View of Le Pantheon and Mercury from the Jardin du Luxembourg.
24. Near the Eiffel Tower.
25. Reflections of the Eiffel Tower in the lake of the Champ de Mars.
26. Livestock at Le Chatelet.
27. The Square Babylone off the Boulevard Raspail.
28. Lovers on the banks of the Seine, 1960.

V The Homeless, Beggars & Tramps

29. Paris by the Seine.
30. Paris.
31. Barcelona.
32. London, the pavement artist by the National Gallery, 1940s.
33. Paris by the entrance to Notre Dame.
34. Paris, Notre Dame in the background.
35. Italy, Vatican City column, 1946.
36. Paris.

VI London Docks, 1950s
(when they still existed)

37. View from Tower Bridge towards London Bridge.
38. The busy London Dock.
39. The London Dry Dock.
40. The busy London Docks.
41. Not a Henry Moore or Barbara Hepworth sculpture in the foreground.
42. Timber in the Russia Dock.
43. A boatload of timber from Scandinavia.
44. A timber warehouse.
45. One half of a swing bridge.

XIII Fireworks and Surrealism

82/87. These photographs were taken from one of the Thames bridges facing east but I am not sure *when*. Presumably it was a fireworks display linked to the Festival of Britain in 1951.

XIV La Escala on the Costa Brava

88/96. La Escala was my favourite village on the Costa (2000 inhabitants) and I took many photographs. This is not a reportage of La Escala but a small collection of photos taken there and included for what I *like about them as photographs*. Which is after all what this volume is supposed to be about! But it's an opportunity to send greetings to all those friends I made in the late 50s and early 60s in La Escala.

88/89. Can the camera lie? In picture 88, did the old man in the beret really love the old boy and did the man in 89 hit the chap opposite him? I can confirm that he didn't and that in both pictures they were talking about fish prices!

90. Unloading nets that have been repaired outside the village on the cliff top (see 93).

91. The fish auction.

92. Two retired fishermen.

93. Interlude. The women repaired the nets and the smiling fishermen, hands in pockets, look on!

94. Even the children join in the fish auction.

95. There were poor folk in La Escala as everywhere.

96. La Escala in evening sunshine.

XV Naples 1946

97/115 All these photographs were taken in October 1946, Naples was still suffering from the war, military occupation and poverty.

97. These two children are the same two as in 100. I have included them as 'proof' that 100 had not been posed by me!

98. One of the sad abandoned children.

99. The 'scugnizzi' – gambling and enjoying it.

100. The man is selling black market cigarettes. The little girls are not ballet dancers, they are victims of poverty and war – but with natural grace.

101/104. This group shows how transport depended on who were your friends or protectors. And if you had none you went barefoot with a mule and cart. The man in the beret (104) is a member of the occupying forces (British/American). The lady looks very Italian!

105. To my mind (apart from the photograph *per se!*) this picture sums up Naples in 1946. Only the boy is wide awake!

106/108. In spite of widespread poverty, the people of Naples were celebrating the festival of Piedigrotta. The meanest *vicolo* (passage) was decorated and the children of the well-to-do bourgeois were parading their beautiful costumes (106). But even the handsome mother (with her blackmarket cigarettes on the stool alongside hoping to make an honest penny) was getting her offspring ready for Piedigrotta (108). And in the darkest backstreet they were admiring their little girl dressed for the *festa* (109).

110/115. But neither Piedigrotta or the black market could hide the poverty in Italy after the war, surely summed up by the barefoot boy (110) standing on the railway track ballast (not in Naples but as the train from Paris crossed into Italy. Hundreds of people approached the train hoping for some crumbs of hope). In Naples they were everywhere. The blind beggar (111) and the emaciated women with her child (112). Note the way she protected the 'decencies' with her left hand! In 113/115 one cannot but feel the desperation of children and adults. And what did the sad beautiful child (114) have in that bag?

XVI Animals

How many people know of this resting place in London for the pets of the rich? I bury mine under trees just as I hope my ashes will be distributed likewise! 128. A translation of what is Romanian since it reads almost like Spanish or Italian: "Gioia. Farewell, Farewell, Once again Farewell. Your disappearance is my suffering." And you notice that 'Spot' gets an anglo-French epitaph. Far from making fun, I can easily imagine the loneliness that the death of an animal can have on the elderly and old. Part of me hopes that our 'Tessa' dog outlives us. She will be 9 this year and Peta and I will be 81. The other part hopes that I will outlive Tessa and bury her under the tree where 'Jack' was buried before her.

XVII Trees and Tree Stumps

XVIII Abstracts, Still Life, etc.!

144. While I was sitting waiting for my companion to do her shopping in Le Printemps stores in Paris (1936?) I happened to look up and this is what I saw!

145. The black circle is the lamp in this meccano type pylon somewhere in this country 1940s.

146. A view from Brighton Pier sometime in the 1930s.

147. The Lake of Geneva in the winter, some time in the 1960s.

148. On the way to Leningrad and near Kronstadt.

149. View of Corfu (Greece) from the cliff road connecting the port to the town of Corfu.

150. The Canal at Westbourne Grove, London, 1950?

151. Shop window, Interlaken.

152. Roundabout horse, Barcelona.

153. Gerona, Spain.

154. The snowbound crucifix, Switzerland.

155. The grim end. Where have the souls gone? Switzerland/Austria.

156. Two Men in a Boat and 5 scamps! Brighton, 1930s.

157. A Russian ship in the London Dock when it still existed, 1950s.

158. The intrepid fisherman, Paris Seine.

159. The placid fisherman, La Escala, 1950s.

160-62. Hanging out the washing and drying off the clogs, Costa Brava, 1960.

163. Shadows in Rosas, Costa Brava, 1960.

164. Study in black and white, Notting Hill Gate.

165. At the CND Easter march. Will the bomb be or not be part of his future, 1958.

166/8. Stone heads. 166 in Pompei, 1946; a Gandhi bust by Claire Sherivan gets an airing at her home in Sussex, 1950; and 168, an unknown supercilious bigwig looks out onto Charles II Street, London, 1950.

169. Skittle alley in Barcelona, 1958.

170. The End! Bollards in the City of London, 1940s.

Freedom Press are also the publishers of

The Blue Cow
and her fantastic exploits

by John Olday

In his introduction to this collection of 41 brilliant drawings and a truly surrealist text, the author writes:

'Now don't say: whoever heard of a blue cow? It's true you won't find her in the Zoo. Farmers don't know anything about her and she is not mentioned in the books by Darwin. But that doesn't prove that there are no blue cows.

Of course, if you ask one of those people who know an answer to everything, they too will say "Blue cow? There are no blue cows!.

But if you ask an artist or a poet – if you happen to know any – or ask somebody who is called a dreamer by his friends, and he'll tell you different.
Perhaps you are a dreamer yourself. You are? In that case I can speak to you as one dreamer to another.

Ever hear of "blue hours"? Blue hours are dreamers' best hours. Not those sunny hours when one dreams in the blue sky. No, I mean the twilight, the fireside hours. When the outside world begins to quieten down, when the crickets chirp in the fields, when the dawn comes and the shadows fall. Those are the blue hours.

You look up at the ceiling and it is as if you are looking at a sky of floating clouds. Your mind begins to wander from the present to the past, from the past into the future. And then ... your room seems to be filled with blue mist and shadows, developing into forms. You watch them coming into life and disappearing. You see figures, people, in old-fashioned dresses. You see Indians, pirates, soldiers, princes, magicians, golden castles and silver mountains, flying witches and dragons. You even hear them'.

66 pages ISBN 0 900 384 86 7 **£3.50**

from your bookseller or direct from

Freedom Press, 84b Whitechapel High Street, London E1 7QX
(post free inland)

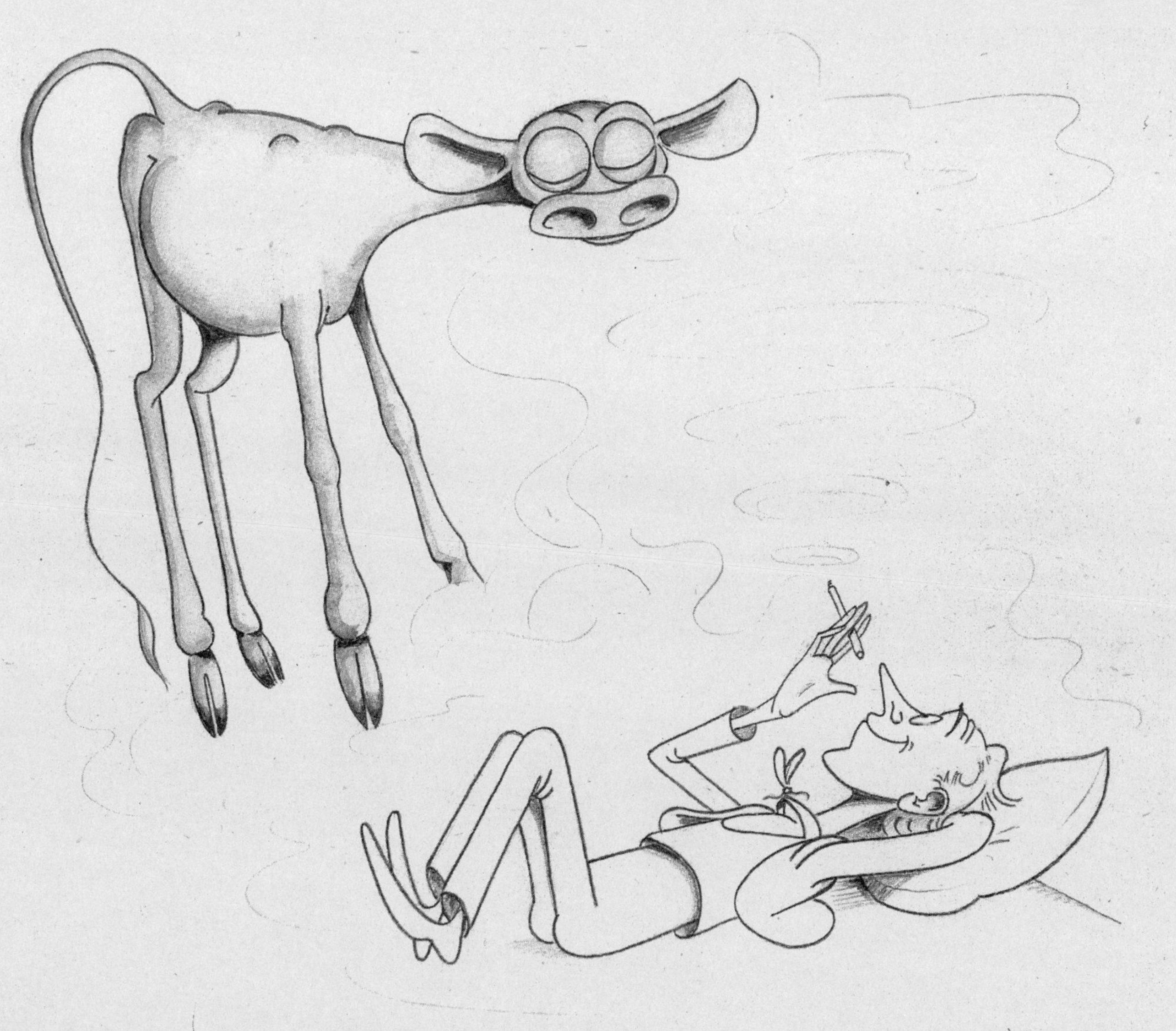

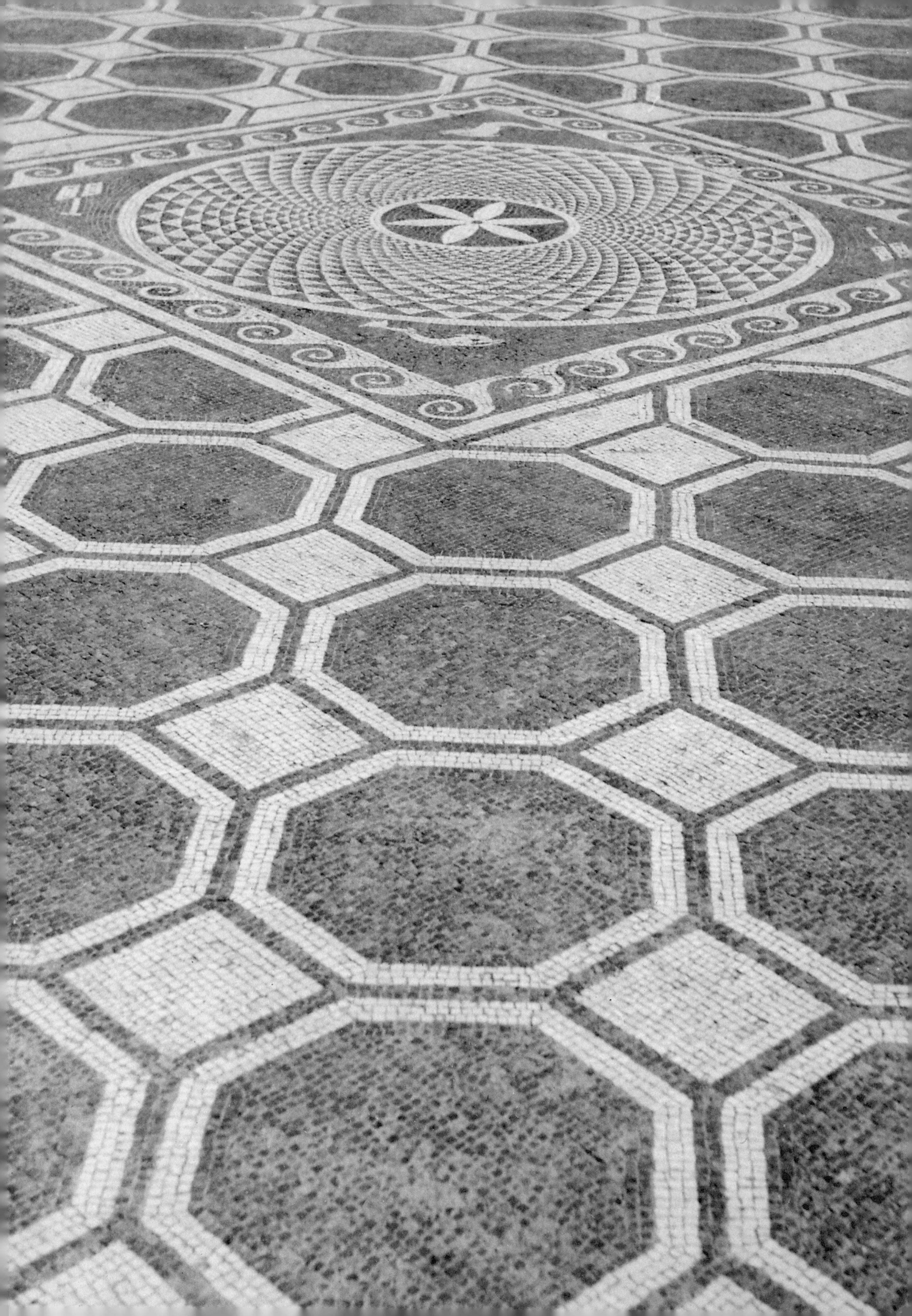